Principles of Vocational Training

Principles of Vocational Training

Gautam Sinha

RANDOM
RANDOM PUBLICATIONS
NEW DELHI (INDIA)

Principles of Vocational Training

ISBN 978-93-5111-439-0

Published in 2014 in India by

RANDOM PUBLICATIONS

4376-A/4B, Gali Murari Lal, Ansari Road
New Delhi-110 002
Phone : +91-11-43580356, +91-11-23289044
e-mail: randomexports@gmail.com, sales@randompublications.com, info@randompublications.com

Reprint 2021

Type Setting by: Friends Media, Delhi-110089
Printed at : Replika Press Pvt. Ltd.

Preface

Vocational Training is education that prepares people for specific trades, crafts and careers at various levels from a trade, a craft, technician, or a professional position in engineering, accountancy, nursing, medicine, architecture, pharmacy, law etc. Craft vocations are usually based on manual or practical activities, traditionally non-academic, related to a specific trade, occupation, or vocation. It is sometimes referred to as technical education as the trainee directly develops expertise in a particular group of techniques. In the UK some higher technician engineering positions that require 4-5 year apprenticeship require academic study to HNC / HND or higher City & Guilds level. Vocational education may be classified as teaching procedural knowledge. This can be contrasted with declarative knowledge, as used in education in a usually broader scientific field, which might concentrate on theory and abstract conceptual knowledge, characteristic of tertiary education. Vocational education can be at the secondary, post-secondary level, further education level and can interact with the apprenticeship system. Increasingly, vocational education can be recognised in terms of recognition of prior learning and partial academic credit towards tertiary education (e.g., at auniversity) as credit; however, it is rarely considered in its own form to fall under the traditional definition of higher education.

Vocational education is related to the age-old apprenticeship system of learning. Apprenticeships are designed for many levels of work from manual trades to high knowledge work. However, as the labour market becomes more specialized and economies demand higher levels of skill, governments and businesses are increasingly investing in the future of vocational education through publicly funded training organizations and subsidized apprenticeship or traineeship initiatives for businesses. At the post-secondary level vocational education is typically provided by an institute of technology, university, or by a local community college. Vocational education has diversified over the 20th century and now exists in industries such as retail, tourism, information technology, funeral services and cosmetics, as well as in the traditional crafts and cottage industries.

The book will be an indispensable source for all professionals, researchers and students in this subject and for anyone working in the related areas for acquiring an up-to-date overviews.

I thank all members of my team who have helped in the preparation of the book. My special thanks go to "Random Publications" who have published the book.

—Gautam Sinha

Contents

1

Introduction

Vocational Education

Introduction

This paper deals with the definition, evolution, and the validity of the education system known as vocational education.

It is the hope of this writer that the reader will gain an understanding of the topic and formulate their own conclusions as to the validity of the topic.

Definition and Background

Vocational education as defined by Webster's dictionary as – *"training for a specific vocation in industry or agriculture or trade"* (Webster, 1993). This brings up the question as to when was this practice started, if it is still in practice today, in what form, and if it is a necessary practice needed in today's advanced society.

This education practice dates back to the ancient Egyptians, Babylonians, and Orientals. In these times the ruling leaders or government felt little or no need for organized education, yet there was still a need for skilled tradesmen. Skills were learned in the form of an apprenticeship, usually from a father or master craftsman.

The goal of the apprentice was to become skilled enough to prove valuable. Valued workers were able to attain secure jobs and were considered to be successful whatever their job may have been.

This process continued for hundreds of years, making skilled tradesmen valued and respected in their community. This was until the social marker known as the FIRST RIFT (Davis, 2005).

The First Rift

The *"First Rift"* began around 350 BC in Greece. This was a time of enlightenment and social reform. Through the teachings of Aristotle and Plato, the definition of "education" was changed. No longer was learning a physical trade considered education. Aristotle believed the people who "do" are too burdened with their hands to learn how to read or write. He believed that academics should be separate from the hand. This marks one of the first times in history that education was split in to a class system, those who work and those who are educated. Although severely degraded the apprentice system still existed and continued to serve its purpose. Those who could afford the luxury to go to school were gifted, and those who worked were placed at a level similar to that of slaves. This educational split continued unchallenged until the beginning of the Renaissance (Smith, 1998).

Academics & Trades

In the year 1500, Martin Luther began to challenge the Catholic Church (the dominating authority on education at the time) and began introducing the concept of merging academics and trade education. Martin Luther believed that there was a need for both academic and hands-on education, and that with one alone a child could not truly be educated. Martin Luther saw the need for skilled and educated society. He put great respect in those who chose the job of teacher.

> *"If I could leave the preaching office and my other duties, or had to do so, there is no other office I would rather have than that of schoolmaster or teacher ... for I know that next to that of preaching, this is the best, greatest, and most useful office there is ... It surely has to be one of the supreme virtues on earth faithfully to train other people's children...."*

Martin Luther set the ground work for merging vocational training into a public educational system. This merging or blending of the educational system was to be seen for the next few hundred years. People began to realize that there was a lot of validity in the apprentice style learning, learning by doing, and we began to see this evolution in the educational system (GANSS, 1910).

Hands-on Learning

A man by the name of Comenius in the country of Czechoslovakia in the 1600's picked up on Martin Luther's ideas and continued to integrate them into his model of children's education. Comenius believed that learning and hands on training should begin at an early age. He realized that a student's education is only as good as his teachings. Comenius's teachings came about during the time of the 30 Year War in Europe. Teachers were hard to find much less trained teachers qualified to teach both academics and hands-on training (Remko, 2004).

Pestalozzi Training for Children

Johann Heinrich Pestalozzi set forth to solve this problem in 1805 when he created his own school. Pestalozzi was born in Zurich and championed the poor and under privileged. He believed that if a child were to grow up to be a valuable member of society he must be educated as such.

> *"I wish to wrest education from the outworn order of doddering old teaching hacks as well as from the new-fangled order of cheap, artificial teaching tricks, and entrust it to the eternal powers of nature herself, to the light which God has kindled and kept alive in the hearts of fathers and mothers, to the interests of parents who desire their children grow up in favour with God and with men" (Pestalozzi, quoted in Silber* ***1965: 134****).*

The Pestalozzi Method used a series of hands on activities to involve children in training for everyday life. This method set the tone for the next 300 years. No longer was using your hands looked at as a negative. Students were encouraged to do hands-on activities as part of visual learning, a method which has been proven to be far more effective. This style of learning continued through educators such as John Locke (1632-1704), Jean-Jacques Rousseau (1712 – 1778), and into the Jean-Jacques Rousseau (Krusi, 2005).

Where was Vocational Education Going?

Vocational education seemed to be taking a less than predictable path throughout its evolution; As defined earlier vocational education is- *training for a specific vocation in industry or agriculture or trade"*, but what was this trade? What were we training ourselves for? In the early 1800s America began to define itself as a country and over the next 100 years we had a pendulum swing like none the world had ever seen before. With the invention of the Newcomen steam engine, the locomotive and steam boat, and new manufacturing techniques, America began a change from farming to an industrial era. With this change we saw the growth of cities. The small town farming communities were being replaced by large cities, mainly due to the ability to transport goods from one area to another. No longer did towns have to be entirely self-sufficient. With the change in lifestyle, we saw a dramatic change in education. An educated labour force was needed to fuel this growing industrial machine. Workers needed to know not only how to read and write, but how to operate the mechanical machinery of the time. Society believed that it was the public school's responsibility to provide skilled workers to the new and growing industrial community. Many people believed that in order for our nation to grow and survive we needed to place more emphasis on vocational education. One man who believed this was Vermont senator, Justin Smith Morrill.

Morrill Act of 1862

Born in Strafford, Vermont, the son of a blacksmith, Justin Morrill ran a general store in Strafford (1831-48), turned to farming, then went to the US House of Representatives (Whig, Republican 1855-67). A member of the Ways and Means Committee, he sponsored the Land-Grant College Act later known as the Morrill Act of 1862, providing public lands for agricultural colleges. In the Senate (Republican, 1867-98) he provided funds for their survival in the Second Morrill Act of 1880. Justin Smith Morrill stated the importance of this bill.

"This bill proposes to establish at least one college in every State upon a sure and perpetual foundation, accessible to all, but especially to the sons of toil, where all of needful science for the practical avocations of life shall be taught, where neither the higher graces of classical studies nor that military drill our country now so greatly appreciates will be entirely ignored, and where agriculture, the foundation of all present and future prosperity, may look for troops of earnest friends, studying its familiar and recondite economies, and at last elevating it to that higher level where it may fearlessly invoke comparison with the most advanced standards of the world."—1862, as quoted by William Belmont Parker, The Life and Public Services of Justin Smith Morrill (NDSU, 2005).

The country was in the middle of civil war and many people wondered if our country would survive this great uproar. It was people like Morrill who realized that the only way for our country to survive was to produce workers skilled in the trades that were needed for our growing nation, and educated in the ways to maintain a humane society. His bill provided Federal money to states to build institutions dedicated to keeping up with the educational demands of new factory and social systems. The grant was originally set up to establish institutions in each state that would educate people in agriculture, home economics, mechanical arts, and other professions that were practical at the time.

The idea was to provide higher education at an affordable rate for those who desired it while not deterring or belittling those who desired a more traditional lifestyle. Schools built under this act include:

- Cornell University
- Iowa State University
- Kansas State University
- Michigan State University
- Rutgers University
- Pennsylvania State University
- University of Vermont
- University of Minnesota
- University of Missouri
- University of Wisconsin

With America out of the Civil War, and the government taking an active role in the continuing education of its citizens, we began to look at other ways in which we could improve our growth as a people and a nation. The next major government intervention was the Smith-Hughes Act of 1917 (NDSU 2005).

Smith-Hughes Act of 1917

Between the years of 1900 and 1917, 38 Senate and House bills were offered pertaining to vocational education. The Smith-Hughes Act is one of the most successful for Vocational Education. The Act established vocational education as a federal programme, and provide both the form and much of the substance of vocational education as we have known it over the past 70 years.

Indeed, there is general agreement that the passage of the Smith-Hughes Act of 1917 is the most important single event in the history of vocational and agricultural education in America (Camp & Crunkilton, 1985). A commonly unknown fact is that the Smith-Hughes Act was constructed by four men, Smith and Hughes doing the least of the work but having greater influence.

Charles Poser was the only professional educator among the four principal players. Charles was a leader in industrial education programme development and in 1912 was hired as the secretary for the National Society for the Promotion of Industrial Education (NSPIE). NSPIE had been formed in 1906 for the purpose of securing federal support for industrial education. In this position, Posser's sole purpose was to work on what would eventually be know as the Smith-Hughes Act of 1917 (Barlow, 1967). The Smith Hughes act was broken down into the following:

1. To promote vocational education, provide for cooperation among the states in promoting vocational education, and regulate the expenditure of money appropriated for these purposes.
2. The money appropriated annually under the act was 7.2 million; the appropriation was on a continuing basis.
3. Act stressed cooperation with the states in order to avoid federal control.
4. Home economics was included under the trade and industrial sections of the act.
5. Instruction under the act was under public control.
6. The purpose of instruction was to fit students for useful employment.
7. Education was provided for those over 14 years of age who were preparing to enter work in specific fields (provided at less than college level).
8. State and local community to provide necessary plants and equipment.
9. Teachers and supervisors to possess minimum qualifications.
10. Federal funds matched by state or local funds.
11. Establishment of a federal board for vocational education.
12. Required state boards and state plans.
13. Required the following: six months of supervised practice in agriculture; 30 hours a week for full-time students; 144 hours a year for part-time students in trades and industries and home economics.
14. Provisions later extended to Hawaii and Puerto Rico.

Senator Carroll S. Page, a Republican senator from Vermont, was a disciple of the late Senator Justin Morrill (of the Morrill Acts of 1862 and 1890) which had influenced the development of land grant colleges in the US. It was Senator Page's goal to have a similar legacy follow his name from similar accomplishments. In 1911, Senator Page took responsibility for promoting legislation for vocational education. He formed an alliance with Prosser and began a six year trek to successfully pass vocational education legislation.

Hoke Smith was governor of Georgia and supporter of vocational education, as well as a strong advocate of rural interests, mainly agriculture. Once voted to the Senate, Smith created a Commission on National Aid to Vocational Education and Labour. On December 7, 1915, he introduced Senate Bill 703 (later known as the Smith-Hughes Bill) it was believed that Smith's power and respect in the Senate are what pushed the bill into effect.

Dudley Hughes was a Democratic congressman, also from Georgia. Hughes was well known in his home state for his support of agricultural education, both at the college and secondary levels. In 1905, his efforts were instrumental in the increased use of agricultural clubs as an instructional tool in agricultural education (Hughes 1955).

Vocational Education was now a federally acknowledged and subsided programme. It was recognized as not only important but necessary. This educational trend continued well in to the 20th century, yet became intertwined with the Industrial Arts programme.

The importance of training students to work with their hands was in full effect with the Industrial Arts programme filling public schools. Industrial arts as, defined by Webster's dictionary is *-a course in the methods of using tools and machinery as taught in secondary schools and technical schools.* American schools started pumping out boy and girls (mostly boys) skilled in the art of using tools and machinery, but was this Vocational Education? Industrial Arts trained students in various skills, from woodworking to metals, and prepared them for jobs in industry. However, it was general education and was not for a specific job.

Many people felt that the general education school system was doing a good enough job preparing students for the trades workforce, and vocational education was swallowed up by the programme. The early federal funding of vocational education programmes (Smith-Hughes Act of 1917) removed trade-specific training from the general education mainstream, although a need remained to develop a philosophical base on which the two disciplines could grow. Technology analysis (Wagner, 1947), human needs analysis (Maley, 1978), the Industrial Arts Curriculum Project (Lux & Ray, 1971), and social-cultural analysis (DeVore, 1980), were all attempts to establish a philosophical base for industrial arts education. However, the difference between industrial arts and vocational education was never clearly defined and implemented as a universal practice.

The unit shops survived as a generic reflection of industry; most of them still model specific job training. It was this shifting of Industrial Arts back into a gender based Industrial Training programme that historians in our field marked as "the Second Rift". After the Vietnam War, industrial training in the classroom was beginning to be questioned. The work force was changing and more high tech jobs were being created. This change had been noticed by forward thinking educators such as John Dewey in the late 1800's.

> *"I believe that the subject-matter of the school curriculum should mark a gradual differentiation out of the primitive unconscious unity of social life" (John Dewey, 1897)*

Dewey stated that the educational system needs to be flexible and adapt to the needs of society. Students learn best by doing, but doing does not necessarily have to be training for industrial employment. This philosophy began to take effect in the 1940's. Vocational Education reappeared as Board of Cooperative Educational Services *(BOCES).* Industrial Arts slowly began morphing into Technology Education (Barlow, 1967).

Technology Education – is defined as a study of technology, which provides an opportunity for students to learn about the processes and knowledge related to technology that are needed to solve problems and extend human capabilities (Webster, 1993).

Boces

The Board of Cooperative Educational Services (BOCES) was created in 1948 as part of a broader effort by the New York State Education Department (SED) to reduce costs, improve educational quality and equity, and enable more effective central control of the state's 5,112 school districts, which were then grouped into 181 supervisory districts. The quality of education and the available resources varied widely among school districts, the number of which had already been reduced by almost half since the SED (State Education Department) was created in 1904. Though the 1947 *Master Plan for School District Reorganization in New York State* called for reducing the number of school districts to 560, further consolidation was resisted because of concerns about loss of local control, transportation, expense, and the diminishment of community (Davis, 2005).

A 1948 law created Intermediate Districts (IDs) as formal arrangements by which school districts could share educational and administrative services and costs. IDs were expected to take over the functions of the supervisory districts, reducing their number to 65, each including at least 5,000 students, and to promote consolidation of schools and districts. This legislation also created BOCES as a temporary transition to get wary districts accustomed to working together before forming an ID. BOCES were intended as vehicles for the sharing of specialized staff, such as nurses, and unlike IDs they could not own or lease buildings, did not replace district superintendencies, and had no authority to tax or to expand their functions or domain.

Today BOCES is a technical based educational programme that works alongside the public school system in an effort to provide students who do not wish to attend college, training in a specific job field. In an attempt to attract BOCES students to future education, the Carl D. Perkins Act was passed in 1998.

Perkins Act

The Morrill Act of 1862 created the technical colleges, the Carl D. Perkins Act provided students funding to attend these vocational schools. The Carl D. Perkins Vocational–Technical Education Act Amendments of 1998 (Public Law 105–332) was signed into law on October 31, 1998. This legislation restructured and reformed programmes previously authorized by the Carl D. Perkins Vocational and Applied Technology Education Act, setting out a new vision of vocational and technical education for the 21st century (Davis, 2005).

This Act was signed into law on August 7, 1998, the Workforce Investment Act of 1998 (WIA– –P.L. 105–220) reformed Federal employment, adult education, and vocational rehabilitation programmes to create an integrated, "one–stop" system of workforce investment and education activities for adults and youth. Entities that carry out post-secondary vocational and technical education activities assisted under the Perkins Vocational and Technical Education Act are mandatory partners in this one–stop delivery system (Davis, 2005).

Conclusion

Throughout history, we have realized the importance of working with one's hands. It can be used for future employment or a learning tool for other subjects. What society has not been able to decide are the social implications? Are labourers skilled tradesmen or just placed at a level slightly above slaves; blue collar or white collar; negative or positive? It is because of this question the education pendulum continues to swing and we, as a society, have not decided where it should stop. First working, with ones hands is an honourable trade, next reserved only for those non thinkers. Then what about artists, painters, sculptors: are they not using the same skills as carpenters and masons? It is this thinking which has caused vocational education to take on so many forms, weaving in and out of the general education system. Vocational education is needed this goes without saying, but should it be included as part of the general education system or kept separate? As we enter the 21st century, it will be interesting to see if the trend of promoting BOCES programmes as and alternative secondary education continues in the public educational system. Will more programmes continue to funnel money into vocational education programmes for such a small percentage of the general population, or has the government realized the diminishing returns on its investment.

What is Vocational Education?

Vocational education is any sort of formal training programme that trains students for work in a particular trade. In most cases, training is somewhat short, usually only one to two years. Unlike most college programmes, which focus on providing a broad and varied education, vocational schools — sometimes also called technical schools — are usually geared towards a specific job. Plumbing, dental hygiene, hairstyling, and mechanics are only some of the many trades that can be learned through vocational education.

Career-Oriented Focus

Students choose to undertake vocational training as a way to prepare for a specific career. Upon graduation, students are able to immediately begin work in areas that are often in very high demand. Students train under experts in their chosen field, and participate in a lot of hands-on work. It is often the case that more time is spent in labs or practice studios than in classrooms studying from books.

Students and Basic Requirements

Most vocational education programmes want their students to have a high school diploma or equivalent, but other than this there are very few entry requirements. Applicants may choose programmes in areas in which they have some expertise, but this is not essential. Most programmes are designed to teach students everything they need to know about working in a particular field, and are usually able to transform people who enter with no developed skills into expert-level workers.

As an Alternative to University Education

Many people look to vocational schools as a form of higher education, often in place of college or university coursework. Vocational schools are almost always less expensive than degree programmes, and job prospects are often much more certain. Though much depends on individual students and market dynamics, most people can find stable work within a few months of programme completion. Many of these jobs pay well, and most offer growth potential far into the future.

The on-the-job learning common to vocational programmes is very attractive to most employers. Someone with a vocational certificate or diploma can usually start work immediately with little or no training required.

As a Path to a Second Career

Not everyone who attends a vocational programme is a new high school graduate looking for a way to break into the workforce. Many people see this sort of training as a way to start a new career. Those who have worked for a long time in a job they dislike may see vocational school as a way to re-train for something more exciting. Similarly, those who are unemployed may also see training as a way to re-invent their potential and get back into the job market.

Licensing and Career Counselling Services

Vocational education programmes typically equip students for all aspects of work within a particular trade. This means that the schools often coach or assist with local licensing requirements, either by providing students with information or actually helping them earn their credentials. Many programmes also offer job placement services, which match recent graduates with employers.

Societal Need for Training Programmes

Most communities need a balance of workers with different skills in order to be productive. Mechanics, repairmen, and plumbers are often seen as essential to social order, while dental hygienists, beauticians, and medical aides are important to quality of life. In order to encourage qualified people to enter these trades, many governments help subsidize vocational education programmes. Others work to promote vocational awareness in high schools, and may even offer financial incentives to students who show promise in one or more trades.

What are the Pros and Cons of Vocational Training and Education?

Weighing the pros and cons of vocational education and training may help determine if this type of training programme is right for a particular situation. For people who want to acquire training and get a job as soon as possible, a vocational training and education programme may be just right. Vocational education and training institutions are typically cheaper to attend than a traditional colleges or universities. There are, however, some negative aspects to acquiring this type of training, such as the stigma of attending these schools, non-transferrable credits, and limitation of career or job opportunities. Before making a decision, there are many things to consider, such as tuition costs, transfer of credits, time of completion, and future employment options.

Some of the positive aspects of vocational education and training are the lower cost of courses offered and the shorter period of time needed to complete the required courses and graduate. The cost of a traditional college education may be out of reach for some people, so vocational school may be the only affordable option for acquiring some kind of occupational training, finding a job and making a living. Vocational courses require much less time to complete than a four-year degree. Some can be completed in a few months, and graduates can start looking for a paying job relatively quickly. Vocational training also allows a more flexible schedule for those students needing to take classes while working or raising a family.

One of the negative aspects of vocational training and education is it that it may limit future employment and career opportunities. If your future career plans include moving into higher-ranking positions or even into management, the training received at a vocational school may not provide much help. Vocational training and education also limit the wages and types of companies for which one may work. Those wanting to remain in a particular area of work and who have no desire to move into higher paying managerial or executive positions will benefit from this type of training and education.

There is sometimes a stigma attached to vocational training and education. This may be a negative aspect of this type of training for some people, while others do not seem to be bothered by it. While more expensive and requiring more time to complete, a college degree is considered by some to be better than any sort of training or education received at a vocational school. One final negative aspect is that some vocational training and education credits may only transfer to another vocational or training school and may not transfer to a traditional college or university.

What are the Pros and Cons of a Vocational School Education?

Vocational schools differ from traditional colleges in that they're more career-focused rather than based on academics. The programmes are also typically much shorter in vocational schools, or community colleges, than the four-year standard undergraduate degree ones offered at traditional learning institutions. Before deciding on pursuing a vocational school education, it's worth taking the time to weight the pros and cons of choosing this path over a traditional college programme. Some of the pros of a vocational school education are learning direct skills that can be applied to a career and being able to apply for a job in the field as early as six months in some cases. The cons of choosing vocational school is that the credits usually aren't as prestigious as those from a traditional college and they may not count as prerequisites if the student wishes to attend a traditional college later.

Since vocational schools typically only have minimum academic work and focus on hands-on training, a disadvantage is that their courses aren't considered academically on par with traditional colleges. As an advantage, or pro, though, most vocational school education programmes require high school completion, or its equivalency, plus basic math and English skills rather than top grades. One of the disadvantages, or cons, of vocational schools is that the course credits earned may be transferable at other vocational schools, but not traditional colleges.

An advantage of vocational courses is, just like many college classes today, some of them may be taken online. Online learning via a computer allows students maximum convenience, as they can often schedule their class work around jobs, family and other commitments. An online vocational school education can also save student-parents time and transportation costs, as well as babysitting expenses.

Another big advantage of vocational school education over traditional college is the cost; the programmes are much shorter as well as typically less expensive overall. Plus, as long as community colleges, or vocational schools, are properly accredited, student loans can still be applied in many cases. A con of vocational schools is that they don't have dorm rooms for students needing housing, but on the pro side, as they are community colleges, the daily commute can be much shorter than it is to get to traditional campuses.

A con to vocational eduction can be the competition for jobs against applicants with a traditional college degree. However, as many community colleges include hands-on work experience, this can be an advantage for applicants in getting hired. Vocational school education students typically enter career fields faster than their traditional college counterparts due to shorter programmes. However, a con is that many of the vocational school careers are in lower-paying positions.

What are the Advantages of a Vocational High School?

A vocational high school is a public or private learning institution that differs from traditional secondary schools in many ways. Students at vocational schools typically receive more hands-on, career-minded education than students at traditional schools. Individuals are given the opportunity to explore and identify potential career goals, and are provided with the resources needed to achieve them. Most vocational schools recognize the importance of general academic studies as well as career preparation, and offer fully accredited high school diplomas. Depending on a student's abilities and interests, a vocational high school can provide several advantages.

At a vocational high school, a student can meet with trained guidance counsellors and choose a programme that will best prepare him or her for college, post-secondary technical school, or a career immediately after graduation. Counsellors and school officials help students evaluate their goals and potential, and place them in programmes that best suit their interests. Vocational learning helps individuals learn the tools and techniques that are vital to certain occupations, gain hands-on experience with different technologies and machines, and develop problem-solving skills that will help them in any career path.

Many vocational high schools provide students with career preparation in health care, computer science, education, business, and any number of highly specialized trades. Individuals have the opportunity to gain the knowledge and experience necessary to become carpenters, electricians, machinists, painters, plumbers, or other professionals. Some programmes administer licensing or certification examinations in such programmes that allow students to become eligible for employment immediately after graduation.

While programmes certainly emphasis career development, they do not fail to provide students with well-rounded educations. A typical vocational high school programme splits its curriculum between job-specific courses and classroom instruction on more general subjects, including math, science, language arts, and physical education. Vocational school students are usually required to complete classroom and homework assignments very similar to those given at traditional high schools.

Another major advantage of a vocational high school is the availability of job placement resources. Guidance counsellors at vocational high schools typically have access to career information and a number of different resources for students who want to find immediate work while attending courses or after they graduate. In addition, many employers and labour unions are closely affiliated with vocational schools, and give preference to job applicants who have completed such programmes. With recommendation from guidance counsellors and teachers, many students are able to obtain paid apprenticeships or entry-level jobs with ease.

What Are the Differences Between Technical and Vocational Training?

While the major difference between technical and vocational training may seem somewhat semantic in nature, it is mostly related to the subjects that each focuses on. Vocational training often refers to education and training that focuses more on practical skills and being able to perform tasks related to working in a particular industry. Technical training is similar in nature, but the focus is on technology and developments made in computers and digital information. While both types of training are less academic and more practical, vocational training often focuses on manufacturing and construction while technical training is more computer-oriented.

The difference between these types of training is somewhat subtle, but it is important. Vocational training is more practical than academic and often focuses on skills and abilities a person needs to perform a job. Much of this training has often been aimed at preparing students for work in construction, manufacturing, and similar jobs that require skilled labour. This type of training can often be found in secondary education, such as the high school level in the US, and post-secondary education as an alternative to college.

As opposed to the manufacturing-oriented vocational training, technical training usually involves computers and advanced technology. This is the primary difference between technical and vocational training, since they both tend to focus on skills and practical ability over academic research or knowledge for its own sake. As a great deal of tasks have been automated and increasingly computerized, technical training has become more important than ever before.

The other major difference is the outlook for each type of training in different countries. In countries like the US, for example, a great deal of effort has been expended to reduce the focus on vocational training in schools as manufacturing jobs have largely been outsourced to other countries. Technical training, on the other hand, has become increasingly important as more and more jobs involve using computers for many tasks and training for such positions has become more specialized. In other countries, however, both forms have expanded as greater opportunities for construction and manufacturing work have developed alongside computer-based work.

What is a Vocational School?

Traditionally, a vocational school, also known as technical education, offered training in careers that require practical expertise. This includes specific trades such as welding, blacksmithing, or mechanics, or more general education geared to the retail or beauty industry. Now, however, more and more vocational schools are now offering courses to cover information technology and the tourism industry.

Other careers that are typical at a vocational school include plumbing, electricity, carpentry, professional locksmithing, floral designer, and motorcycle repair technician. Other careers, which may not be so obvious, include medical transcription and medical insurance clerk, home inspection, professional bridal consultant, veterinary assistant, and hotel/restaurant management.

In the United States, a vocational school is usually post-secondary, with classes being offered through community colleges or institutes of technology. In recent years, it has become standard for a vocational school to offer online certifications, especially in areas where practical experience is not essential.

Many vocational schools are private. Although this is not typical, a vocational school can sometimes take the place of a traditional high school education. Courses such as wood and metal shop and home economics are a good example of vocational courses that are sometimes taught in traditional high schools. Other schools, however, may focus more on this type of courses and less in traditional subjects.

A vocational school is sometimes the best way for an adult to reenter the labour market. Adult education programmes, such as the Work Incentive Programme (WIN) and the Job Corps, are in place for unemployed adults that are currently in welfare and in need of an educational push before they can go out and find a new job. The U.S. Department of Education also provides financial aid for adults wishing to attend vocational school.

Whatever your reason for considering a vocational school, always investigate all options before making a final choice. If you are interested in qualifications and quality of classes, a community college is a great option, but if you prefer a small class size and more hands-on experience, a private vocational school may be a better choice.

What Is Government Vocational Training?

Government vocational training provides residents and citizens of a country with assistance in preparing to go to work as well as training for specific trades and professions. The availability of government vocational training depends on the resources that the government has, and eligibility for these programmes varies by programme policy. Typically, government vocational training is made available to people who are unemployed or who must be retrained for new types of work after a disability or their previous job becomes obsolete. In some cases, the training may also take place in institutions such as prisons or schools. Vocational training classes may be provided directly by government employees, or a government may contract with a private or public school or business to provide training to eligible clients.

In some cases, people may find themselves in need of career direction and assistance in preparing for a new job. Governments may seek to assist these individuals by providing government vocational training. The types of training available depends on a number of factors, including the need for workers in a particular trade or profession in a certain geographic area as well as the cost-effectiveness of providing the training. For example, some government vocational training programmes may offer training in vocations, such as plumbing, in which the trainee must spend several years learning the trade or profession before he or she can practice. In other cases, a vocational training programme may focus on preparing people for careers that do not require a long training programme, such as data entry or medical assisting.

A government vocational training centre may specialize in offering its services to individuals who might have difficulty securing employment, such as those who have recently been released from prison or who have been chronically unemployed for most of their lives. In addition to providing practical instruction in a trade or profession, the programme may also assist participants by offering job placement services and training classes that help job hunters learn how to find a job and successfully remain employed.

In areas with high unemployment, government vocational training may also be available to individuals who may need to enhance their existing job skills or train for a new vocation. In such cases, the government may partner with existing vocational schools, colleges, and universities to provide these training services. Candidates for these programmes may be able to receive this training at no or minimal charge so as to increase their chances of being reemployed.

What is a Vocational Training Scheme?

A vocational training scheme is a formalized step-by-step plan developed between a vocational rehabilitation counsellor and a client seeking new employment. In the US, this vocational training scheme and job search services may be mandated by legislation if a large employer leaves a community taking jobs to another country, or made available to welfare recipients and other low-income individuals. States also provide vocational rehabilitation under state-specific workers compensation laws to citizens injured on-the-job if they are unable to return to their previous occupations. Additionally, states provide vocational training to disabled members of their populations. Any of these vocational training, retraining or rehabilitation programmes — public or private — require an individualized vocational training scheme prior to implementation.

New job seekers are not simply placed into positions in which they feel interested. A great deal of data is collected in order to develop a reasonable job placement plan with a good chance of placement and success. Different types of assessments and tests may be administered to the job seeker, depending upon the position or positions sought, to help guide the process. These evaluations may include aptitude tests, personality evaluations, tests to confirm written and numeric literacy, tests to measure eye-hand coordination and even some hands-on problem-solving evaluations. The results of any or all these tests are included in and help to guide the vocational training scheme.

In addition to a complete educational performance history, a detailed job history is included as part of the vocational training scheme development. A job history is not only helpful in showing the types of positions previously favoured by or available to the job seeker, it is necessary to generate a transferable skills analysis. This type of report lists those skills transferable from job to job and may include concrete skills such as the ability to operate an electronic cash register or a skill less tangible such as the ability to multitask. Similar transferable skills may be required by markedly disparate jobs, allowing individuals to change careers without the necessity of learning as many new skills as one would expect.

Sometimes a vocational training scheme will allow a job "tryout." This period of time — from anywhere to a couple of hours to a couple of weeks — gives an individual the opportunity to determine whether or not the particular career he might have in mind meets his expectations. A vocational training scheme must also contain a labour market survey or some information as to job availability in the individual's chosen field. This information is necessary to justify the time, expense and resources utilized to complete it.

What are the Different Types of Vocational Training Equipment?

Vocational training programmes are as diverse and varied as the careers they train workers to perform. Equipment used in these programmes is also quite varied, and has spun off an entire industry to supply the materials needed for students. Various companies now contract with public and private vocational schools to provide all manner of training and practice equipment, depending upon the school or an industry's needs. Vocational training equipment is similar or identical to the equipment, machines and tools used in the actual occupation. Thus, with the exception of books, paper and pens, training equipment will often vary widely.

In clerical occupations, the vocational training equipment typically used includes many types of office machines in addition to personal computers (PCs) and some of the standard business software programmes. Typewriters, fax machines, 10-key adding machines, copy machines, multi-line telephones and laminators are also practiced on and used in preparation for the eventual occupation. Classroom work may include learning about filing systems, general business etiquette and business letter templates.

Certified nursing assistant or licensed vocational nursing programmes will naturally require different kinds of vocational training equipment. These students will work with durable medical equipment items such as wheelchairs, hospital beds and oxygen tanks in addition to machines to measure and monitor patients' conditions and vital signs. Medical mannequins may be used for practicing cardiopulmonary resuscitation (CPR), the Heimlich maneuver or simply repositioning patients. Classroom work and study is usually extensive.

The vocational training equipment necessary for the building trades includes any number of carpentry tools, both hand and electric versions. For carpenters, the tools will also vary as individuals might specialize in initial or finish carpentry. Apprentice plumbers will also work with plastic, copper and iron pipes, valves and other tools of their trade. Flooring specialists will work with ceramic tiles, wooden flooring pieces, stone pieces, linoleum and carpeting and will therefore require expertise in cutting, laying and adhering these materials.

Automobile mechanic and automotive body repair students will work with vocational training equipment necessary to fix mechanical or automotive body defects. These tools include both hand tools and an increasing number of computerized machines to adjust the computer-based systems of many newer automobiles. Automotive body repairers may also specialize in automotive body painting and the specialized equipment and paint required for vehicles.

What is a Vocational Training Assessment?

A vocational training assessment is a type of test used to evaluate the amount of skill or previous training a person has within a particular vocation. This type of test is often used by a job placement agency to determine the skills and abilities a person has, in order to more accurately place that person in a job that he or she can comfortably perform. A vocational training assessment can also be utilized by a vocational training programme to determine what skills a person has developed. Such assessments are often used as pre-testing or post-testing to evaluate growth and personal skill development.

The purpose of a vocational training assessment can vary somewhat, depending on the context in which the test is given. A job placement agency, for example, is likely to use this type of assessment to evaluate the skills of a particular individual. In this situation, someone is likely to take a vocational training assessment based on his or her individual interests and background. Someone with experience working in the information technology (IT) sector, for example, might take an IT assessment to demonstrate his or her abilities, allowing the agency to better place him or her in an appropriate position.

This type of vocational training assessment is typically created by the agency itself, though it may have input from various employers regarding what is expected or needed. Such tests are commonly divided into several sections, often including a basic skills section as well as various sections for specific background or vocational skills. A vocational training assessment can also be utilized by a potential employer, to ensure that a job candidate can demonstrate the skills or abilities he or she claims to have. Such testing may not be necessary if an applicant has sufficient professional experience, though this depends on individual employers.

A vocational training assessment can also be used by a school or vocational training college. It is likely to be used in a class, and is typically designed by the teacher to gauge the abilities of individual students. A pre-test may be given to students at the start of a class or unit to determine what knowledge the students already possess. After completion of a unit or the class, then students might take another vocational training assessment for post-testing purposes, to determine what they have learned and to evaluate their growth and development.

What Happens at a Vocational Training Centre?

A vocational training centre usually functions a lot like a blend between a school and a career counselling office: within its walls, students take lessons, practice skills and get help with finding and holding a job. This usually involves classes on all sorts of things, from actual trades to more general job skills. Students usually must also do some self-reflection about their futures, usually at the direction of a guidance counsellor or job placement specialist.

Vocational training centres usually enroll students who are interested in pursuing career paths that require a lot of hands-on training. They usually focus all of their teaching energy on preparing people for a specific job, usually a trade. For this reason, a vocational college or vocational school might also be called a trade school.

Rather than taking a range of courses, students at a vocational training centre typically study only what is necessary to do a certain job. They usually graduate with a certificate in their chosen field. Degrees usually are offered only through more comprehensive college-level programmes.

Most of the time, a vocational training centre is focused on one sort of job preparation. Common examples are plumbing and electrical skills, auto repair and medical technician services. Much depends on the target audience, however. Choosing a vocational training centre requires some research into the centre's mission and main audience.

Many vocational training centres are designed specifically for students who have learning or intellectual disabilities, for instance. These kinds of programmes often focus on the creation of arts and marketable crafts or basic skills such as cash register operation and making change. Other programmes are intended primarily for disadvantaged people, particularly those who have not received even a basic education. This sort of vocational training centre is very popular in the developing world, and it often teaches skills such as sewing or small business enterprising.

No matter the focus, classwork makes up the bulk of what happens in a vocational training centre. Students usually spend some time listening to lectures and watching demonstrations, then they have a chance to try the skills by participating in workshops. In most cases, hands-on work comprises the bulk of the learning. Students usually work under the close guidance of their instructors to master each step that is needed to perform their chosen vocation.

Each student usually will have his or her own workspace. For mechanics, this usually involves a shop bench, student in sewing classes will use a sewing machine, and so on. Students are graded and are able to advance by mastering basic steps and demonstrating understanding of foundational concepts. Some schools offer exams, and others require comprehensive projects. Much depends on the school's main mission and structure.

Career counselling usually is also a big part of what happens in a vocational training centre. Students who attend vocational skills programmes almost always do so with the intention of entering a workforce. Training is an important part of getting a job, but it is often only a piece of the process. Schools often offer job hunting seminars and job placement counselling services to help graduates find meaningful work in their new field of expertise. Much of this is tailored to the individual learner or the specifics of the local market.

What are the Different Types of Medical Vocational Training?

Medical vocational training is very popular, particularly in the US and Canada, as healthcare is one of the fastest growing occupational sectors. It is expected to continue its growth rate as the baby boomer population ages and experiences more healthcare needs. Any of these medical or healthcare-related occupations provide excellent opportunities for employment, offer generally average to above-average wages, and only rarely require education beyond an associate's degree. Most fields can be entered with a high school diploma and limited education or training for a certificate. Different types of medical vocational training are usually classified as clerical careers or clinical positions, depending upon the amount of expected patient contact and can include medical records technicians, certified nursing assistants, phlebotomists or medical practice receptionists.

Clerical positions that can form the focus of medical vocational training may range from a hospital telephone operator to a clinical coder specializing in medical insurance reimbursements. Many of these positions can be acquired with a high school diploma and a period of supervised on-the-job training (OJT). Clerical positions that require little educational preparation can include hospital telephone operators, medical practice receptionists or medical practice appointment secretaries. Other positions may require some background in medical terminology; this is the case, for example, for medical records transcribers or physician note recorders. A medical records technician, on the other hand, often requires classes from a community college for certification, and some institutions offer associate's degrees in the field.

Medical vocational training programmes for careers in the clinical fields are quite numerous and all require some type of more specialized training, certification and education because of patient contact and safety issues. These positions range from those requiring a high school diploma and certification to those needing an associate's degree to enter the field. Clinical careers available through medical vocational training that require the least amount of education include certified nursing assistants (CNAs), home health aides, personal trainers and laboratory phlebotomists. Positions such as electrocardiograph (EKG) technicians, medical sonographers, surgical assistants or physical therapy assistants often require some additional training and a certification in the field. The careers requiring the greatest medical vocational training and education to begin include pharmacy technicians, radiological technicians and nuclear medicine technologists.

In the US, some of these careers require licensure by examination following the specified and prerequisite medical vocational training.

Most clinical positions related to patient care also require a satisfactory criminal background check. All educational, training, certification and licensure requirements are readily available from the occupation's national association.

What is a Vocational Training Certificate?

A vocational training certificate is a document that is given upon completion of a training programme that focuses on a more skills-based or vocational education. This type of programme is usually intended for someone who is interested in learning particular skills and abilities needed for certain careers. Rather than completing an education that culminates in a degree, which usually focuses on broad learning with some focus on particular skills, a student can pursue an education from a vocational school. These schools offer programmes that usually culminate in a vocational training certificate and focus more on the specific skills and abilities a person needs to perform a certain job.

The purpose of vocational education in general, and a vocational training certificate specifically, is to demonstrate mastery of certain skills. This has increasingly become accepted as an effective way for a student to receive training in certain fields, though this often depends on the career chosen. A programme that results in a vocational training certificate is usually shorter than other degree-granting curricula, though an associate's degree might be received in about the same amount of time. The focus of such a programme, however, can be quite different and may be a better choice for some students.

A vocational education usually focuses on the skills necessary to be employed within a certain career. Students pursuing a degree usually enroll at a school that offers a curriculum that focuses on overall education, to ensure that someone has a broad and well-rounded understanding of scholarly subjects. While this is certainly effective for many students, others may find it difficult to stay focused on their chosen field while studying other subjects. Someone interested in becoming a commercial electrician, for example, may prefer to pursue a vocational training certificate rather than a degree, since the certificate is often faster and more relevant to his or her interests.

While students may receive some additional education in subjects like writing and business, most courses in a vocational programme focus on the skills and knowledge they need to work in their chosen industry. Once this programme is completed to a satisfactory level, as established by a particular school, then a student can graduate and receive a vocational training certificate instead of a diploma. This does not typically grant a particular degree to a student, but instead indicates to potential employers that the graduate has received training necessary to be an effective addition to their workforce. Different schools can set various requirements for completion of a programme and issuing of a vocational training certificate, though it usually involves completing classes and may require some apprenticeship work.

What are the Different Types of Adult Vocational Training?

Adult vocational training prepares an adult to pursue a vocation or job. Welding, computer sciences and culinary arts are all vocations that can be trained for at the adult level. Other popular adult vocational training courses are medical billing and assistant, office skills and professional health care worker, and many of these training programmes qualify for loans and assistance in many areas of the world. Roles such as cosmetologist, dental assistant and pharmacy technician are all vocations covered by the adult training field. Floral design, restaurant manager and truck driver are skills and careers that can be obtained through attending a quality adult vocational training programme.

Unlike a typical college background that educates students in a wide area of knowledge, adult vocational training adheres specifically to the requirements of a single aspect or skill to provide the required knowledge to begin a career in that field. In many cases, the students attending adult vocational training need not have a high-school diploma. The training is commonly seen as an alternative to working an entry-level job that has no promise of advancement. Students typically receive a certificate of completion upon graduating the training and are prepared to enter the workforce as trained specialists.

Many adult students enter adult vocational training in order to pursue a dream of owning their own business. Cosmetology and welding are two fields in which an adult can begin a home-operated business with little overhead. These businesses can quickly develop into a larger interest, requiring an off-site location capable of employing other workers. Other vocational training, such as floral design and culinary arts, can be obtained to both begin a career in the field as well as to simply enjoy and practice the mastered skills around the home. Other vocational fields, such as truck driving, can be a means for the adult student to seek adventure and see more of the world.

Most vocations require a certification to allow a graduate to begin employment. Any adult vocational training programme should be investigated to ensure that the programme offers the proper certification once completed. Vocations, such as cosmetology and pharmacy, also require licensing in order to begin a career and the programme must be accredited in order to provide this licensing in most areas. For many individuals, taking adult vocational training is a way to continue providing for a family in very difficult economic times.

What are the Advantages of a Vocational Curriculum?

A vocational curriculum provides training in a specific field or industry. Rather than focusing on academic education, a vocational curriculum tends to place emphasis on trade skills and preparing to enter the job field. For people absolutely certain of their career goals, a vocational curriculum may be the start to a long term, fulfilling career. Vocational schools can be found for many different fields that require technical skills rather than academic or intellectual knowledge. Often, schools with a vocational emphasis, also known as trade schools, offer certificates of completion upon fulfilling class requirements, rather than an academic degree. Some major industries that rely on vocational training include mechanics, information technology, beauty and fashion, tourism, and secretarial or office work.

A vocational curriculum allows students to focus solely on training for a career in their chosen field. Rather than confuse students with general education requirements or requisite classes outside their major, trade schools and programmes are geared toward turning out competent professionals quickly. For this reason, schools with a vocational curriculum are popular for adults looking to change careers as they often promise quick and directed training meant to result in job qualifications.

Another major advantage to a vocational curriculum is that the programmes are often flexible and available from a variety of sources. Many community colleges offer certificate programmes designed to function as a trade school, which can be far less expensive than a university education or private vocational school. Community colleges are usually very open and welcoming environments with students of all ages, allowing adults taking career training to feel more comfortable in a school atmosphere despite having been away from school for many years.

Private vocational schools often feature flexible class schedules that benefit people with jobs or families to care for. While at a community college, classes may not be available every semester, private schools are more likely to offer a consistent programme to students. In addition, many private schools offer vocational curriculum primarily through online classes, allowing students to complete work at their leisure and on their own schedules.

In the United States, private schools make up the bulk of vocational training programmes, but this is not universal. Many other countries offer trade school as a viable alternative to university and may even offer intense vocational training at the secondary or high school level. Government funding is frequently available for students attending vocational schools, as it is often in the interest of the state to have a base of skilled professionals. Check with state and federal agencies to see if any funds are available to assist with financial aid.

What are Vocational Qualifications?

Vocational qualifications are all the necessary requirements that must be met in order to be permitted to hold certain positions or jobs in society. Credible organizations and legal institutions set these standards for the purposes of maintaining uniformity of a profession, as well as to protect people who may seek out the services of such professionals. Licensing, certification, and educational training are a few general examples of different types of vocational qualifications.

Frequently required as part of vocational qualifications, licensing and certification in certain fields ensure safety of the public, as they prove credibility to serve in a particular capacity. Those working in legal fields as attorneys and barristers pass examinations qualifying them to offer services to people in the countries and regions where they are allowed to practice. Nurses are also licensed and, upon further experience and successful examination, may receive additional certifications in speciality areas of practice such as oncology and pediatrics.

To be able to be a member of a particular occupation, it is necessary to understand what it is that entails the duties of the profession. A thorough breadth of knowledge may be needed depending upon the career field as some require short durations of study, as others want several years of preparation. Schools exist to teach and train individuals to receive vocational qualifications from colleges, universities, and trade institutions all over the world. Undergraduate degrees encompass generalized educational courses along with completion of major studies, while, at the graduate level, the student is expected to build upon previous knowledge as study becomes more specialized.

Professional schools offer speciality training at the graduate level, typically included in vocational qualifications for lawyers, doctors, and business occupations. These particular educational institutions outline certain guidelines for entrance, most of which require applicants to already possess a bachelor's degree, above-average grades, and sometimes completion of prerequisite courses. Additionally, professional schools expect students to demonstrate their academic aptitude and ability by taking an examination as a part of qualifying for admission. The General Record Examination (GRE) and the Medical College Admissions Test (MCAT) are examples of such assessments.

Provided by organizations responsible for oversight and setting standards for vocations, including various healthcare professions, a specific type of programme accreditation is essential for meeting certain vocational obligations. For example, to receive a nursing license in certain countries like the U.S. and Canada, candidates must have been trained at an educational institution accredited by the Commission on Collegiate Nursing Education (CCNE) or Canadian Association of Schools of Nursing (CASN), respectively. Without the required type of accreditation, licensing is typically unobtainable.

Vocation

A vocation is an occupation to which a person is specially drawn or for which he or she is suited, trained, or qualified. Though now often used in non-religious contexts, the meanings of the term originated in Christianity.

Senses

Use of the word "vocation" before the sixteenth century referred firstly to the "call" by God to the individual, or calling of all humankind to salvation, particularly in the Vulgate, and more specifically to the "vocation to the priesthood", which is still the usual sense in Roman Catholicism. Roman Catholicism recognizes marriage and virginity or celibacy as the two vocations. Martin Luther, followed by John Calvin, placed a particular emphasis on vocations, or divine callings, as potentially including most secular occupations, though this idea was by no means new.

Calvinism developed complex ideas about different types of vocations of the first type, connected with the concepts of Predestination, Irresistible grace, and the elect. There are the *vocatio universalis*, the *vocatio specialis*, only extended to some. There were also complex distinctions between internal and external, and the "vocatio efficax" and "inefficax" types of callings. Hyper-Calvinism, unusually, rejects the idea of a "universal call" to repent and believe, held by virtually all other Christian groups.

In Protestantism the call from God to devote one's life to him by joining the clergy is often covered by the English equivalent term "call", whereas in Roman Catholicism "vocation" is still used.

Both senses of the word "call" are used in 1 Corinthians 7:20, where Paul says "Let every man abide in the same calling wherein he was called" (KJV).

Concept

The idea of vocation is central to the Christian belief that God has created each person with gifts and talents oriented toward specific purposes and a way of life. In the broadest sense, as stated in the Catechism of the Catholic Church, "*Love* is the fundamental and innate vocation of every human being" (CCC 2392). More specifically, in the Orthodox and Catholic Churches, this idea of vocation is especially associated with a divine call to service to the Church and humanity through particular vocational life commitments such as marriage to a particular person, consecration as a religious, ordination to priestly ministry in the Church and even a holy life as a single person. In the broader sense, Christian vocation includes the use of one's gifts in their profession, family life, church and civic commitments for the sake of the greater common good.

Christian Views on Work

Many Christian theologians appeal to the Old Testment Book of Genesis in regards to work. According to Genesis 1, human beings were created in the image of God, and according to Genesis 2, Adam was placed in the Garden of Eden to "work it and keep it" (2:15, ESV). Dorothy L. Sayers has argued that "work is the natural exercise and function of man – the creature who is made in the image of his Creator." Likewise, John Paul II said in *Laborem Exercens* that by his work, man shares in the image of his Creator.

Christian theologians see the Fall of man profoundly affecting human work. In Genesis 3:17, God said to Adam, "cursed is the ground because of you; in pain you shall eat of it all the days of your life" (ESV). Leland Ryken points out that, because of the Fall, "many of the tasks we perform in a fallen world are inherently distasteful and wearisome." Through the Fall, work has become toil, but John Paul II says that work is a good thing for man in spite of this toil, and "perhaps, in a sense, because of it" because work is something that corresponds to man's dignity and through it he achieves fulfilment as a human being. The Fall also means that a work ethic is needed. As a result of the Fall work has become subject to the abuses of idleness on the one hand, and overwork on the other. Drawing on Aristotle, Ryken suggests that the moral ideal is the golden mean between the two extremes of being lazy and being a workaholic.

Some Christian theologians also draw on the doctrine of redemption to discuss the concept of work. Oliver O'Donovan points out that although work is a gift of creation, it is "ennobled into mutual service in the fellowship of Christ."

Leland Ryken argues for seeing the call of God to a particular occupation as a reflection of the gospel call, and suggests that this implies vocational loyalty – "modern notions of job become deficient" and "the element of arbitrariness of one's choice of work" is removed.

Apprenticeship

Apprenticeship is a system of training a new generation of practitioners of a structured competency a basic set of skills. Apprenticeships ranged from craft occupations or trades to those seeking a professional license to practice in a regulated profession. Apprentices (or in early modern usage "prentices") or protégés build their careers from apprenticeships. Most of their training is done while working for an employer who helps the apprentices learn their trade or profession, in exchange for their continuing labour for an agreed period after they have achieved measurable competencies. For more advanced apprenticeships, theoretical education was also involved, with jobs and farming over a period of 4–6 years.

To be successful, the individual must have perseverance, ambition, and initiative. Like a college education, the successful completion of an apprenticeship term does not come easily, but is the result of hard work on the part of the apprentice. In practically every skilled occupation, more than fundamental knowledge of arithmetic is essential. The ability to read, write and speak well is beneficial in any walk of life, but in some apprenticeship occupations it is more important than in others.

Development

The system of apprenticeship first developed in the later Middle Ages and came to be supervised by craft guilds and town governments. A master craftsman was entitled to employ young people as an inexpensive form of labour in exchange for providing food, lodging and formal training in the craft. Most apprentices were males, but female apprentices were found in crafts such as seamstress, tailor, cordwainer, baker and stationer. Apprentices usually began at ten to fifteen years of age, and would live in the master craftsman's household. Most apprentices aspired to becoming master craftsmen themselves on completion of their contract (usually a term of seven years), but some would spend time as a journeyman and a significant proportion would never acquire their own workshop.

In Coventry those completing seven-year apprenticeships with stuff merchants were entitled to become freemen of the city.

Subsequently governmental regulation and the licensing of technical colleges and vocational education formalized and bureaucratized the details of apprenticeship.

Analogs at Universities and Professional Development

The modern concept of an internship is similar to an apprenticeship. Universities still use apprenticeship schemes in their production of scholars: bachelors are promoted to masters and then produce a thesis under the oversight of a supervisor before the corporate body of the university recognises the achievement of the standard of a doctorate. Another view of this system is of graduate students in the role of apprentices, post-doctoral fellows as journeymen, and professors as masters.

Also similar to apprenticeships are the professional development arrangements for new graduates in the professions of accountancy, Chartered Engineer and the law. A British example was training contracts known as 'articles of clerkship'. The learning curve in modern professional service firms, such as law firms or accountancies, generally resembles the traditional master-apprentice model: the newcomer to the firm is assigned to one or several more experienced colleagues (ideally partners in the firm) and learns his skills on the job.

Australia

Australian Apprenticeships encompass all apprenticeships and traineeships. They cover all industry sectors in Australia and are used to achieve both 'entry-level' and career 'upskilling' objectives. There were 470,000 Australian Apprentices in-training as at 31 March 2012, an increase of 2.4% from the previous year. Australian Government employer and employee incentives may be applicable, while State and Territory Governments may provide public funding support for the training element of the initiative. Australian Apprenticeships combine time at work with formal training and can be full-time, part-time or school-based.

Information and resources on potential apprenticeship and traineeship occupations are available in over sixty industries.

The distinction between the terms apprentices and trainees lies mainly around traditional trades and the time it takes to gain a qualification. The Australian government uses Australian Apprenticeships Centres to administer and facilitate Australian Apprenticeships so that funding can be disseminated to eligible businesses and apprentices and trainees and to support the whole process as it underpins the future skills of Australian industry. Australia also has a fairly unique safety net in place for businesses and Australian Apprentices with its Group Training scheme. This is where businesses that are not able to employ the Australian Apprentice for the full period until they qualify, are able to lease or hire the Australian Apprentice from a Group Training Organisation. It is a safety net, because the Group Training Organisation is the employer and provides continuity of employment and training for the Australian Apprentice.

In addition to a safety net, Group Training Organisations (GTO) have other benefits such as additional support for both the Host employer and the trainee/apprentice through an industry consultant who visits regularly to make sure that the trainee/apprentice are fulfilling their work and training obligations with their Host employer. There is the additional benefit of the trainee/apprentice being employed by the GTO reducing the Payroll/Superannuation and other legislative requirements on the Host employer who pays as invoiced per agreement.

Austria

Apprenticeship Training in Austria is organized in a Dual education system: company-based training of apprentices is complemented by compulsory attendance of a part-time vocational school for apprentices (Berufsschule). It lasts two to four years – the duration varies among the 250 legally recognized apprenticeship trades.

About 40 percent of all Austrian teenagers enter apprenticeship training upon completion of compulsory education (at age 15). This number has been stable since the 1950s.

The five most popular trades are: Retail Salesperson (5,000 people complete this apprenticeship per year), Clerk (3,500 / year), Car

Mechanic (2,000 / year), Hairdresser (1,700 / year), Cook (1,600 / year). There are many smaller trades with small numbers of apprentices, like "EDV-Systemtechniker" (Sysadmin) which is completed by fewer than 100 people a year.

The Apprenticeship Leave Certificate provides the apprentice with access to two different vocational careers. On the one hand, it is a prerequisite for the admission to the Master Craftsman Exam and for qualification tests, and on the other hand it gives access to higher education via the TVE-Exam or the Higher Education Entrance Exam which are prerequisites for taking up studies at colleges, universities, "Fachhochschulen", post-secondary courses and post-secondary colleges.

The person responsible for overseeing the training inside the company is called "Lehrherr" or "Ausbilder". An Ausbilder must prove he has the professional qualifications needed to educate another person. The "Ausbilder" must also prove he does not have a criminal record and is an otherwise respectable person. According to the laws: *the person wanting to educate a young apprentice must prove that he has an ethical way of living and the civic qualities of a good citizen.*

Switzerland

Switzerland has an apprenticeship similarly to Germany and Austria. The educational system is ternar, which is basically Dual education system with mandatory practical courses. The length of an apprenticeship can be 2, 3 or 4 years.

Length

Apprenticeship with a length of 2 years are for persons with weaker school results. The certificated after successfully completing an 2 year apprenticeship is called "Eidgenössisches Berufsattest" (EBA).

Apprenticeship with a length of 3 or 4 years are the most common ones. The certificated after successfully completing an 3 or 4 year apprenticeship is called "Certificat Fédérale de Capacité" (CFC) or "Eidgenössisches Fähigkeitszeugnis" (EFZ).

Some crafts like Electrician are educated in length of 3 and 4 years. In this case, an Electrician with 4 years apprenticeship gets more theoretical background than one with 3 years apprenticeship. Also, but that is easily lost in translation, the profession has a different name.

Each of the over 300 nationwide defined vocational profiles has defined framework - conditions as length of education, theoreticla and practical learning goals and certification conditions.

Age of the Apprentices

Typically an apprenticeship is started at age of 15 and 18 after finishing general education. Some apprenticeships have a recommend or required age of 18, which obviously leads to a higher average age. There is formally no maximum age, however for persons above 21 it is hard to find company.

Canada

In Canada, each province has its own apprenticeship programme. At the completion of the provincial exam they may write the Interprovincal Standard exam. British Columbia is one province that uses these exams as the provincial exam. This means a qualification for the province will satisfy the whole country. The interprovincal exam questions are agreed upon by all provinces.

France

In France, apprenticeships also developed between the ninth and thirteenth centuries, with guilds structured around apprentices, journeymen and master craftsmen, continuing in this way until 1791, when the guilds were suppressed.

The first laws regarding apprenticeships were passed in 1851. From 1919, young people had to take 150 hours of theory and general lessons in their subject a year. This minimum training time rose to 360 hours a year in 1961, then 400 in 1986.

The first training centres for apprentices (*centres de formation d'apprentis*, CFAs) appeared in 1961, and in 1971 apprenticeships were legally made part of professional training. In 1986 the age limit for beginning an apprenticeship was raised from 20 to 25. From 1987 the range of qualifications achieveable through an apprenticeship was widened to include the *brevet professionnel* (certificate of vocational aptitude), the *bac professionnel* (vocational baccalaureate diploma), the *brevet de technicien supérieur* (advanced technician's certificate), engineering diplomas, masters degree and more.

On January 18, 2005, President Jacques Chirac announced the introduction of a law on a programme for social cohesion comprising the three pillars of employment, housing and equal opportunities. The French government pledged to further develop apprenticeship as a path to success at school and to employment, based on its success: in 2005, 80% of young French people who had completed an apprenticeship entered employment. In France, the term apprenticeship often denotes manual labour but it also include other jobs like secretary, manager, engineer, shop assistant... The plan aimed to raise the number of apprentices from 365,000 in 2005 to 500,000 in 2009. To achieve this aim, the government is, for example, granting tax relief for companies when they take on apprentices. (Since 1925 a tax has been levied to pay for apprenticeships.)

The minister in charge of the campaign, Jean-Louis Borloo, also hoped to improve the image of apprenticeships with an information campaign, as they are often connected with academic failure at school and an ability to grasp only practical skills and not theory. After the civil unrest end of 2005, the government, led by prime minister Dominique de Villepin, announced a new law. Dubbed "law on equality of chances", it created the First Employment Contract as well as manual apprenticeship from as early as 14 years of age. From this age, students are allowed to quit the compulsory school system in order to quickly learn a vocation. This measure has long been a policy of conservative French political parties, and was met by tough opposition from trade unions and students.

Germany

Apprenticeships are part of Germany's dual education system, and as such form an integral part of many people's working life. Finding employment without having completed an apprenticeship is almost impossible. For some particular technical university professions, such as food technology, a completed apprenticeship is often recommended; for some, such as marine engineering it may even be mandatory.

In Germany, there are 342 recognized trades (*Ausbildungsberufe*) where an apprenticeship can be completed. They include for example doctor's assistant, banker, dispensing optician, plumber or oven builder. The dual system means that apprentices spend about 50-70% of their time in companies and the rest in formal education. Depending on the profession, they may work for three to four days a week in the company and then spend one or two days at a vocational school (*Berufsschule*). This is usually the case for trade and craftspeople. For other professions, usually which require more theoretical learning, the working and school times take place blockwise e.g. in a 12–18 weeks interval. These *Berufsschulen* have been part of the education system since the 19th century.

In 2001, two thirds of young people aged under 22 began an apprenticeship, and 78% of them completed it, meaning that approximately 51% of all young people under 22 have completed an apprenticeship. One in three companies offered apprenticeships in 2003, in 2004 the government signed a pledge with industrial unions that all companies except very small ones must take on apprentices.

The latent decrease of the German population due to low birth rates is now causing a lack of young people available to start an apprenticeship.

Apprenticeship After General Education

After graduation from school at the age of fifteen to nineteen (depending on type of school), students start an apprenticeship in their chosen professions. Realschule and Gymnasium graduates usually have better chances for being accepted as an apprentice for sophisticated craft professions or apprenticeships in white-collar jobs in finance or administration. An apprenticeship takes between 2.5 and 3.5 years. Originally, at the beginning of the 20th century, less than 1% of German students attended the Gymnasium (the 8-9 year university-preparatory school) to obtain the Abitur graduation which was the only way to university back then. In the 1950 still only 5% of German youngsters entered university and in 1960 only 6% did. Due to the risen social wealth and the increased demand for academic professionals in Germany, about 24% of the youngsters entered college/university in 2000. Of those, who did not enter university many started an apprenticeship. The apprenticeships usually end a person's education by age 18-20, but also older apprentices are accepted by the employers under certain conditions. This is frequently the case for immigrants from countries without a compatible professional training system.

History

In 1969, a law (the *Berufsbildungsgesetz*) was passed which regulated and unified the vocational training system and codified the shared responsibility of the state, the unions, associations and the chambers of trade and industry. The dual system was successful in both parts of the divided Germany. In the GDR, three quarters of the working population had completed apprenticeships.

Business and Administrative Professions

The precise skills and theory taught on German apprenticeships are strictly regulated. The employer is responsible for the entire education programme coordinated by the German chamber of commerce. Apprentices obtain a special apprenticeship contract until the end of the education programme. During the programme it is not allowed to assign the apprentice to a regularly employment and he is well protected from abrupt dismissal until the programme ends. The defined content and skillset of the apprentice profession must be fully provided and taught by the employer. The time taken is also regulated. Each profession takes a different time, usually between 24 and 36 months.

Thus, everyone who had completed an apprenticeship e.g. as an industrial manager (*Industriekaufmann*) has learned the same skills and has attended the same courses in procurement and stocking up, controlling, staffing, accounting procedures, production planning, terms of trade and transport logistics and various other subjects. Someone who has not taken this apprenticeship or did not pass the final examinations at the chamber of industry and commerce is not allowed to call himself an *Industriekaufmann*. Most job titles are legally standardized and restricted. An employment in such function in any company would require this completed degree.

Trade and Craft Professions

The rules and laws for the trade and craftswork apprentices such as mechanics, bakers, joiners, etc. are as strict as and even broader than for the business professions. The involved procedures, titles and traditions still strongly reflect the medieval origin of the system. Here, the average duration is about 36 months, some specialized crafts even take up to 42 months.

After completion of the dual education, e.g. a baker is allowed to call himself a bakery journeyman (*Bäckergeselle*). After the apprenticeship the journeyman can enter the master's school (*Meisterschule*) and continue his education at evening courses for 3–4 years or full-time for about one year. The graduation from the master's school leads to the title of a master craftsman (*Meister*) of his profession, so e.g. a bakery master is entitled as *Bäckermeister*. A master is officially entered in the local trade register, the craftspeople's roll (*Handwerksrolle*). A master craftsman is allowed to employ and to train new apprentices. In some mostly safety-related professions, e.g. that of electricians only a master is allowed to found his own company.

License for Educating Apprentices

To employ and to educate apprentices requires a specific license. The AdA - *Ausbildung der Ausbilder* - "Education of the Educators" license needs to be acquired by a training at the chamber of industry and commerce.

The masters complete this license course within their own master's coursework. The training and examination of new masters is only possible for masters who have been working several years in their profession and who have been accepted by the chambers as a trainer and examiner.

Academic professionals, e.g. engineers, seeking this license need to complete the AdA during or after their university studies, usually by a one-year evening course.

The holder of the license is only allowed to train apprentices within his own field of expertise. For example a mechanical engineer would be able to educate industrial mechanics, but not e.g. laboratory assistants or civil builders.

After the Apprenticeship of Trade and Craft Professions

When the apprenticeship is ended, the former apprentice now is considered a journeyman. He may choose to go on his journeyman years-travels.

India

In India, the Apprentices Act was enacted in 1961. It regulates the programme of training of apprentices in the industry so as to conform to the syllabi, period of training etc. as laid down by the Central Apprenticeship Council and to utilise fully the facilities available in industry for imparting practical training with a view to meeting the requirements of skilled manpower for industry. The Apprentices Act enacted in 1961 and was implemented effectively in 1962. Initially the Act envisaged training of trade apprentices. The Act was amended in 1973 to include training of graduate and diploma engineers as "Graduate" & "Technician" Apprentices. The Act was further amended in 1986 to bring within its purview the training of the 10+2 vocational stream as "Technician (Vocational)" Apprentices.

Overall responsibility is with the Directorate General of Employment & Training (DGE&T) in the Union Ministry of Labour. DGE&T is also responsible for implementation of the Act in respect of Trade Apprentices in the Central Govt. Undertakings & Departments. This is done through six Regional Directorates of Apprenticeship Training located at Kolkata, Mumbai, Chennai, Hyderabad, Kanpur & Faridabad.

State Apprenticeship Advisers are responsible for implementation of the Act in respect of Trade Apprentices in State Government Undertakings/ Departments and Private Establishments. Department of Education in the Ministry of HRD is responsible for implementation of the Act in respect of Graduate, Technician & Technician (Vocational) Apprentices. This is done through four Boards of Apprenticeship Training located at Kanpur, Kolkata, Mumbai & Chennai.1

Pakistan

In Pakistan, special apprenticeship programmes running to fulfill the needs of IT industry in the coming years. So, for this purpose Pakistan Software Export Board formerly PSEB has launched a very attractive programme for young IT graduates.

Under the IT Industry Apprenticeship Programme, PSEB offers financial subsidy for the companies to recruit graduates possessing the basic skills and knowledge in Information Technology and other related disciplines to provide IT/ITeS services.

These recruits, generally graduates with some experience rather than traditional apprentices, are hired by companies as full-time employees and put through a 12-month programme, consisting of in-company training, on-the-job training and mentoring. Since its launch, the IT Industry Apprenticeship Programme has been awarded to 7 companies, approved by PSEB and ICT R&D Fund's Project Committee, which will result in the creation of over 700 job opportunities in the IT industry.

Turkey

In Turkey, apprenticeship has been part of the small business culture for centuries since the time of Seljuk Turks who claimed Anatolia as their homeland in 11th century.

There are three levels of apprenticeship. First level is the apprentice, i.e. the "çýrak" in Turkish. The second level is pre-master which is called, "kalfa" in Turkish. The mastery level is called as "usta" and is the highest level of achievement. An 'usta' is eligible to take in and accept new 'ciraks' to train and bring them up.

The training process usually starts when the small boy is of age 10-11 and becomes a full grown master at the age of 20-25. Many years of hard work and disciplining under the authority of the master is the key to the young apprentice's education and learning process.

In Turkey today there are many vocational schools that train children to gain skills to learn a new profession. The student after graduation looks for a job at the nearest local marketplace usually under the authority of a master.

United Kingdom

Early History: Apprenticeships have a long tradition in the United Kingdom, dating back to around the 12th century and flourishing by the 14th century. The parents or guardians of a minor would agree with a Guild's Master craftsman the conditions for an apprenticeship which would bind the minor for 5–9 years (e.g. from age 14 to 21). They would pay a premium to the craftsman and the contract would be recorded in an indenture. In 1563, the Statute of Artificers and Apprentices was passed to regulate and protect the apprenticeship system, forbidding anyone from practising a trade or craft without first serving a 7-year period as an apprentice to a master (though in practice Freemen's sons could negotiate shorter terms).

From 1601, 'parish' apprenticeships under the Elizabethan Poor Law came to be used as a way of providing for poor, illegitimate and orphaned children of both sexes alongside the regular system of skilled apprenticeships, which tended to provide for boys from slightly more affluent backgrounds. These parish apprenticeships, which could be created with the assent of two Justices of the Peace, supplied apprentices for occupations of lower status such as farm labouring, brickmaking and menial household service.

In the early years of the Industrial Revolution entrepreneurs began to resist the restrictions of the apprenticeship system, and a legal ruling established that the Statute of Apprentices did not apply to trades that were not in existence when it was passed in 1563, thus excluding many new 18th century industries. In 1814 compulsory apprenticeship by indenture was abolished.

System Introduced in 1964

The mainstay of training in industry has been the apprenticeship system, and the main concern has been to avoid skill shortages in traditionally skilled occupations and higher technician and engineering professionals, e.g. through the UK Industry Training Boards (ITBs) set up under the 1964 Act. The aims were to ensure an adequate supply of training at all levels; to improve the quality and quantity of training; and to share the costs of training among employers. The ITBs were empowered to publish training recommendations, which contained full details of the tasks to be learned, the syllabus to be followed, the standards to be reached and vocational courses to be followed. These were often accompanied by training manuals, which were in effect practitioners' guides to apprentice training, and some ITBs provide training in their own centres. The ITBs did much to formalize what could have been a haphazard training experience and greatly improved its quality. The years from the mid-1960s to the mid-1970s saw the highest levels of apprentice recruitment, yet even so, out of a school leaving cohort of about 750,000, only about 110,000 (mostly boys) became apprentices. The apprenticeship system aimed at highly developed craft and higher technician skills for an elite minority of the workforce, the majority of whom were trained in industries that declined rapidly from 1973 onwards, and by the 1980s it was clear that in manufacturing this decline was permanent.

Since the 1950s the UK high technology industry (Aerospace, Nuclear, Oil & Gas, Automotive, Telecommunications, Power Generation and Distribution etc.) trained its higher technicians and professional engineers via the traditional indentured apprenticeship system of learning - usually a 4 - 6 year process from age 16–21.

There were 4 types of traditional apprenticeship; craft, technician, higher technician, and graduate. Craft, technician and higher technician apprenticeships usually took 4 to 5 years while a graduate apprenticeship was a short 2 year experience usually while at university or post graduate experience. Non graduate technician apprenticeships were often referred to as technical apprenticeships.

The traditional Apprenticeship Framework in the 1950s, 60's and 70's was designed to allow young people (16 years old) an alternative path to GCE A Levels to achieve both an academic qualification at level 4 or 5 NVQ along with competency based skills for knowledge work. Often referred to as the "Golden Age" of work and employment for bright young people, the traditional technical apprenticeship framework was open to young people who had a minimum of 4 GCE "O" Levels to enroll in an Ordinary National Certificate or Diploma or a City & Guilds engineering technician course. Apprentices could progress to the Higher National Certificate, Higher National Diploma or advanced City and Guilds course such as Full Technological Certification.

Apprenticeship positions at elite companies often had hundreds of applications for a placement. Academic learning during an apprenticeship was achieved either via block release or day release at a local technical institute. An OND or HND were usually obtained via the block release approach whereby an apprentice would be released for periods of up to 3 months to study academic courses full-time and then return to the employer for applied work experience. For entrance into the higher technical engineering apprenticeships "O"Levels had to include Mathematics, Physics, and English language. The academic level of subjects such as mathematics, physics, chemistry on ONC / OND and some City & Guilds advanced technicians courses was equivalent to A level mathematics, physics and chemistry. The academic science subjects were based on applied science in subjects such as thermodynamics, fluid mechanics, mechanics of machines, dynamics and statics, electrical science and electronics.

These are often referred to as the engineering sciences . HNC and HND were broadly equivalent to subjects in the first year of a Bachelors degree in engineering but not studied to the same intensity or mathematical depth. HNC was accepted as entrance into the first year of an engineering degree and high performance on an HND course could allow a student direct entry into the second year of a degree. Few apprentices followed this path since it would have meant 10 –12 years in further and higher education. For the few that did follow this path they accomplished a solid foundation of competency based work training via apprenticeship and attained a higher academic qualifications at a university or Polytechnic combining both forms of education; vocational plus academic. During the 1970s City and Guilds assumed responsibility for the administration of HNC and HND courses.

The City and Guilds of London Institute the forerunner of Imperial College engineering school has been offering vocational education through apprenticeships since the 1870s from basic craft skills (mechanic, hairdresser, chef, plumbing, carpentry, bricklaying etc.) all the way up to qualifications equivalent to university masters degrees and doctorates. The City and Guilds diploma of fellowship is awarded to individuals who are nationally recognized through peer review as having achieved the very highest level in competency based achievement. The first award of FCGI was approved by Council in December 1892 and awarded in 1893 to Mr H A Humphrey, Engineering Manager of the Refined Bicarbonate and Crystal Plant Departments of Messrs Brunner, Mond & Co. His award was for material improvements in the manufacture of bicarbonate of soda. The system of nomination was administered within Imperial College, with recommendations being passed to the Council of the Institute for approval. Approximately 500 plus people have been awarded Fellowship since its inception.

The traditional apprenticeship framework's purpose was to provide a supply of young people seeking to enter work-based learning via apprenticeships by offering structured high value learning and transferable skills and knowledge. Apprenticeship training was enabled by linking industry with local technical colleges and professional engineering institutions. The apprenticeship framework offered a clear pathway and competency outcomes that addressed the issues facing the industry sector and specific companies. This system was in place since the 1950s. The system provided young people with an alternative to staying in full-time education post- 16/18 to gain purely academic qualifications without work-based learning. The apprenticeship system of the 1950s 60's and 70's provided the necessary preparation for young people to qualify as a Craft trade (Machinist, Toolmaker, Fitter, Plumber, Welder, Mechanic, Millwright etc.), or Technician (quality inspector, draughtsman, designer, planner, work study, programmer,or Technician Engineer (tool design, product design, methods, stress and structural analysis, machine design etc.) and even enabled a path to full Chartered Engineer registration (Mechanical, Electrical, Civil. Aeronautical, Chemical, Manufacturing etc.). Chartered Engineer registration was usually achieved in the late 20's early 30's. Apprentices undertook a variety of job roles in numerous shop floor and office technical functions to assist the work of master craftsmen, technicians, engineers, and managers in the design, development, manufacture and maintenance of products and production systems.

It was possible for apprentices to progress from national certificates and diplomas to engineering degrees if they had the aptitude. Reference "The social production of technical work: the case of British engineers" Peter Whalley, SUNY Press 1986. The system allowed young people to find their level and still achieve milestones along the path from apprenticeship into higher education via a polytechnic or university. Though rare, it was possible for an apprentice to advance from vocational studies, to undergraduate degree, to graduate study and earn a masters degree or a PhD. The system was effective; industry was assured of a supply of well educated and fit for work staff, local technical colleges offered industry relevant courses that had a high measure of academic content and an apprentice was prepared for professional life or higher education by the age of 21. With the exception of advanced technology companies particularly in aerospace (BAE systems, Rolls Royce, Bombardier) this system declined with the decline of general manufacturing industry in the UK.

Traditional apprenticeships reached their lowest point in the 1980s: by that time, training programmes declined. The exception to this was in the high technology engineering areas of aerospace, chemicals, nuclear, automotive, power and energy systems where apprentices continued to served the structured four- to five-year programmes of both practical and academic study to qualify as engineering technician or Incorporate Engineer (engineering technologist) and even go on to earn a master of engineering degree and qualify as a Chartered Engineer; the UK gold standard engineering qualification. Engineering technicians and technologists continued in the traditional approach from the golden age attended the local technical college (1 day and 2 evenings per week) on a City & Guilds programme or Ordinary National Certificate / Higher National Certificate course. In effect becoming a chartered engineer via the apprenticeship route involved 10 – 12 years of both academic and vocational training at an employer, college of further education and university. In 1986 National Vocational Qualifications (NVQs) were introduced, in an attempt to revitalize vocational training. Still, by 1990, apprenticeship took up only two-thirds of one percent of total employment.

Revitalisation From 1990s on

In 1994, the Government introduced Modern Apprenticeships (since renamed 'Apprenticeships' in England, Wales and Northern Ireland; Scotland has retained Modern Apprenticeship), based on frameworks that are now devised by Sector Skills Councils. Apprenticeship frameworks contain a number of separately certified elements:

- a knowledge-based element, typically certified through a qualification known as a 'Technical Certificate' (this component is not mandatory in the Scottish Modern Apprenticeship);
- a competence-based element, typically certified through an NVQ (in Scotland this can be through an SVQ or an alternative Competence Based Qualification);
- Key Skills (in Scotland, Core Skills); and
- Employment Rights and Responsibilities (known as ERR) to show that the Apprentice has had a full induction to the company or training programme, and is aware of those right and responsibilities that are essential in the workplace; this usually requires the creation of a personal portfolio of activities, reading and instruction sessions, but is not examined.

In Scotland, Modern Apprenticeship Frameworks are approved by the Modern Apprenticeship Group (MAG) and it, with the support of the Scottish Government, has determined that from January 2010, all Frameworks submitted to it for approval, must have the mandatory elements credit rated for the Scottish Credit and Qualifications Framework (SCQF).

As of 2009 there are over 180 apprenticeship frameworks. The current scheme extends beyond manufacturing and high technology industry to parts of the service sector with no apprenticeship tradition. In 2008 Creative & Cultural Skills, the Sector Skills Council, introduced a set of Creative Apprenticeships awarded by EDI. A freelance apprenticeship framework was also approved and uses freelance professionals to mentor freelance apprentices. The Freelance Apprenticeship was first written and proposed by Karen Akroyd (Access To Music) in 2008. In 2011 Freelance Music Apprenticeships are available in music colleges in Birmingham, Manchester and London. The Department for Children, Schools and Families has stated its intention to make apprenticeships a "mainstream" part of England's education system.

Employers who offer apprenticeship places have an employment contract with their apprentices, but off-the-job training and assessment is wholly funded by the state for apprentices aged between 16 and 18. In England, Government only contributes 50% of the cost of training for apprentices aged 19 – 24. Employers of apprentices over the age of 25 may only get a contribution.

Government funding agencies (in England, the Learning and Skills Council) contract with 'learning providers' to deliver apprenticeships, and may accredit them as a Centre of Vocational Excellence or National Skills Academy. These organisations provide off-the-job tuition and manage the bureaucratic workload associated with the apprenticeships. Providers are usually private training companies but might also be Further Education colleges, voluntary sector organisations, Chambers of Commerce or employers themselves.

United States

Apprenticeship programmes in the United States are regulated by the Smith-Hughes Act (1917), The National Industrial Recovery Act (1933), and National Apprenticeship Act, also known as the "Fitzgerald Act." In the modern era, the number of apprenticeships have declined greatly in the United States. Free traditional apprenticeship job training has largely been replaced with on-the-job training (pay as you work), vocational classes, or college courses, which requires the student or an organization to pay for tuition.

American Apprenticeship Educational Regime

In the United States, education officials and nonprofit organizations who seek to emulate the apprenticeship system in other nations have created school to work education reforms. They seek to link academic education to careers. Some programmes include job shadowing, watching a real worker for a short period of time, or actually spending significant time at a job at no or reduced pay that would otherwise be spent in academic classes or working at a local business. Some legislators raised the issue of child labour laws for unpaid labour or jobs with hazards.

In the United States, school to work programmes usually occur only in high school. American high schools were introduced in the early 20th century to educate students of all ability and interests in one learning community rather than prepare a small number for college. Traditionally, American students are tracked within a wide choice of courses based on ability, with vocational courses (such as auto repair and carpentry) tending to be at the lower end of academic ability and trigonometry and pre-calculus at the upper end.

American education reformers have sought to end such tracking, which is seen as a barrier to opportunity. By contrast, the system studied by the NCEE (National Centre on Education and the Economy) actually relies much more heavily on tracking. Education officials in the U.S., based largely on school redesign proposals by NCEE and other organizations, have chosen to use criterion-referenced tests that define one high standard that must be achieved by all students to receive a uniform diploma. American education policy under the "No Child Left Behind Act" has as an official goal the elimination of the achievement gap between populations. This has often led to the need for remedial classes in college.

Many U.S. states now require passing a high school graduation examination to ensure that students across all ethnic, gender and income groups possess the same skills. In states such as Washington, critics have questioned whether this ensures success for all or just creates massive failure (as only half of all 10th graders have demonstrated they can meet the standards).

The construction industry is perhaps the heaviest user of apprenticeship programmes in the United States, with the US Department of Labour reporting 74,164 new apprentices accepted in 2007 at the height of the construction boom. Most of these apprentices participated in what are called "joint" apprenticeship programmes, administered jointly by construction employers and construction labour unions. For example, the International Union of Painters and Allied Trades (IUPAT) has opened the Finishing Trades Institute (FTI).

The FTI is working towards national accreditation so that it may offer associate and bachelor degrees that integrate academics with a more traditional apprentice programmes.

The IUPAT has joined forces with the Professional Decorative Painters Association (PDPA) to build educational standards using a model of apprenticeship created by the PDPA.

Example of a U.S. Apprenticeship Programme

Persons interested in learning to become electricians can join one of several apprenticeship programmes offered jointly by the International Brotherhood of Electrical Workers and the National Electrical Contractors Association. No background in electrical work is required. A minimum age of 18 is required. There is no maximum age. Men and women are equally invited to participate. The organization in charge of the programme is called the National Joint Apprenticeship and Training Committee.

Apprentice electricians work 32 to 40+ hours per week at the trade under the supervision of a journeyman wireman and receive pay and benefits. They spend an additional 8 hours every other week in classroom training. At the conclusion of training (five years for inside wireman and outside lineman, less for telecommunications), apprentices reach the level of journeyman wireman.

All of this is offered at no charge, except for the cost of books (which is approximately $200–600 per year (depending on grades). Persons completing this programme are considered highly skilled by employers and command high pay and benefits.

Other unions such as the United Brotherhood of Carpenters and Joiners of America, United Association of Plumbers, Fitters, Welders and HVAC Service Techs, Operating Engineers, Ironworkers, Sheet Metal Workers, Plasterers, Bricklayers and others offer similar programmes.

Trade associations such as the Independent Electrical Contractors and Associated Builders and Contractors also offer a variety of apprentice training programmes. Registered programmes also are offered by the Aerospace Joint Apprenticeship Committee (AJAC) to fill a shortage of aerospace and advanced manufacturing workers in Washington State.

Example of a Professional U.S. Apprenticeship

A modified form of apprenticeship is required for before an engineer is licensed as a Professional Engineer in any of the states of the United States. In the United States, regulation of professional engineering licenses is the right and responsibility of the federated state. That is, each of the 50 states sets its own licensing requirements and issues (and, if needed, revokes) licenses to practice engineering in that state.

Although the requirements can vary slightly from state to state, in general to obtain a Professional Engineering License in a given state, one must a graduate with Bachelor of Science in Engineering from an accredited college or university, pass the Engineer-in-Training (Engineer Intern) exam, work in that discipline for at least four years under a Licensed Professional Engineer, and then pass the Professional Engineers exam.

In most cases the states have reciprocity agreements so that once an individual becomes licensed in one state can also become licensed in other states with relative ease.

School-to-work Transition

School-to-work transition is a phrase referring to on-the-job training, apprenticeships, cooperative education agreements or other programmes designed to prepare students to enter the job market. This education system is primarily employed in the United States, partially as a response to work training as it is done in Asia.

School to Work is a system to introduce the philosophy of school-based, work-based, and connecting activities as early as kindergarten to expose students to potential future careers. School to Work emphasizes lifelong learning.

School to Work is funded and sponsored at the federal level by the U.S. Department of Labour and U.S. Department of Education. At the state level in states like Arizona, the grant is administered by the Arizona Department of Commerce, School to Work Division. This grant was funded for a maximum of five years with decreasing funds years three through five;

An example of county level involvement is the Cochise County School to Work Consortia in Arizona. It is composed of more than fifty Cochise County public and private schools, kindergarten through four-year university level, local and community-based organizations, and more than one hundred supporting business partners.

STW is part of a comprehensive education reform movement which includes formulating new standards which emphasize higher order thinking skills, new standards based assessments, and graduation exams, such as the Certificate of Initial Mastery which insure that students are ready for job training or college prep by age 16.

Reformers believe that it is important and egalitarian that all students graduate ready for jobs and ready for college, rather than tracking students one way or the other.

Critics

"Back to basics" traditionalists observe that in Europe, apprenticeships typically mean that the worker essentially ends their formal education after age 16, and works full-time at reduced pay in exchange for learning "job skills" such as assembling automobiles. Some believe that it was better to have students who were not bound for college concentrate on career schools, while academic students should spend class time learning core academic subjects such as history or science rather than job-shadowing at a hospital or auto dealer.

A student in North Dakota would have little opportunity to learn to be an auto designer, while one in Alabama would have little opportunity to do job shadowing at a major software company if job training were allocated according to local human resource needs, as many programmes are structured.

Local businesses also need to structure their operations to accommodate student workers, and transportation since typically schools are situated close to homes, and not businesses which are typically a car or transit commute away from homes.

The Michigan STW Initiative states "students work without pay for two to three hours each day" and "students are able to perform what might otherwise be hazardous order work." which would contradict child labour laws. Data would be shared with state STW partnership network and local labour market areas which might be an invasion of privacy.

The state would utilize the national industry-recognized skill certificates when developed, which would be the Certificate of Initial Mastery. Critics call this a government-controlled passport to work.

Michigan Rep. Harold J. Voorhees expressed concern that, with full implementation, a child would not be employed without this Certificate.

Standards-based Education Reform in the United States

Education reform in the United States since the 1980s has been largely driven by the setting of academic standards for what students should know and be able to do. These standards can then be used to guide all other system components. The SBE (standards-based education) reform movement calls for clear, measurable standards for all school students. Rather than norm-referenced rankings, a standards-based system measures each student against the concrete standard. Curriculum, assessments, and professional development are aligned to the standards.

Outcomes-based Education

Standards are an evolution of the earlier OBE (outcomes-based education) which was largely rejected in the United States as unworkable in the 1990s, and is still being implemented by some and abandoned by other governments in Australia by the hito completely change the structure of education and grading by massively individualizing instruction. In contrast, the more modest "standards" reform has been limited to the core goals of the OBE programmes:

- the creation of curriculum frameworks which outline specific knowledge or skills which students must acquire,
- an emphasis on criterion-referenced assessments which are aligned to the frameworks, and
- the imposition of some high-stakes tests, such as graduation examinations requiring a high standard of performance to receive a diploma.

In the process of establishing standards for each individual curriculum area, such as mathematics and science, many other reforms, such as enquiry-based science may be implemented, but these are not core aspects of the standards programme.

The standards movement can be traced to the efforts of Marc Tucker's NCEE which adapted aspects of William Spady's OBE movement into a system based on creating standards and assessments for a Certificate of Initial Mastery. This credential has since been abandoned by every state which first adopted the concept, including Washington and Oregon and largely replaced by graduation examinations.

His organization had contracts with states and districts covering as many as half of all American school children by their own claims, and many states enacted education reform legislation in the early 1990s based on this model, which was also known at the time as "performance-based education" as OBE (and the non-OBE progressive reforms co-marketed with it) had been too widely attacked to be saleable under that name. Though the standards movement has a stronger backing from conservatives than OBE by adopting a platform of raising higher academic standards, other conservatives believe that it is merely a re-labelling of a failed, unrealistic vision. It is believed to be the educational equivalent of a planned economy which attempts to require all children to perform at world-class levels merely by raising expectations and imposing punishments and sanctions on schools and children who fall short of the new standards.

Vision

The vision of the standards-based education reform movement is that every teenager will receive a meaningful high school diploma that serves essentially as a public guarantee that they can read, write, and do basic mathematics (typically through first-year algebra) at a level which might be useful to an employer. To avoid a surprising failure at the end of high school, standards trickle down through all the lower grades, with regular assessments through a variety of means.

No student, by virtue of poverty, age, race, gender, cultural or ethnic background, disabilities, or family situation will ultimately be exempt from learning the required material, although it is acknowledged that individual students may learn in different ways and at different rates.

Standards are chosen through political discussions that focus on what students will need to learn to be competitive in the job market, instead of by textbook publishers or education professors or tradition. Standards are normally published and freely available to parents and taxpayers as well as professional educators and textbook writers.

Standards focus on the goal of a literate and economically competitive workforce.

- Standards outline *what students need to know, understand, and be able to do.*
- Standards should be developmentally appropriate and relevant to future employment and education needs. Standards should generally be written so that all students are capable of achieving them, and so that talented students will exceed them.

- All students are believed to be capable of learning and of meeting high expectations. Both advanced and struggling students can learn new things in their own ways and at their own rates.
- Instruction that helps an individual student learn the information and skills listed in the standards is emphasized.
- Both *excellence and equity* are valued. Subgroups are carefully measured to identify and reduce systemic racism, bias, and the tyranny of low expectations.
- Professional teachers are empowered to make the decisions essential for effective learning, rather than having a teaching style prescribed under traditional education models.
- Social promotion is discouraged. Students advance or are retained based on their actual learning achievements instead of based on their age, their friends' achievements, or tradition.

Components

Some of the common components of standards-based education reform are:

- Creation of specific, concrete, measurable standards in an integrated curriculum framework. These standards apply to all schools in a state or country, regardless of race or relative wealth.
- Criterion-referenced tests based on these standards rather than norm-based relative rankings (which compare one student with another).
- An assertion that the new standards are higher than the pre-reform expectations for middle-class or upper-middle-class students.
- A requirement that attention be paid to narrowing academic gaps between groups such as races, income, or gender.
- High school graduation examinations, which are a form of high-stakes testing that denies diplomas to students who do not meet the stated standards, such as being able to read at the eighth-grade level or do pre-algebra mathematics.

  The Regents Examination in New York, first given in 1878, is the oldest high school graduation exam in the U.S. In most educational systems, students who can not pass the test are given a certificate of attendance instead of a normal diploma.

History

Standards-based education reform in the United States began with the publication of *A Nation at Risk* in 1983.

In 1989, an education summit involving all fifty state governors and President George H. W. Bush resulted in the adoption of national education goals for the year 2000; the goals included content standards. That same year, the National Council of Teachers of Mathematics published the *Curriculum and Evaluation Standards for School Mathematics*, a standards-based document.

A standards based vision was enacted under the Clinton Administration in 1994. A reauthorization of the Elementary and Secondary Education Act (ESEA) was passed to ensure that all states had rigorous standards for all subject areas and grade levels. This vision was then carried forward by the Bush Administration in 2001 with the passing of No Child Left Behind (NCLB).

Standards-based school reform has become a predominant issue facing public schools. By the 1996 National Education Summit, 44 governors and 50 corporate CEOs set the priorities (Achieve, 1998)

- High academic standards and expectations for all students.
- Tests that are more rigorous and more challenging, to measure whether students are meeting those standards.
- Accountability systems that provide incentives and rewards for educators, students, and parents to work together to help students reach these standards.

By 1998, almost every state had implemented or was in the process of implementing academic standards for their students in math and reading. Principals and teachers have received bonuses or been fired, students have been promoted or retained in their current grade, and legislation has been passed so that high school students will graduate or be denied a diploma based on whether or not they had met the standards, usually as measured by a criterion-referenced test.

The standards-based National Education Goals (Goals 2000) were set by the U.S. Congress in the 1990s. Many of these goals were based on the principles of outcomes-based education, and not all of the goals were attained by the year 2000 as was intended. The movement resulted in the No Child Left Behind Act of 2001, which as of 2009 is still an active nation-wide mandate in the United States.

Critics

Some aspects of standards-based reform have come under scrutiny. Some education researchers such as UCLA's Gary Orfield disagree that all students should pass a rigorous test just to get a high school diploma. Others such as Mathematically Correct have questioned the NCTM standards approach to teaching mathematics.

Some state standards have been criticized for either not being specific as to academic content, or not implementing curricula which follow the new standards.

Advocates of traditional education believe it is not realistic to expect all students to perform at the same level as the best students, nor to punish students simply because they do not perform as well as the most academically talented.

2

Educational Theory of Apprenticeship

The Apprentice Perspective is an educational theory of apprenticeship concerning the process of learning through physical integration into the practices associated with the subject, such as workplace training. By developing similar performance to other practitioners, an apprentice will come to understand the tacit (informally taught) duties of the position. In the process of creating this awareness, the learner also affect their environment; as they are accepted by master practitioners, their specific talents and contributions within the field are taken into account and integrated into the overall practice.

The Apprenticeship Perspective can be used to teach procedures to students. For example, tying a shoe, building a fire, and taking blood can all use the Apprenticeship Perspective to teach students these skills. However, it can be used to develop master practitioners in fields that involve increased complexity, numerous webs of interaction, or shifting environments demanding constant attention. Driver education, flight training and sports training all use the Apprenticeship Perspective for learners to learn a specific skill.

Definition

Apprenticeship learning has several formal definitions. Here are the most popular definitions:

- According to Pratt (1998) the Apprenticeship Perspective involves the learner within an actual, physical context of practice.
- Apprentices work side by side with an expert in order to learn a specific task (Barab & Hay, 2001).

- Apprenticeships include: "(1) the development of learning contexts that model proficiency, (2) providing coaching and scaffolding as students become immersed in authentic activities, (3) independent practice so that students gain an appreciation of the use of domain-related principles across multiple contexts" (Barab & Hay, p. 72, 2001)
- Apprenticeship is a teaching method utilized by educators to teach students how to solve problems, understand tasks, perform specific tasks, and deal with difficult situations (Collins, Brown, and Newman 1989).
- Furthermore, apprenticeship learning can be a useful supplement for adult educators with other types of instruction (Brandt, Farmer Jr., & Buckmaster, 1993).

In summary, apprenticeship learning is a method used by teachers to teach students about a specific task. It is utilized in a problematic situation so students know how to react when faced with a similar situation. Students work very closely with an expert at learning a specific skill. Apprenticeship learning is very beneficial to the learner.

Educational Theory of Apprenticeship

Unlike most other perspectives of education, the Apprenticeship Perspective is rarely formally taught. This is because the concepts communicated through apprenticeship are often practical, tacit strategies for achieving goals that do not always conform to standard procedure. For example, in an office environment lunch breaks may be limited to thirty minutes, but through apprenticeship one learns that up to forty-five minutes is acceptable. It would be inconvenient for the company to formally allow that allotment, but through informal training the message may still be communicated.

Educational theories of apprenticeship often involve the combination of formal and information training for the development of schema, mental structures that represent individual understanding of experiences that frame a person's conceptualization of reality. For example, a bicycle mechanic accustomed to road cycling may study texts covering mountain biking, but he will probably find it difficult to apply that formal training on a rough course. Educational theory's response to this is apprenticeship; by riding with a friend on the mountain side, the cyclist can watch and learn, constantly reiterating his performance to meet the demands of the sport. In this way he is developing his schema through formal and informal training.

The Apprentice Perspective is a holistic field of learning because it involves the education of both the student and the teacher. As the learner develops a schema that begins to incorporate the intricacies of the environment, they will be more capable of performing similarly to their peers. Once this is recognized by the trainer, the student will become accepted as a peer; at this point, as the new worker tackles problems through their new and previously existing schema, their individual talents may start to be applied within the group practices. In this way, apprenticeship retains fresh information and ideas within a common body of knowledge.

Factors of Success in Apprenticeship

According to Pratt (1998), successful development through apprenticeship involves three key factors. To become a master of the field, the learning process must be active, social, and authentic. These points will lead to the learner's greater understanding of the field and improved future contributions:

- Activity concerns the level to which the learner is physically and mentally stimulated within the environment. Successful trainers allow the student to be highly involved in the processes of decision making and action because they know that it is the doing that will have the most effect on the student's schema. In training to drive an automobile, students will never be able to pass without a physical examination of driving ability. To prepare for this, learners are given the opportunity to drive in safe areas. This active use of the tool prepares the student for its later, tested use.
- Second is the concept of sociality. Students must interact constantly with the tools for success, the teachers and the beneficiaries of the work. This holistic approach will further integrate the student into the interrelated web of action and consequence within the field. For example, a server training at a restaurant will not only follow a more experienced server, but interact with the customers, fellow employees, and management in the same time frame. The server will thus establish connections between all these groups and the personnel that embody them, preparing the server for day to day activities.
- Finally, authenticity is essential to apprenticeship. This is the establishment of a mental connection between the work of the

student in a particular field and the comprehension of the greater public. An electrical engineer may understand the intricacies and challenges of computer panels, but this is only half of the required knowledge. They must also learn how most people perceive these panels and their interaction with them. From this understanding of the other end of spectrum, the engineer will better understand the achievement and thus authenticity of the community of electrical engineering.

Apprenticeship Phases

The Apprenticeship Perspective includes a series of phases that help articulate the roles of the learner and teacher during the process of observing and enacting concepts.

- Phase I: Modelling - The complete act is observed and contemplated. This means that the smaller parts that make up the whole are not yet examined in depth. The observer first frames the larger experience and will be able to specify from there(). "Modelling occurs in two parts: behavioural modelling allows learners to observe performance of an activity by experienced members to share "tricks of the trade" with news members" (Hansman, 2001, p. 47). The learner is using articulation and domain-specific heuristics in this phase (Brandt et al., 1993).
- Phase II: Approximating - In private or in non-critical scenarios, the observer begins to mimic the actions of the teacher. Through close guidance, the learner begins to articulate more clearly the teacher's actions. This phase allows the learner to try the activity and lets them think about what they plan to do and why they plan to do it. Then after the activity the learner reflects about the activity. They examine what the did in comparison to what the expert did.
- Phase III: Fading - The learner, still within the safety net, starts operating in a more detailed manner, playing within the structure that has been taught. The learner's capabilities are increased as the experts assistance decreases (Hansman, 2001).
- Phase IV: Self-directed Learning - The learner attempts the actions within real society, limiting him/herself to the scope of actions in the field that are well-understood(). The learner is performing the actual task and only seeking assistance when needed from the expert (Hansman, 2001).

- Phase V: Generalizing - The learner generalizes what has been learned, trying to apply those skills to multiple scenarios and continuing to grow in ability in the field. The learner uses discussion in this phase to relate that they have learned to other relevant situations (Hansman, 2001).

Goals of Apprenticeship

There are three main goals of apprenticeship learning according to Brandt et al. (1993).

- The first goal is for the adult learner to discover what works. This does not mean for the learner to use problem solving learning and figure out the situation on their own. There is guidance provided. The learner uses skills learned from the expert in order to successfully solve a problem.
- Secondly, the learner recognizes tasks, problems or situations and knows how to handle them. The learner learns the appropriate practical and theoretical knowledge. Learners are not learning this knowledge in isolation from other students. Students are working in a social setting with lifelike scenarios in order to learn a specific task.
- Finally, the learner is able to perform at an acceptable level. The learner is not learning basic skills at a novice level but working with an expert in order to perform at an acceptable level. Students are not learning skills at a basic level but rather at a level that is accepted in the specific industry.

These three goals have been accomplished based on published literature, learners feel apprenticeship "learning experience expands their awareness of the factors that should be considered' helps them organize and pay attention to their thought processes while handling difficult tasks, problems, and problematic situations; and emphasizes the importance of particular aspects of such tasks, problems, and problematic situations previously ignored or regarded as unimportant" (Brandt et al., 1993).

Clearly the three goals of apprenticeship learning have been accomplished. Learners have been able to discover what works in situations, and knows how to handles problems and finally the learner can perform at a satisfactory level.

Apprentices Mobility

Apprentices mobility is the movement of students and teachers in Vocational education or training (VET) to another institution inside or outside their own country to study or teach for a limited time. The term is usually used in the context of European Union (EU) policy.

Under the EU Lisbon agenda attempts have been made to lower cultural, socio-economical and academic barriers to mobility. Mobile learners are usually divided into two groups: *free-movers* are learners who travel entirely on their own initiative, while *programme students* use exchange programmes at department, faculty, institution or national level (such as Leonardo da Vinci II).

Terminology

The practice of going abroad to learn has been denoted by different terms in different contexts over the years, such as "exchange" or "transnational mobility". For the specific practice of sending people abroad on placements in public and private enterprise, the more neutral term of "placements abroad" has been preferred.

Many different practices use the term "placement" as a denominator for their activities, and some form of definition is necessary to distinguish between these, and to mark it off from ordinary employment abroad as well as other forms of transnational mobility. Placements may be set up by an organiser who has made the necessary arrangements for a placement, defined the intended learning outcome, and thought out the pedagogic implications. Placements may also be self-organised by the participant.

When a student organises a work stay in another country during holidays or a study break, this may or may not qualify as a placement according to the criterion of intent. If the purpose is to acquire vocational skills and/or improve language and intercultural skills in general, it should be seen as a placement, and count it as such, rather than a holiday job. It may be inscribed in an educational context through accreditation of prior experiential learning (APEL), if the organisation can be convinced that the person in question has sought out learning situations during the stay rather than just focused on having a good time or earning as much money as possible.

Other activities in this borderline category are au pair placements and voluntary work in charitable institutions and organisations, e.g. as financed under the European Voluntary Service. The practice of some companies to send employees abroad in foreign subsidiaries for a period of time in order to acquire specific competences may also be considered under this label. It should be distinguished from employment abroad in general, which is another matter.

The line is blurred, and different definitions may collide here. Any labour market activity where the participant draws some kind of wages or salary is juridically considered as employment. But payment is not necessarily a way of distinguishing between placements and proper jobs; placements may be paid or unpaid, even though the learning role of participants is often signified by the fact that they receive no – or a considerably reduced – payment.

History

Mobility of VET learners can be traced to the tradition of the travelling journeyman of the medieval guilds. Dedicated transnational placement programmes appeared after the Second World War when the organisations AIESEC and IAESTE were set up under the auspices of Unesco in 1948 to facilitate placements for students of commerce and technology in higher education.

Another placement programme was set up in 1964 by the Commission of the European Communities in the shape of the Young workers' exchange programme (YWEP). In 1981 a binational Franco-German programme for placements (exchanges) in VET was established within the framework of the Franco-German Treaty of 1963.

The Comett programme from 1987 – also set up by the European Commission – grant aided placements of students in higher education in order to promote cooperation between universities and industry and to facilitate transfer of technology. Action 4 of the Lingua programme from 1990 contained funding provisions for young people in VET to undertake placement periods abroad in order to improve foreign language proficiency.

Up to the early 1990s, however, mobility in VET – and in particular in initial VET and for young workers – was very limited and certainly not a realistic proposition except for a very small minority of the total population engaged in VET. Mobility took a quantum leap upwards on the agenda of European and national VET-policies more or less precisely a decade ago, notably with the introduction of the enlarged Petra programme (Petra II) in 1992. That year, 8500 placements were grant-aided through the programme, and by the end of the programme period in 1995, the total number approached 35 000 for the then 12 EU Member States. A significant development at national level was the establishment by the Danish government in 1992 of the PIU programme, which gave people in initial vocational training not just the opportunity but the right to undertake all or part of their mandatory work placements in another EU or EFTA country. Funding was provided by Danish employers through the Employers' reimbursement scheme for apprentices and trainees (AER). This was the first of several national programmes for placements abroad that have since been set up in various countries.

Criteria for Defining Placements Abroad in VET

Criteria have been established to define what a work placement is, in order to differentiate it from other activities. A placement:

1. is carried out in an authentic work environment. The placement period is not an artificially created situation, where the central feature is the learning of the participant. The most important thing here is continuing production, and learning is placed second or third or even lower down on the scale of priorities;
2. implies involvement in concrete work processes. The participants are not merely onlookers to the activities, but are given an active role;
3. is for a limited time. Placements are planned and carried out as a period abroad that is set in a (national) learning context – i.e. surrounded by this on both sides. They are not open-ended. Duration, however, may vary considerably, from two weeks to two years. To this we may add another features, which we should term characteristics rather than criteria, since they need not always be applicable.

A placement thus as a rule:

1. demands professional experience as the "entry ticket". Workplaces where it is possible to become integrated in work processes immediately without any prior training or experience are few and far between. Therefore participation in most placement projects is contingent upon either a wholly or partly completed training course or solid practical experience;
2. is not under the supervision of trained pedagogical staff. Contrary to a school environment or youth exchanges, there are usually no pedagogically trained staff (teachers) or experienced youth leaders around to offer guidance and practical support during the placement period. Mentors may be appointed, but the supervision of the participants is only a secondary task for them;
3. does not take place among peer groups. In school stays or youth exchanges, the participants will often be surrounded by people in the same age bracket and societal position who are

in a similar life situation. At the workplace, however, there is a broad spectrum of colleagues, who are largely in a different position from the participant and have different dreams, expectations and interests.

Some activities are excluded from the definition, For example "work camps" organised to improve intercultural understanding bring together young people from many countries to accomplish a practical task such as building a playground, or restoring a building to be used by the local community. However, the work situation is an artificially created one, there are trained supervisors present, and the group is composed of young people in the same age bracket. Study visits are also excluded: even though they may be in authentic work environments, the participants are merely engaged as onlookers.

A definition of the term "placement abroad" is "a shorter or longer period spent abroad in a public or private enterprise, which has been consciously organised for learning purposes, which implies active involvement in concrete work processes, and which can be paid or unpaid". The phenomenon is often associated with past and present programmes of the European Commission. These have grant-aided placements abroad, represent the largest single programmes and initiatives, and provide the best statistical material. Currently, the Leonardo da Vinci programme is much in evidence in discussions on mobility in VET for exactly these reasons. The practice goes well beyond these programmes, however, and encompasses also programmes and initiatives at binational, national and regional level, as well as the activities of organisations and individuals, which are undertaken without any recourse to programme funding.

Benefits

Placements abroad can be a pedagogical exercise. Mobility in a context of education and training differs substantially from other types of mobility in that it is primarily a pedagogical exercise: it is a tool used to produce certain kinds of learning of an affective and/or cognitive nature in the participant.

Placements abroad can be a means for achieving intercultural understanding, learning how to live peacefully together in Europe and in the world and develop a sense of "European Citizenship" as opposed to a strictly nationalist outlook (corresponding to the initial thoughts of Jean Monnet when forging the European Coal and Steel Union in 1951 - as a means to promote peace and understanding in a war-torn Europe). Latterly, this discourse has also been used in connection with the fight against racism and xenophobia. An example refers the activities of the Franco-German Youth Office.

Placements abroad can be a method for acquiring 'new basic skills' and developing 'employability'. The world has changed fundamentally in the last decade. The world is flattening. We can focus on the many differences between apprentices and placements in Europe. And we can continue to question the importance of experience abroad for apprentices and other young people in IVET, who often work in small and medium sized enterprises with a regional focus. However, the reality is that experience of mobility provides apprentices and IVET students with particular competences over and above those obtained from the vocational curriculum including communicative, social, meaning-related and change-related skills. These critical competences benefit the individual apprentice and IVET student personally and they are also likely to make them more employable.

Within this discourse, the rationale for the activity lies in the use of placements abroad as a didactic tool to equip participants with so called "key skills" that enable them to cope with the constant changes in occupational profiles, work organisation and career paths arising as a consequence of globalisation and technological change. This corresponds to a focus on education and training as a motor for economic growth, and the aims of the Lisbon-declaration concerning the creation of a 'Europe of knowledge'.

Placements abroad can be an activity linked to internationalisation of education and training in Europe. In this case they are the response of national educational systems to the perceived negative effects of globalisation. At the level of the individual, it enables the future workforce to acquire foreign language skills and intercultural skills so that they can deal with increased foreign contacts at the workplace. At systemic level, it allows national educational systems to fill in temporary gaps in training provision by sending trainees abroad to where such opportunities exist.

Increasingly, employees from all levels need to be able to operate in an environment that deals with international customers and suppliers. Those companies and sectors who earn their money abroad, or work with foreign suppliers, are more likely to be engaged in mobility. Although right now less than 50% of small and medium enterprises (SMEs) are internationalised, figures by the World Trade Organisation, show that more and more economies are dependent on external and foreign trade. It is likely that this will increase the pressure on employers to hire people with a 'worldly mindset'. In the best tradition of 'Master craftsmen' who only got their credentials after having been abroad, sectors can use this changing environment to train their future employees. To facilitate knowledge-transfer between sectors, economies and generations, education should continue to play its role here.

Placements abroad can be a method for promoting the free movement of workers in Europe. In this case they are concerned with learning how to live and work in another country, how to become a 'migrant worker' willing and able to move across borders and thereby allay skills shortages in other Member States (corresponding to the thoughts in the Treaty of Rome from 1957 creating the European Economic Communities, where the free circulation of labour across borders was seen as an essential element in the economic development of Europe).

The rationales for mobility may differ for each actor. At EU level, several reasons for stimulating mobility are mentioned, i.e. more mobility between regions and jobs represents an essential part of the Lisbon Agenda, mobility is a tool for acquiring language skills and mobility contributes to increasing stability and peace of the EU.

More exposure to other countries leads to increased intercultural awareness and good feelings about host nation/culture. Mobility implies acquiring international skills, which become increasingly important with the liberalization of trade and commerce. For individuals, mobility implies developing personal skills and competencies

For vocational schools and training centres hosting students and apprentices and other young people in IVET from abroad creates an international atmosphere that brings benefits for the whole institution (e.g. inspiration of other students, learning language). Transnational mobility projects can serve as a launch pad for transnational partnerships and for a proactive internationalisation strategy and policy. For employers, reasons for engaging in mobility can be a faster diffusion and acquisition of knowledge and skills.

Benefits for Employers

- Mobility is a means to address both short-term and long-term shortages in skills.
- Greater use of mobile workers and trainees is an important measure to cope with recruitment difficulties. In the long run,

companies can include recruitment for young people in their human resource policies.

- While time for adaptation to key technologies is becoming shorter, the mobility of employees can facilitate a fast diffusion of knowledge.
- Hiring of trainees implies low costs. The risk of hiring trainees for the sole purpose of lowering the labour costs needs to be mitigated by some forms of control and accreditation by the education system.

Benefits for the Individual

- Mobility implies acquiring of international skills, what becomes increasingly important with the liberalization of trade and commerce.
- Mobility implies developing of personal skills and competencies such as change-related, relational, learning-related, and meaning-related skills.

Benefits for vocational schools and training centres

- Hosting students and apprentices from abroad creates an international atmosphere that brings benefit for the whole institution (e.g. inspiration of other students, learning language).
- VET-institutions have the possibility to benchmark their course contents and pedagogic practices.
- Involvement of a VET-institution in mobility activities makes it attractive for students in comparison with other 'not-towards-mobility-oriented' institutions.
- Transnational mobility projects can serve as a launch pad for transnational partnerships and for a proactive internationalization strategy and policy.
- The role of VET-institutions is gradually changing from a traditional 'school' towards a regional knowledge centre. There is a need to reflect internationalization in their array of competences and skills.
- Mobility projects might imply income-generating activities.

Take-up Statistics

Initially, we should distinguish between placements abroad organised within the framework of programmes and spontaneous placement activities happening outside of these. We have only very limited ability to measure the placements abroad that are undertaken outside of dedicated programmes, or in programmes or initiatives that deal with wider issues and where placements abroad are only a possibility, and not a distinct programme activity. Anything concerning this must thus be based on guesswork.

Even when concentrating on dedicated mobility programmes (or programmes where mobility is a distinct activity) are we faced with problems. First, problems of definition can make comparability difficult. Second (and partly as a consequence of this), the way in which information is gathered (and what is gathered) may differ from programme to programme, which makes it yet more difficult to come up with robust and comparable information. It is not possible to see from the statistical material available whether some activities were undertaken as placements or as another form of mobility. Moreover, mobility programmes (or programmes incorporating mobility activities) are undertaken in many different contexts, and there is virtually no national level overview of all mobility activities.

The annual Dutch BISON monitoring report of international mobility within education and training remains an isolated initiative, but it includes only mobility taking place within the framework of educational establishments. In addition, all the information available is concerned with outgoing mobility (the sending aspect), and there is no indication of incoming mobility (hosting). This lack of quantitative data makes it very difficult to arrive at any figures concerning both the participation rates and financing involved.

For the Leonardo da Vinci programme, we can give very precise indications on participation rates and the amount of funding in the programme, but we do not have figures on funding that also involves national cofinancing. Given the different ways of calculating this from project to project, and the varying percentage of Commission funding, a conservative estimate would put this at a level equal to the Commission's contribution (e.g. for the second phase of the Leonardo da Vinci programme, approximately EUR 600 million).

Take-up Through Programmes

The Leonardo da Vinci programme remains the biggest single funding mechanism for transnational mobility in VET in Europe, and in some countries it is more or less the only programme within VET that can be used for funding placements abroad on any significant scale. In other countries there are more funding opportunities.

In the Netherlands 1 230 people benefited from a Leonardo mobility grant in the year 1999-2000 (total figure, including short study tours undertaken by teachers, instructors and human resource specialists).

The total number of people participating in transnational mobility activities in VET in the same period, however, is registered by the BISON monitoring report as close to 7000 (6877). Of these, 204 come from the Lingua programme (i.e. another EU programme), but 5158 were financed through the national Onbegrensd talent programme. Unfortunately we cannot assess the exact amount spent on placements abroad from this programme, since the funds are allocated as lump sums to educational establishments for broad 'internationalisation' purposes.

Also, we cannot compare factors like length of stay and target countries. Even without information on mobility financed through other sources than the established programmes, it would seem that Leonardo accounts for less than one fifth of the total figure for mobility within VET in the Netherlands. It is problematic, however, to transpose this figure to the rest of Europe for want of a reliable yardstick for measurement and comparison. In many instances, grant allocations and/or numbers involved are used as indicators. Another complication is that a mere headcount will not give a correct picture of the scope of mobility in VET.

In the Danish PIU programme, the participants (apprentices) stay abroad for eight to nine months on average, which has greater effect than, for example, a two-week stay financed under Lingua/ Socrates. Similarly, Danish apprentices are paid the appropriate apprentice wage by their employer in the host country, which means that programme costs measured by grant allocation only will not give a real picture of the total costs involved. However, some countries have only the Leonardo programme to finance mobility, which tips the scales in the other direction when trying to figure out a European average for participation and funding of mobility.

Take-up throughnspontaneous Mobility

Quantifiable information on spontaneous mobility is virtually non-existent, even though we have anecdotal evidence of its existence as a factor. We might have got an indication of sorts from the German Sprungbrett programme; a national-level mobility programme which started in 2003, which gave grants to individuals within initial VET undertaking placement periods in other European countries.

Unfortunately this programme was discontinued at the end of 2003 due to budget cuts.

Measuring the factors such as the numbers of applications received may give us a rough estimate of this activity in at least one Member State, but only in initial vocational training, where spontaneous mobility is likely to be low for reasons of age. Almost equally impossible to assess are the activities that are undertaken as pilot projects within programmes that on the surface have nothing to do with the issue of placements abroad.

An example of this is the Eurojoker project, which was financed out of funds from the EU Konver II initiative. In this project (duration March 1999 – May 2000) young unemployed persons from the Brandenburg region in Germany were sent on one year placements in other European countries with a view to increasing their employability.

Locating such projects mainly relies on the unofficial network of the person collecting the data, or happens by chance. It follows that any estimate of the numbers and amounts involved will doubtless be inaccurate. The scarcity of data is equally pronounced for the qualitative aspects of the phenomenon. Given the scope of activities, it is strange to note that studies on the qualitative aspects of placements abroad as a didactic tool in the context of VET are sparse.

Evaluations of Programmes

Very few evaluations of mobility programmes and projects have been undertaken at European or national level, and even fewer of these concentrate on the learning aspects.

Most of the evaluations undertaken are summative evaluations carried out by or for programme administrators with a view to justifying expenses and administrative practices, and have little to say about learning. After the conclusion of the first phase of the Leonardo da Vinci programme, a 'valorisation' exercise was carried out on selected aspects of the programme, both at national and at European level.

Valorisation is not the same as traditional evaluation or impact assessment, but focuses mainly on the achievements of the programme with a view to formulating recommendations for improvements and future priorities. It is not a very well defined methodology, and valorisation exercises consequently vary greatly from country to country, as well as in quality. Each country was given the possibility to choose between certain themes, and mobility was an issue in several countries covered by this study (Denmark, France, Iceland, Norway, and the UK) as well as an element in European-level valorisation.

Other than these evaluations, research-based treatment of the theme of placements abroad is virtually non-existent. Some work, however, has been done on organisational matters, notably on legal and administrative barriers, culminating with the Commission's Green Paper on obstacles to mobility from 1996.

The main source of funding for development activities (in the majority of countries the only source) is the strand for pilot-projects under the Leonardo da Vinci programme. The recognition of qualifications acquired abroad is a major issue here. However, only 57 projects dealing with mobility-related subjects could be identified (out of a total project number of over 3000) in the first phase of the programme (1995–99). Prominent themes were placement finding, preparation, and quality assurance.

Registered Apprenticeship

Registered Apprenticeship is a programme of the United States Department of Labour that connects job seekers looking to learn new skills with employers looking for qualified workers. Employers, employer associations, and joint labour-management organizations, known collectively as "sponsors", provide apprentices with paid on-the-job learning and academic instruction that reflects industry needs. The goal of such instruction is to provide workers with advanced skillsets that meet the specific needs of their employers.

History

Following the creation of the first Registered Apprenticeship system in Wisconsin in 1911, the United States Congress passed the National Apprenticeship Act (known as the "Fitzgerald Act") in 1937, establishing federal Registered Apprenticeship. Initially, Registered Apprenticeship programmes consisted mainly of the manufacturing, construction and utilities industries. After World War II, Registered Apprenticeship began to expand into training of health and safety workers, including firefighters, police, and emergency medical technicians. Recently, the programme guidelines were revised in late 2008 to allow for greater flexibility in serving apprentices and programme sponsors in prevailing economic conditions. Currently, Registered Apprenticeship includes 29,000 programmes impacting 250,000 employers, involving approximately 450,000 apprentices.

Role of the U.S. Government

The National Apprenticeship Act authorizes the Federal government, in cooperation with the states, to oversee the nation's apprenticeship system. The U.S. Department of Labour's Office of Apprenticeship works in conjunction with both the Bureau of Apprenticeship and Training states that report directly to the Federal government as well independent State Apprenticeship Agencies to administer the programme. These agencies are responsible for:

- Registering apprenticeship programmes that meet Federal and State standards
- Protecting the safety and welfare of apprentices
- Issuing nationally recognized and portable Certificates of Completion to apprentices
- Promoting the development of new programmes through marketing and technical assistance
- Assuring that all programmes provide high quality training
- Assuring that all programmes produce skilled competent workers.

Programme Benefits and Requirements

Registered Apprenticeship provides a wide array of benefits to employers, employees, unions, and other stakeholders. For employers, the programme provides a pipeline of skilled workers enrolled in customized programmes that meet a variety of the employer's needs, e.g., increased competitiveness or higher worker retention rates. For workers, enrolled apprentices receive a paycheck that is guaranteed to increase as their training and skill levels increase. Apprentices also complete a combination of industry-specific classroom education and hands-on career training leading to nationally recognized, portable Certificates of Completion.

Registered Apprenticeship programme sponsors identify the minimum qualifications to apply into their apprenticeship programme. The eligible starting age can be no less than 16 years of age; however, individuals must usually be 18 to be an apprentice in hazardous occupations. Programme sponsors may also identify additional minimum qualifications and credentials to apply, e.g., education, ability to physically perform the essential functions of the occupation, proof of age. Based on the selection method utilized by the sponsor, additional qualification standards, such as fair aptitude tests and interviews, school grades, and previous work experience may be identified.

Dual Education System

A dual education system combines apprenticeships in a company and vocational education at a vocational school in one course. This system is practiced in several countries, notably Germany, Austria, Bosnia and Herzegovina, Croatia, Serbia, Slovenia, Macedonia, Montenegro and Switzerland, but also Denmark, the Netherlands and France, and for some years now in China and other countries in Asia.

In the *Duales Ausbildungssystem* young German people can learn one of 356 (2005) apprenticeship occupations (*Ausbildungsberufe*), such as e.g. Doctor's Assistant, Dispensing Optician or Oven Builder. The precise skills and theory taught are strictly regulated and defined by national standards:

An *Industriekaufmann* (Industrial Manager) has always acquired the same skills and taken the same courses in production planning, accounting and controlling, marketing, HR management, trade laws, etc.

Especially in southern Germany this model is also used for a special college system called *Duale Hochschule.*

In France, dual education (*formation en alternance*) has undergone a boom since the 1990s, with information technology being the greatest draw.

Apprenticeship Section

As one part of the dual education course, students are trained in a company for three to five days a week. The company is responsible for ensuring that students get the standard quantity and quality of training set down in the training descriptions for each trade.

In Germany, this practical training may be complemented by more practical lessons at workshops run by the guilds and chamber of commerce, in order to compensate for the bias caused by training at only one company. These extra courses usually take three or four weeks a year. The time spent at vocational school is approximately 60 days a year, in blocks of one or two weeks at a time spread out over the year.

In France, the same amount of time is spent in practical training and theory, with the following possible systems:

- 2.5 days in a company, 2.5 days at school,
- one week in a company, one week at school,
- six months in a company, six months at school.

French companies must provide a tutor or other person responsible for the students, or a human resources officer to deal with them. Their duties may involve daily tutoring and/or targeted training. French apprentices on the dual education course are paid a certain percentage of the minimum wage for the job they are learning.

School Section

The other part of the dual education course involves lessons at a vocational school (German: *Berufsschule*). The responsibility for this part of the course lies with the school authorities in every German state or Swiss canton. Both general lessons (for example German, politics, economics, religion or even sport) and trade-specific theory are taught.

Lessons may be taught part-time (one or two days a week) or in blocks of several weeks. The latter is preferred for trades learned by only a small number of students, where students may have to travel long distances to get to the nearest vocational school which teaches their subject.

Testing

In Germany, for most trades, the first examination takes place about half-way through the vocational training and is only to test how well the student is doing so far: the marks do not go towards the final exam. Both exams are organised by the small business trade group and chamber of commerce and industry. Examinations for trained artisans are traditionally known as journeyman's tests (*Gesellenprüfung*).

Examinations for trades which have been recognised more recently are organised slightly differently. Here, the first examination counts as 40% of the total result, with the final examination making up the other 60%.

Those who fail the exam can apply to have their training extended until the following year when they can retake it. Only one extension is allowed.

Advantages of Dual Education

The student is an employee of the company from the beginning and receives tasks according to his growing abilities. If a company is willing to make a employment-contract with the student after his dual education time, the company will get an employee who knows the company's workflow. The student can also benefit from the knowledge about hard skills and soft skills of more experienced co-workers. The student develops under real conditions. Therefore, he can see if he is not able or willing to do this job quite early and not after exams. Furthermore the student earns money from the beginning.

Problems with Dual Education

Germany: Although the dual education system is generally considered to be exemplary, an increasing number of young people are taking vocational education and training (VET) courses at training sites and schools rather than in real companies, as for various reasons, companies are becoming less willing to take on apprentices. To counter this, the government considered making it compulsory for firms to take on apprentices. This idea, however, was dropped when the trade associations agreed to a voluntary training pact.

The reasons behind the lack of places on dual education courses include:

- companies which take on apprentices have to follow a large number of regulations
- the training itself is very expensive
- the requirements for several positions have become more complex and many school graduates do not provide a fitting level of education
- for the less complex positions only graduates with a very low level of education are willing to do it, but they are not able to keep up with the course
- companies are often highly specialized and unable to train apprentices in all the required areas

Recently some attempts have been made to overcome these difficulties, but as yet with no success. Two solutions put forward so far are "contractual education" (*Auftragsausbildung*) and state-run courses. The former would involve companies training apprentices which they do not plan to employ; the contract would also not be an employment contract. The latter solution would involve training outside of companies, in schools and colleges.

Switzerland

In Switzerland too, more and more young people are finding it hard to get a place in a company of their choice. In 2004, a conference took place on this subject, attended by all the parties in the Swiss Federal Council; as no agreement could be reached on which measures to take, the only result was a call for all companies to take on apprentices.

The lack of places has changed the conditions in which apprentices are taken on. In 2004, one newly-founded company even advertised apprenticeships in IT where the apprentices had to pay for the training themselves. The uproar was so great, however, that the company was not able to start up. Today, most apprentices have to take aptitude tests before they are accepted, and there are usually several candidates for a company to choose from.

Commercial Advancement Training Scheme

Commercial Advancement Training Scheme (CATS) is a dual education system adopted from the German Dual System and introduced in Namibia in 2005, and South Africa in 1985. It combines apprenticeships in a company and technical education at a University in one course. It is accepted and recognized by the European Union through the German Chamber of Commerce and Industry. The programme is also accredited by the South African Qualifications Authority (SAQA) evaluation level 5 /NQF level 5.

Namibia

Introduced in 2005 in Namibia, classes are offered by the Centre for Enterprise Development (CED) at the Polytechnic of Namibia and practical training is provided by partner companies such as Manica, Namport, Agra, TransNamib, Wesbank Transport, Cymot and others.

South Africa

The system was introduced in South Africa in 1985, thereafter graduating more than 1,600 students in the two countries, with the contribution of 360 companies and institutions.

Advantages of Dual Education

The student works as an employee of the company from the beginning and receives tasks according to his growing abilities. Companies who employ the student after his education, the company gets a well-trained employee. The student develops both hard and soft skills. The student develops under real conditions, getting an earlier look at what the work entails, earning money in the process.

Cognitive Apprenticeship

Cognitive apprenticeship is a theory of the process where a master of a skill teaches that skill to an apprentice. Constructivist approaches to human learning have led to the development of a theory of cognitive apprenticeship. This theory holds that masters of a skill often fail to take into account the implicit processes involved in carrying out complex skills when they are teaching novices. To combat these tendencies, cognitive apprenticeships "...are designed, among other things, to bring these tacit processes into the open, where students can observe, enact, and practice them with help from the teacher...". This model is supported by Albert Bandura's (1997) theory of modelling, which posits that in order for modelling to be successful, the learner must be attentive, must have access to and retain the information presented, must be motivated to learn, and must be able to accurately reproduce the desired skill.

Overview

Part of the effectiveness of the cognitive apprenticeship model comes from learning in context and is based on theories of situated cognition. Cognitive scientists maintain that the context in which learning takes place is critical (e.g., Godden & Baddeley, 1975). Based on findings such as these, Collins, Duguid, and Brown (1989) argue that cognitive apprenticeships are less effective when skills and concepts are taught independent of their real-world context and situation. As they state, "Situations might be said to co-produce knowledge through activity. Learning and cognition, it is now possible to argue, are fundamentally situated". In cognitive apprenticeships, the activity being taught is modelled in real-world situations.

By using processes such as modelling and coaching, cognitive apprenticeships also support the three stages of skill acquisition described in the expertise literature: the cognitive stage, the associative stage, and the autonomous stage. In the cognitive stage, learners develop declarative understanding of the skill. In the associative stage, mistakes and misinterpretations learned in the cognitive stage are detected and eliminated while associations between the critical elements involved in the skill are strengthened. Finally, in the autonomous stage, the learner's skill becomes honed and perfected until it is executed at an expert level.

Like traditional apprenticeships, in which the apprentice learns a trade such as tailoring or woodworking by working under a master teacher, cognitive apprenticeships allow the master to model behaviours in a real-world context with cognitive modelling. By listening to the master explain exactly what she is doing and thinking as she models the skill, the apprentice can identify relevant behaviours and develop a conceptual model of the processes involved. The apprentice then attempts to imitate those behaviours with the master observing and providing coaching. Coaching provides assistance at the most critical level – the skill level just beyond what the learner/apprentice could accomplish by herself. Vygotsky (1978) referred to this as the Zone of Proximal Development and believed that fostering development within this zone leads to the most rapid development. The coaching process includes additional modelling as necessary, corrective feedback, and reminders, all intended to bring the apprentice's performance closer to that of the master's. As the apprentice becomes more skilled through the repetition of this process, the feedback and instruction provided by the master "fades" until the apprentice is, ideally, performing the skill at a close approximation of the master level.

[This entry is an excerpt from R. Shawn Edmondson's doctoral dissertation, entitled Evaluating the Effectiveness of a Telepresence-Enabled Cognitive Apprenticeship Model of Teacher Professional Development (2006).]

Teaching Methods

Collins, Brown, and Newman developed six teaching methods rooted in cognitive apprenticeship theory and claim these methods help students attain cognitive and metacognitive strategies for "using, managing, and discovering knowledge". The first three (modelling, coaching, scaffolding) are at the core of cognitive apprenticeship and help with cognitive and metacognitive development. The next two (articulation and reflection) are designed to help novices with awareness of problem-solving strategies and execution similar to that of an expert. The final step (exploration) intends to guide the novice towards independence and the ability to solve and identify problems within the domain on their own. The authors note, however, that this is not an exhaustive list of methods and that the successful execution of these methods is highly dependent on the domain.

Modelling

Modelling is when an expert, usually a teacher, within the cognitive domain or subject area demonstrates a task explicitly so that novices, usually a student, can experience and build a conceptual model of the task at hand. For example, a math teacher might write out explicit steps and work through a problem aloud, demonstrating her heuristics and procedural knowledge. Modelling can include modelling of expert performance or processes in the world.

Coaching

Coaching involves observing novice task performance and offering feedback and hints to sculpt the novice's performance to that of an expert's. The expert oversees the novice's tasks and may structure the task accordingly to assist in the novice's development.

Scaffolding

Instructional scaffolding is the act of putting into place strategies and methods to support the student's learning. These supports can be teaching manipulatives, activities, and group work. The teacher may have to execute parts of the task that the student is not yet able to do. This requires the teacher to have the skill to analyze and assess student abilities in the moment.

Articulation

Articulation includes "any method of getting students to articulate their knowledge, reasoning, or problem-solving process in a domain" (p. 482). Three types of articulation are enquiry teaching, thinking aloud, and critical student role. Through enquiry teaching (Collins & Stevens, 1982), teachers ask students a series of questions that allows them to refine and restate their learned knowledge and to form explicit conceptual models.

Thinking aloud requires students to articulate their thoughts while solving problems. Students assuming a critical role monitor others in cooperative activities and draw conclusions based on the problem-solving activities.

Articulation is described by McLellan as consisting of two aspects: separating component knowledge and skills to learn them more effectively and, more common verbalizing or demonstrating knowledge and thinking processes in order to expose and clarify them.

Reflection

Reflection allows students to "compare their own problem-solving processes with those of an expert, another student, and ultimately, an internal cognitive model of expertise" (p. 483). A technique for reflection could be to examine the past performances of both expert and novice and to highlight similarities and differences.

The goal of reflection is for students to look back and analyze their performances with a desire for understanding and improvement towards the behaviour of an expert.

Exploration

Exploration involves giving students room to problem solve on their own and teaching students exploration strategies. The former requires the teacher to slowly withdraw the use of supports and scaffolds not only in problem solving methods, but problem setting methods as well. The latter requires the teacher to show students how to explore, research, and develop hypotheses. Exploration allows the student to frame interesting problems within the domain for themselves and then take the initiative to solve these problems.

Engineering Apprentice

An engineering apprenticeship in the UK is an apprenticeship in mechanical engineering or electrical engineering to train craftsmen, technicians, senior technicians, and Incorporated Engineers for vocational oriented work and professional practice. modern Chartered Engineers are usually formed through a university degree programme at the Masters Engineering level and may undertake a short form of post graduate apprenticeship. A typical example is the apprenticeships formerly available at the BTH and EEC at Rugby in England. Subjects covered included limits and fits, metallurgy, foundry technology, engineering drawing, materials science for engineering materials, metalworking by hand, operating machine tools, and basic features of engineering design. Also refer to apprenticeship and the UK and German section.

3

Learning Enterprises

Learning Enterprises is the type of learning which reflected capabilities that combine types of learning into more general expertise developed by Gangné and Merrill (1990). This is additional type of learning to Gagnè's types of learning: declarative knowledge, intellectual skills, cognitive strategies, attitudes, and psychomotor skills. Learning goal not always include one learning outcome. The multiple objectives are frequently occurred when instruction handled not just single topic or lesson to the course. Integration of multiple objectives may usefully be conceived in terms of the more comprehensive activity in which the human performer is engaged, which we call an enterprise. An enterprise is a purposive activity that may depend for its execution on some combination of verbal information, intellectual skills, and cognitive strategies, all related by their involvement in the common goal. Given such an integrative goal of performance resulting from instruction, the various single objectives are viewed as being integrated as constituents of an enterprise schema.

Gangné 's Types of Learning Outcomes

Robert M. Gagné (1985) divided possible learning outcomes into five large "Domains"; declarative knowledge, intellectual skill, cognitive strategies, psychomotor skills and attitude. In1990, Gangne and Merrill added new type of learning which is learning enterprises.

- *Declarative knowledge* :Also called as verbal information. This type of learning requires a learner to recall in verbatim, paraphrased, or summarized form facts, lists, names, or organized information. It requires recall, recognize, or state contents in learner's own words.

- *Intellectual skills* :Intellectual skills are typified by application of rules to previously unencountered examples or information. This type of learning outcome differs from declarative knowledge because learners learn how to not only recall, but also to apply knowledge to instances not encountered during instruction. The four most common types of intellectual skills are making discriminations, forming concepts, applying rules, and solving problems.
- *Cognitive strategies* :This is "learning how to learn". Cognitive strategies are the metaprocesses that we use to manage our thinking about thins and manage our own learning. A more complex cognitive strategy would be figuring out how to organize, cluster, remember, and apply new information.
- *Psychomotor skills* :This is the learning about how to performance. Coordinated muscular movements that are typified by smoothness and precise timing are called psychomotor skills (R.Gagné, 1985)
- *Attitude* :An attitude is a mental state that predisposes a learner to choose to behave in a certain way (R. Gagné, 1985). Attitudes affects the learner's choice, and this play a strong role in motivational aspect.
- *Learning Enterprise* :types of activities that require students to collaborate and use a variety of capabilities; translate those activities into a class project; translate the project into objectives by identifying the component skills

From each of the single categories of learning outcome, the instructional designer is able to analyze and prescribe the instructional conditions necessary for effective learning. When instruction is considered in the more comprehensive sense of a module, section, or course, in a macro level, it becomes apparent that multiple objectives commonly occur.

Base of Learning Enterprises

Macro Strategy: First of all, micro strategies are ways to approach instruction on particular topics of learning goals. Typically, an instructional design and development task for either education or training involves more than one goal or topic. Therefore we need to approach with Macro level. Developing instruction at the macro level is frequently referred to as curriculum development or design which is concerned with making decisions about the scope, organization, and sequence of content at the macro level. Posner and coworkers (Posner&Strike, 1976; Poser & Rudnitsky, 1994) classified curriculum sequencing structures, which is used in curriculum development, into five major categories:

world related structure, learning-related structure, utilization-related structure, enquiry-related structure, and concept-related structure. Learning enterprise is based on macro strategy, because it is beyond the single topic, or goal. Especially it is connected with learning-related structure.

Learning-Related Structure

Learning-related structures organize information in such a way that new learning builds on relevant prior knowledge. We use this into two ways. One is prerequisite-based structure which is based on prerequisite relationship of all the information and skills in the course. The other is Knowledge structure. The knowledge structure idea is seen in learning enterprises. The unifying element in an enterprise is a declarative knowledge representation of enterprise itself. A strong emphasis is placed on the purposeful and interrelated qualities of the knowledge, and hence, various theories related to schema. The declarative knowledge of the enterprise is referred to as an enterprise schema.

Components of Learning Enterprises

Each kind of enterprise is represented in memory by a schema that reflects the purpose or goal of the enterprise category, the various knowledge and skills required to engage in the enterprise, and a scenario which indicates when and how each piece of knowledge or skill is required by the enterprise.

Enterprise Schema

the enterprise schema is expected to contain a number of knowledge and skill constituents which become associated in the service of the integrated goal. These include verbal labels, connected-discourse forms of verbal information, intellectual skills, and cognitive strategies. Depending upon the enterprise, motor skills, and attitudes may also be involved.

There are different kinds of enterprise schemas, just as there are different kinds of application forms. Each such schema contains slots to be filled by the details of any specific enterprise. There appear to be several categories of integrative goals that are useful to distinguish as different kinds of enterprise schemas. Three varieties of enterprise and their associated enterprise schemas are described, designated by their goals as denoting, manifesting, and discovering.

Denoting An entity (thing, place, event) or class of entities may be denoted by giving its name, the class to which it belongs, and the function it serves. The denoting communication may also include identification of the parts of the entity, their locations, and functions. As an example, a hawser is denoted as a large rope (its class) for towing or moving a ship (its function). Denoting may also proceed to indicate parts, such as the hawser bend (used for connecting two hawsers) and a hawser clamp (a device for gripping a hawser). Entities other than objects may be denoted, such as persons, places, or events. Examples might be the U. S. Attorney General, the city of St. Louis, the 1988 baseball World Series. An enterprise of this sort is a part of many human occupations such as teaching, explaining, orienting, counselling, and giving directions.

Manifesting Actions involving entities as actors or objects may be arranged in a series of steps leading to a particular result. Such a series is called a process, and it is this that is the object of a manifesting enterprise. Learners must gain knowledge of the steps in the process. A manifesting enterprise consists of making a process evident to other people (e.g., students, co-workers) by indicating its stages and their sequence. Manifesting a process implies going beyond employing a simple verbal communication; it may require the use of pictures or props, as is commonly done in a demonstration. An example of manifesting a process occurs when a student can indicate the stages in the life cycle of an insect and can show how these stages vary under different environmental conditions.

Discovering The enterprise of discovering reveals (to observers) a previously unknown novel entity or process. Often, entities and the procedures for manipulating them are inventions. One of the most creative types of enterprise involves the capability to design or discover a novel entity or procedure. For example, to remove tight covers from jars, a learner might discover the design of an object that grips the cover tightly, making possible its unscrewing from the jar. Alternatively, a learner might discover a procedure that would cause the cover to loosen its grip on the jar by metal expansion. As another example, having knowledge of control mechanisms in mechanical systems, a learner may discover a hypothesis about biological control mechanisms which trigger phases of the life cycle of insects.

Enterprise Scenario in Learning Transfer

Verbal information in the form of an enterprise scenario is typically a prominent part of an enterprise schema. It is this declarative knowledge that relates particular singular objectives that compose the expected behaviour to the purposive activity that is the enterprise. The enterprise scenario "tells" the learners that the concept they are identifying, or the procedure they are following, is actually an essential part of a purposeful enterprise.

For example, an enterprise scenario may remind students of arithmetic that they are going to encounter future situations requiring them to perform mental subtraction in order to verify the change from a purchase made with a paper-money bill of fixed value. Or, an enterprise scenario may help a student of physics to bring to mind the relation between the practice of electric heating and the cost of electric power. The enterprise schema is likely to be a factor of considerable prominence in the mediation of transfer of learning from one task to another, or from a learning task to a later performance. As contrasted with factors pertaining to the quality of learning content such as amount and variety of practice, the enterprise frame is a metacognitive feature.

The implication it carries for instructional design is to ensure transfer from training to the job, provision must be made for learner acquisition of an enterprise schema in addition to the specific knowledges and skills that the performance requires. The enterprise scenario of this schema is one that relates each component of knowledge and skill to the goal, and thus to the enterprise that embodies this goal.

Conclusion

Course with enterprise goals might have a first tier of organization structured by the enterprises themselves, organized according to their schemata and sequenced accordingly. The second tier of organization might employ an enquiry or utilization structure. (Smith & Ragan)

Vocational-technical School

A vocational-technical school, often called a voc-tech school, is a high school in the United States and Canada designed to bring vocational and technical training to its students. Such skills become highly valuable to students entering into a vocational or technical field without first obtaining higher education. Proponents claim that students bound for college may be able to use such skills to realize a distinct educational advantage over other students in their major. Additionally, vocational-technical schools often provide training to adults from the surrounding communities. The training, offered for a cost, may range from a single course to an entire programme of ten or more courses.

Vocational-technical schools are licensed, registered, or accredited like any other high school.

Types

Though less common, some vocational-technical schools are *full-time*. Not only do they provide vocational and technical training, but they also provide traditional academics that students would typically receive during high school, all within one school district or building. Such schools often expose students to their academic classes during one half of the day, and to their vocational and technical classes during the other half.

Most vocational-technical schools, however, are *part-time*. This means that they only provide vocational and technical training, while the academic portion of their education is obtained from their home school district. Students engaged in such schools often spend one half of the school year at their home school for academic classes and the other half of the school year at the vocational-technical school for training, alternatively they may go to their home school in the morning and their vocational-technical school after lunch.

Professional Technical School

A professional technical school– "professionalno-tehnicheskoye uchilishche" is a type of vocational education facility established in the former Soviet Union to train qualified industrial workers and servicemen. Such schools are widespread in all post-Soviet countries (usually in every city).

PTUs formed a government-funded USSR-wide system for school graduates who didn't intend to receive a university degree. Instead, they were both educated generally and trained for non-academic occupations. There were PTUs specializing in almost all such professions, but the most common were construction and machinery positions. Specializations also included secretaries (girls only), cooks, waiters and even mosaic artists (needed drawing talents to apply). The usual entering age for students was 15 - after 8 years of ordinary school, with students coming from peasant backgrounds, the lower working class, orphanages and the like. Two or three years of learning were typical, though some students would enter after 10 years of ordinary school and learn during 1 year.

PTUs required no entering examination and provided students with free hostels and meals. Parents were also attracted by the 24-hour presence of "upbringers" - mentors tasked with preventing students from engaging in deviant behaviour. Further employment was also guaranteed, as well as the possibility of continuing education at university level. PTUs played an important role in urbanizing rural communities and forming the Soviet working class.

History

In the 1920–1930s, the forerunners of PTU's included "schools of factory and plant apprenticeship", which were partly inherited from the vocational school system of the Russian Empire. In 1940, they were reorganized to "vocational schools", and in 1959 to PTUs.

During the transformation to a market economy, PTUs suffered a huge blow as their graduates lost socialist employment guarantees. Many PTUs were closed or merged and the number of students declined dramatically. Some PTUs were renamed and reformed into "lyceums" in an attempt to gain higher status and establish tuition fees.

Industry-oriented Education

Industry Oriented Education has been applied to vocational education. It was only offered to sub-degree education and industry training until 2004. Since 2004 Industry Oriented Education has been introduced to undergraduate degree and Master's degree.

Definition

Industry oriented education is an approach to learning from an industry perspective. With traditional technical teaching methodologies in educational environments, the conventional pathway is to build the foundation learning through subject based teaching of maths, physics and science independently. Subjects based on the knowledge required for the discipline usually follow on from this. The problem with this traditional methodology of learning is that there is no close relationship with industry requirements.

Examples

Students may well graduate with no industrial oriented learning experience prior to their first job. Industrial oriented methodology is an approach to learning from an industry perspective. As an example, the course of Electronics Technology in the Bachelor of Applied

Technology is directly linked to industry and the focus is on an industrial product such as a Switch-mode power supply. Initially students will receive a demonstration and the product enclosure will be opened to investigate inside.

The internal components form the topics for study: this includes the mechanical design for the enclosure, electronic design including the PCB (Printed Circuit Board) and embedded software design.

The focus for learning is product design, application and operation of electronic components and circuitry. The industrial product will be activated under simulated industry conditions where students will gain invaluable insight of design technology, operational procedure and programming techniques.

All foundation skills can be achieved within these studies and the students are well prepared to develop further knowledge and skills required for their industry project required in their final year through cooperative education with industry. Mathematics is not taught here as an independent course of study, but totally integrated into the compulsory technical courses.

As an example, the course of Electronics Technology taught in the Bachelor of Applied Technology uses Fast Fourier Transform series to explore the method of Electromagnetic Interference (EMI) in Switch-mode power supplies.

Initially students will receive a demonstration and the product which is a commercial product, will be opened for internal investigation of the enclosure.

The internal components form the topics for study: this includes the mechanical design for the enclosure, electronic design including the PCB (Printed Circuit Board) and embedded software design. The focus for learning is product design, application and operation of electronic components and circuitry.

An example in post-graduate programme is a "bridge" technology course designed for the first year students in Master of Design programme before they start their projects. It is to enable a Bachelor of Design graduate to entry this technology oriented programme.

Advanced Level Mathematics

Advanced Level (A-Level) Mathematics is a qualification of further education taken in the United Kingdom and occasionally in other countries as well. In the UK A-Level exams are traditionally taken by 18-year-olds after a two-year course at a sixth form or college. Advanced Level Further Mathematics is often taken by students who wish to study a mathematics based degree at university.

Like other A-level subjects, mathematics has been assessed in a modular system since the introduction of Curriculum 2000, whereby each candidate must take six modules, with the best achieved score in each of these modules (after any retakes) contributing to the final grade.

Most students will complete three modules in one year, which will create an AS-level qualification in their own right and will complete the A-level course the following year with three more modules.

Overview

The basic A-Level course consists of six modules, four standard (C1, C2, C3, and C4) and two modules that can be chosen by the student or school/college, etc. The C1 through C4 modules are referred to by A-level textbooks as "Core" modules, encompassing the major topics of mathematics such as logarithms, differentiation/integration and geometric/arithmetic progressions, to name but a few.

The two chosen modules for the final two parts of the A-Level are determined either by a student's personal choices or the course choice of their school/college, but commonly take the form of S1 (Statistics) and M1 (Mechanics)

Further Mathematics

Some mathematics students will choose to take an A-level in Further Mathematics which requires taking a further 6 modules to give a second qualification. The grades of the two A-levels will be independent of each other. Further Mathematics requires students to take a minimum of two Further Pure modules, one of which must be FP1, and the other either FP2 or FP3, which are simply extensions of the four Core modules from the normal Maths A-Level. Four more modules need to be taken; those available vary with different specifications.

Not all schools are able to offer Further Mathematics, due to teachers not being qualified, so to fulfill the demand extra tutoring such as from the Further Mathematics Support Programme is available.

Some students can also take a third maths qualification, "Additional Further Mathematics", which adds more modules from those not used for Mathematics or Further Mathematics. Schools that offer this qualification usually only take this to AS-level, taking three modules, but some students can go further, taking the extra six modules to gain another full A-Level qualification.

Additional Further Mathematics is offered by Edexcel and OCR only. Lastly, a Pure Mathematics A-level is available for those students who (on the Edexcel exam board) take the modules C1, C2, C3, C4, FP1 and either FP2 or FP3.

Results and Statistics

Each module carries a maximum of 100 points towards the total grade and each module is also given a separate grade depending on its score. The number of points required for different grades are defined below:

Grade	*Module (Out of 100)*	*AS level (Out of 300)*	*A level (Out of 600)*
*A**	-	-	*480 (With 180/ 200 from C3 + C4)*
A	80	240	480
B	70	210	420
C	60	180	360
D	50	150	300
E	40	120	240

The proportion of candidates acquiring these grades in 2007 are below :

Mathematics

	Male	*Female*	*Combined*
Entries			60093
Grade A	42.6%	45.5%	43.7%
Grade B	20.8%	22.2%	21.4%
Grade C	15.8%	15.1%	15.6%
Grade D	10.9%	10.0%	10.4%
Grade E	6.4%	5.0%	5.9%

Criticisms

It has been suggested by The Department for Education that the high proportion of candidates who obtain grade A makes it difficult for universities to distinguish between the most able candidates. The 2010 exam session has introduced an A* grade that distinguishes between better candidates.

The A* grade in maths is awarded to candidates who achieve an A (480/600) in their overall A Level as well as achieving a combined score of 180/200 in modules Core 3 and Core 4.

The A* grade in further maths is awarded slightly differently. The same minimum score of 480/600 is required across all six modules, however a 90% average (or a score of 270/300) must be obtained across the candidate's best 'A2' modules. A2 modules include any modules other than those with a '1' (C1, S1, M1 are not A2 modules, whereas S2, S3, S4, FP3 and FP2 are).

4

Applied Academics

Applied academics is an approach to learning and teaching that focuses on how academic subjects (communications, mathematics, science, and basic literacy) can apply to the real world. Further, applied academics can be viewed as theoretical knowledge supporting practical applications.

Definition

Applied Academics is an approach to learning which focuses on motivating and challenging students to connect what they learn with the world they experience and with what interests them. The basic premise is that if academic content is made more relevant, participatory and concrete, students learn better, retain more and apply learning in their lives.

Teaching in this model uses hands-on innovative teaching methods sometimes called contextual learning. Teachers help students understand the reasons for studying their subject matter and capitalize on students' natural learning inclinations and problem-solving approaches they can use well beyond the classroom throughout their lives.

Applied Academics is an attempt to break from disconnected learning (where students go to different classes for different subjects for specified periods of time and don't gain a sense of the interconnectedness of learning) that has become a part of traditional approaches to education. This approach attempts to reintegrate learning by doing such things (for example) as teaching math and/or science and/or writing and/or speech within other contexts such as a learning experience dealing with some form of technology training.

Research in Cognitive Science

Research in cognitive science has shown that learners are not passive receptacles into which knowledge may be "poured". Learning occurs when the learner constructs, invents, and solves problems. Studies have shown that students taught theoretical principles, processes and skills in isolation without practice do not transfer these skills and knowledge as well to real life situations. Although "learning to know," "learning to do," and their "application" are often separated, there is no effective learning or understanding of one kind without the other two.

Relating to the SCANS Competencies

In the United States the Secretary's Commission on Achieving Necessary Skills (SCANS) states that "good jobs require people who can put knowledge to work", and listed the knowledge (academics) that it considered critical for all students to possess.

These competencies include:

- Knowing how to effectively allocate time, money, materials, space, and staff
- The ability to work on a team, teach, serve customers, lead, negotiate and work with people from culturally diverse backgrounds
- Understanding how to effectively acquire, evaluate, and use data
- Understanding and ability to design and improve social, organizational, and technological systems
- The ability to effectively use technology

Relating to Action Research

The concept of action research is related to Applied Academics, as one tenet of action research is to discover theory through practice, and then implement using the foundation of theory.

Bachelor of Vocational Education

Bachelor of Vocational Education (B.V.E., BVE, or BVEd) is a specialized undergraduate bachelor's degree which qualifies the graduate as a vocational teacher in public schools or trainer for private companies. Some universities offer a Bachelor of Vocational Education and Training, or a Bachelor of Career and Technical Education degree, which are basically equivalent to a BVE. Further, many universities have specific vocational education bachelor degrees to prepare agricultural, business, computer, health occupations, marketing, and industrial arts teachers as well as degrees for Adult and Continuing Education.

History

Vocational educators have existed since the first vocations existed. One of the main systems of vocational education was through masters and apprentices. As traditional academic institutions started to recognize the need for vocational education, there became a need to accredit potential vocational teachers within the traditional academic system.

This can be seen in California through their requirement that all community college tenured vocational instructors have a bachelor's degree In Australia the Bachelor of Vocational Education and Training grew out of "an expressed need for a programme of study for training and vocational educators"

Requirements

California: While each colleges specific curriculum and courses may vary, nearly every college in California that offers a Bachelor of Vocational Education degree includes courses in Characteristics and Management of Education for Adult Students, Assessment and Instruction, Teaching Diverse Learners, Advanced Instructional Design, Programme Evaluation and Leadership, and School Health Care as these are generally required for a Designated Subjects Vocational Education Teaching Credential.

Further, BVE students may generally complete a SWAN Portfolio that allows them to get college credit for experience they have had from their specific vocations.

Value and Effectiveness

A study done by the Department of Education of Newfoundland and Labrador, Canada found that 94% of BVE graduates were working in a field related to their degree compared with 80% for all graduates with an undergraduate degree. Further, BVE graduates earned on average \$18.01-\$20.00 per hour compared to \$14.01-\$16.00 for the general graduating population.

Community College

A community college is a type of educational institution. The term can have different meanings in different countries.

Australia

In Australia, the term community college is not used. Analogous to community colleges are colleges or institutes of Technical and Further Education (TAFEs); public institutions mostly regulated at state and territory level. There are also an increasing number of private providers of varying social esteem; often these are colloquially called 'colleges'.

TAFEs and other providers carry on the tradition of adult education, which was established in Australia around mid 19th century when evening classes were held to help adults enhance their numeracy and literacy skills. The majority of Australian universities can also be traced back to such forerunners, although obtaining a university charter has always changed their nature. I

n TAFEs and colleges today, courses are designed for personal development of an individual and/or for employment outcomes. Educational programmes cover a variety of topics such as arts, languages, business and lifestyle; and are usually timetabled to be conducted in the evenings or weekends to accommodate people working full-time. Funding for colleges may come from government grants and course fees; and many are not-for-profit organisations. There are located in metropolitan, regional and rural locations of Australia.

Learning offered by TAFEs and colleges has changed over the years. By the 1980s many colleges had recognised a community need for computer training and since then thousands of people have been up-skilled through IT courses. The majority of colleges by the late 20th century had also become Registered Training Organisations; recognising the need to offer individuals a nurturing, non-traditional education venue to gain skills that would better prepare them for the workplace and potential job openings. TAFEs and colleges do not grant bachelor's degrees, although an increasing number have arrangements with universities to provide pathways towards degrees. The American innovation of the associate degree is emerging at some institutions. Certificate courses I to IV, diplomas and advanced diplomas are typically offered, the latter deemed equivalent to bachelor degrees, albeit typically in more vocational areas.

Canada

In Canada, the term community college is not widely used. There are 150 institutions that could be roughly equivalent of the US community college in certain contexts. They are usually referred to simply as "colleges" since in common usage a degree granting institution is almost exclusively a university. In the province of Quebec, even when speaking in English, all colleges are incorrectly called Cégeps, the french acronym for the public system: "Collège d'enseignement général et professionnel", meaning "College of General and Vocational Education". (The word College can also refer to a private High School in Quebec).

Colleges are educational institutions providing higher education and tertiary education, granting certificates, and diplomas. Associate's degrees and bachelor's degrees are granted by universities, but, in some courses of study, there may be an agreement between colleges and universities to collaborate on the education requirements toward a degree. Only in Western Canada is the term Associates degree used as in the United States. In other parts of Canada a degree is usually attained as a 4 year study programme, and to a much lesser degree now (except in Quebec, where it is the norm), in 3 years.

Each province has its own educational system reflecting the decentralization of the Canadian provinces and therefore of the education system. However, most of the colleges began in the mid-1960s to provide education and training for the then-emerging baby boom generation and for immigrants from around the world who were starting to enter the country.

Malaysia

Community colleges in Malaysia are a network of educational institutions whereby vocational and technical skills training could be provided at all levels for school leavers before they entered the workforce. The community colleges also provide an infrastructure for rural communities to gain skills training through short courses as well as providing access to a post-secondary education.

At the moment, most community colleges award qualifications up to Level 3 in the Malaysian Qualifications Framework (Certificate 3) in both the Skills sector (Sijil Kemahiran Malaysia or the Malaysian Skills Certificate) as well as the Vocational and Training sector but the number of community colleges that are starting to award Level 4 qualifications (Diploma) are increasing. This is two levels below a Bachelor's degree (Level 6 in the MQF) and students within the system who intend to further their studies to that level will usually seek entry into Advanced Diploma programmes in public universities, polytechnics or accredited private providers.

Philippines

In the Philippines, a community school functions as elementary or secondary school at daytime and towards the end of the day convert into a community college. This type of institution offers night classes under the supervision of the same principal, and the same faculty members who are given part-time college teaching load.

The concept of community college dates back to the time of the former Minister of Education, Culture and Sports (MECS) that had under its wings the Bureaus of Elementary Education, Secondary Education, Higher Education and Vocational-Technical Education. MECS Secretary, Dr. Cecilio Putong, who in 1971 wrote that a community school is a school established in the community, by the community, and for the community itself. Dr. Pedro T. Orata of Pangasinan shared the same idea, hence the establishment of a Community College, now called the City College of Urdaneta.

A community college like the one in Abuyog, Leyte can operate with only PHP 124,000 annual budget in a 2-storey structure housing more than 700 students.

United Kingdom (Excluding Scotland)

In the United Kingdom, except for Scotland, a community college is a school which not only provides education for the school age population (11-18) of the locality, but also additional services and education to adults and other members of the community. This education includes but is not limited to sports, adult literacy and lifestyle education. Usually at the age of 16 when students finish their secondary school studies, they move on to a sixth form college where they study for their A-levels (although some secondary schools have integrated sixth forms). After the 2 year A-level period, they may then proceed to a college of further education or a university.

United States

In the United States, community colleges, sometimes called junior colleges, technical colleges, or city colleges, are primarily two-year public institutions providing higher education and lower-level tertiary education, granting certificates, diplomas, and associate's degrees. Many also offer continuing and adult education.

After graduating from a community college, some students transfer to a four-year liberal arts college or university for two to three years to complete a bachelor's degree.

Before the 1970s, community colleges in the United States were more commonly referred to as junior colleges, and that term is still used at some institutions. However, the term "junior college" has evolved to describe private two-year institutions, whereas the term "community college" has evolved to describe publicly funded two-year institutions. The name derives from the fact that community colleges primarily attract and accept students from the local community, and are often supported by local tax revenue.

Comprehensive Community Colleges

Many schools have evolved into and adapted the term *comprehensive* to describe their institutions. These schools typically offer six facets of education:

1. Transfer education – The traditional two-year student who will then transfer to a four-year institution to pursue a BS/BA degree.
2. Career education – The traditional two-year student that will graduate with an Associate Degree and directly enter the workforce.
3. Developmental – Remedial education for high school graduates who are not academically ready to enroll in college-level courses.
4. Continuing – Non-Credit courses offered to the community for personal development and interest.
5. Industry training – Contracted training and education wherein a local company pays the college to provide specific training or courses for their employees.
6. eLearning - Distance learning occurs online using one's computer and proctored exams. Pell grants and federal aid apply to eLearning also. For example, studying Spanish in an eLearning environment is possible when a student is in another state and federal aid is applied to out-of-state tuition.

Within the transfer education category, comprehensive schools typically have articulation agreements in place that provide prearranged acceptance into specific four-year institutions. At some community colleges, the partnering four-year institution teaches the third and fourth year courses at the community college location and thereby allows a student to obtain a four-year degree without having to physically move to the four-year school.

There is a number of institutions and organizations which provide community college research to inform practice and policy.

For background on U.S. community college libraries, see "Disposed to Consolidation and Innovation: Criteria for the Community College Specialization."

Research

There are a number of research organizations and publications who focus upon the activities of community college, junior college, and technical college institutions.

Many of these institutions and organizations present the most current research and practical outcomes at annual community college conferences.

- The American Association of Community Colleges has provided oversight on community college research since the 1920s. AACC publishes a research journal called the Community College Journal.
- The Association of Community College Trustees (ACCT) has provided education for community college boards of directors and advocacy for community colleges since 1972. ACCT President and CEO J. Noah Brown has authored a book about the past, present, and future of community colleges called Charting a New Course for Community Colleges: Aligning Policies with Practice.
- The mission of the Community College Research Centre from Teachers College at Columbia University is to "conduct research on the major issues affecting community colleges in the United States and to contribute to the development of practice and policy that expands access to higher education and promotes success for all students."
- The Centre for Community College Student Engagement at the University of Texas at Austin administers surveys and provides data analysis support to member colleges regarding various factors of student engagement and involvement in community colleges in the United States and Canada.
- The Community College Futures Assembly is an annual conference to showcase the best practices in community college administration. Focus groups convene at the conference to serve as a "think tank" to inform practice of community college board of trustees, presidents, and policy makers.

Additionally, several peer-reviewed journals extensively publish research on community colleges:

- Community College Journal of Research and Practice
- New Directions for Community Colleges
- Community College Review
- Journal of Applied Research in the Community College
- Journal of Transformative Leadership and Policy Studies

Corporate Education

Corporate Education refers to a system of professional development activities provided to educate employees. It may consist of formal university or college training or informal training provided by non-collegiate institutions. The simplest form of corporate education may be training programmes designed "in-house" for an organization that may wish to train their employees on specific aspects of their job processes or responsibilities. More formal relationships may further exist where corporate training is provided to employees through contracts or relationships with educational institutions who may award credit, either at the institution or through a system of CEUs (Continuing Education Units).

Many institutions or trainers offering corporate education will provide certificates or diplomas verifying the attendance of the employee. Some employers use corporate and continuing education as part of a holistic human resources effort to determine the performance of the employee and as part of their review systems.

Increasingly organisations appear to be using corporate education and training as an incentive to retain managers and key employees within their organisation. This win-win arrangement creates better educated managers for the organisation and provides the employees with a more marketable portfolio of skills and, in many cases, recognised qualifications.

The Difference Between Corporate Education and Corporate Training

Most organisations tend to think of corporate education as corporate training. Corporate training programmes are often competency based and related to the essential training employees need to operate certain equipment or perform certain tasks in a competent, safe and effective manner. The outcome of a corporate training programme is a participant who is either able to operate a piece of equipment or perform a specific task in an effective manner according to pre-determined training criteria.

The primary role of corporate training is to ensure an employee has the knowledge and skills to undertake a specific operation to enable an organisation can continue to operate. Fundamentally, corporate training is centred on knowledge transfer, with an instructor teaching or demonstrating a particular function and the student learning and demonstrating they can apply what they have learnt to a particular operation.

Corporate education, however, adds another dimension and depth to training by involving learners as participants in generating new knowledge that assists an organisation to develop and evolve, rather than maintain the status quo. Corporate education focuses on developing the capability of an organisation to be able to do things and, in particular, the right things in order to be a sustainable and successful organisation.

Corporate education involves a facilitator, rather than an instructor or trainer, to engage participants and encourage them to think about the what, how and why of what they are doing and to challenge their current paradigms. Corporate education is centred on introducing learning techniques to stimulate employees to think about what their organisation does, where it is heading, potential new opportunities for the organisation and new and better ways of doing things. While the role of corporate training is to develop the operational competency of individuals, the purpose of corporate education is to promote the development of capability of both an individual and their organisation.

Increasingly organisations appear to be using corporate education as an incentive to retain managers and key employees within their organisation. This win-win arrangement creates better educated managers and employees for the organisation and gives individual employees a more marketable portfolio of skills and, in many cases, recognised qualifications.

Dual Sector Education

Dual sector education is a system of tertiary education that includes substantial amounts of both vocational (skills-based) and higher (academic-based) education in the same institution. Dual sector education is offered by colleges and universities worldwide, most prominently in Australia, Austria, Germany, Ireland, New Zealand, Switzerland and the United Kingdom. It differs from, and/or can also encompass, the similarly termed dual education system - which combines both vocational education within a school and an apprenticeship within a workplace. Moodie distinguishes between single sector institutions which offer 97% of their teaching in one sector, mixed sector institutions which teach from 3% to 20% of their students in their smaller sector, and dual sector institutions which have substantial (> 20% of their load) in each of vocational and higher education.

Further Education

Further education (often abbreviated FE; called continuing education in U.S. English) is a term mainly used in connection with education in the United Kingdom and Ireland. It is post-compulsory education (in addition to that received at secondary school), that is distinct from the education offered in universities (higher education). It may be at any level above compulsory secondary education, from basic skills training to higher vocational education such as; City and Guilds, Higher National Diploma or Foundation Degree.

A distinction is usually made between FE and higher education ("HE") which is education at a higher level than secondary school, usually provided in distinct institutions such as universities. FE in the United Kingdom therefore includes education for people over 16, usually excluding universities. It is primarily taught in FE colleges (which are similar in concept to United States community colleges, and sometimes use "community college" in their title), work-based learning, and adult and community learning institutions. This includes post-16 courses similar to those taught at schools and sub-degree courses similar to those taught at higher education (HE) colleges (which also teach degree-level courses) and at some universities.

Further Education by Country

Australia: In Australia, technical and further education or TAFE institutions provide a wide range of predominantly vocational tertiary education courses, mostly qualifying courses under the National Training System/Australian Qualifications Framework/Australian Quality Training Framework. Fields covered include hospitality, tourism, construction, engineering, secretarial skills, visual arts, information technology and community work.

Individual TAFE institutions (usually with many campuses) are known as either colleges or institutes, depending on the state or territory. TAFE colleges are owned, operated and financed by the various state and territory governments. This is in contrast to the higher education sector, whose funding is predominantly the domain of the Commonwealth government and whose universities are predominantly owned by the state governments.

United Kingdom

England: From 2001-2010 FE in England was managed by the Learning and Skills Council (LSC), the then largest government agency funding education provision. The LSC had a budget of some £13 billion and is organised on a regional basis through around 47 local councils. The LSC had a particular mission to improve and expand further education provision, driven by the UK government's desire to increase standards in post-16 student retention and achievement, particularly in skills-based vocational provision in FE colleges. Recent government-driven LSC and Department for Children, Schools and Families policies, such as Success for All and the Skills Strategy, articulate this vision.

Colleges in England that are regarded as part of the FE sector include:

- General FE (GFE) and tertiary colleges
- Sixth form colleges
- Specialist colleges (mainly colleges of agriculture and horticulture and colleges of drama and dance)
- Adult education institutes

In addition, FE courses may be offered in the school sector, both in sixth form (16-19) schools, or, more commonly, sixth forms within secondary schools.

The Learning and Skills Improvement Service (LSIS - formerly the Quality Improvement Agency and Centre for Excellence in Leadership) is the sector owned body supporting the development of excellent and sustainable FE provision across the learning and skills sector. Its aim is to accelerate the drive for excellence and, working in partnership with all parts of the sector, builds on the sector's own capacity to design, commission and deliver improvement and strategic change.

For technology support and advice, JISC provides a network of regional support centres, free at the point of use to anyone working in colleges in the UK.

From September 2007, teachers working in FE in England are required to gain professional status, known as Qualified Teacher Learning and Skills (QTLS). The first stage of QTLS is an initial 'passport to teaching' module. The second stage is full teacher training, which would typically take up to five years to complete. The qualification covers both taught and practical skills, and also requires teachers to undertake 30 hours of continuous professional development per year.

Good quality support for employers is indicated by the award of the Training Quality Standard, an initiative to improve the quality of provision for vocational education, while all colleges and FE providers are subject to regular inspections by Ofsted.

Lifelong Learning UK is the independent sector skills council responsible for the qualifications and standards for teachers working in FE. The trade unions for FE staff are the University and College Union and the Association of Teachers and Lecturers. Teachers working in the sixth form colleges, sixth form schools and sixth forms of secondary schools are eligible to join the teaching unions which recruit in the secondary school sector

In England, further education is often seen as forming one part of a wider learning and skills sector, alongside workplace education, prison education, and other types of non-school, non-university education and training. Since June 2009, the sector is overseen by the new Department for Business, Innovation and Skills, although some parts (such as education and training for 14-19 year olds) fall within the Department for Children, Schools and Families.

Northern Ireland

Further education in Northern Ireland is provided through six multi-campus colleges. Northern Ireland's Department for Employment and Learning has the responsibility for providing FE in the province.

- Belfast Metropolitan College
- North West Regional College
- Northern Regional College
- South Eastern Regional College
- South West College
- Southern Regional College

Most secondary schools also provide a Sixth Form scheme whereby a student can choose to attend said school for 2 additional years to complete their AS and A-levels.

Scotland

Scotland's further education colleges provide education for those young people who follow a vocational route after the end of compulsory education at age 16. They offer a wide range of vocational qualifications to young people and older adults, including SVQs, Higher National Certificates and Higher National Diplomas. Frequently, the first two years of higher education, usually in the form of an HND can be taken in an FE college, followed by attendance at university.

Wales

Further education in Wales is provided through:

- Sixth form colleges
- FE colleges
- High school sixth form within secondary schools

Further education in Wales comes under the remit of the Welsh Assembly Government and was formerly funded by ELWa before its merger with the Assembly.

Ireland

Ireland has further education colleges.

Job Rotation

Job rotation is a management technique that assigns trainees to various jobs and departments over a period of a few years. Surveys show that an increasing number of companies are using job rotation to train employees. There are both positive and negative effects involved with job rotation that need to be taken into consideration when a company makes the decision to use this technique.

Job rotation is also a control to detect errors and frauds. It reduces the risk of collusion between individuals. Organizations dealing with sensitive information or system (e.g. bank) where there is an opportunity for personal gain can benefit by job rotation. Job rotation also helps in business continuity as multiple people are equally equipped to perform a job function. If an employee is not available other can handle his/her position with similar efficiency.

Job Rotation is frequently used with new college graduates who are just entering the workforce. Trainees gain perspective on various areas of the organization. This provides an opportunity to work with higher management and different departments. Job rotation helps trainees to best apply their:

- knowledge
- abilities
- Interests

Positive Effects

There are different reasons a company may choose to use job rotation such as using job rotation as a learning mechanism. Research suggests that there are significant benefits that may out weigh the costs involved with training employees for diversified positions. As a learning mechanism, employees are given the opportunity to learn necessary skills which can help them to advance within a company. This employment opportunity also has the effect of boosting morale and self efficacy. The company may benefit from using job rotation by having the ability to staff key positions within a company. This practice may allow a company to run more efficiently, and as a result, become more productive and profitable.

Job rotation can also be used to alleviate the physical and mental stresses endured by employees when working the same position, year after year. By allowing employees to rotate to other positions, the risk factors for some types of musculoskeletal disorders may be reduced. Job Rotation is also believed to have the ability to decrease the amount of boredom and monotony experienced by employees who work the same position for extended periods of time.

Conclusion

In conclusion, when a company decides to use job rotation, it is a decision which needs to be thoroughly evaluated based on the positive and negative aspects a company may face during the utilization process.

5

Vocational Qualification Transfer System

The Vocational Qualification Transfer System (VQTS) model is a proposal for a structured description of work-related competences. The core elements are the Competence Matrix and the Competence Profiles. A Competence Matrix displays competences structurally in a table according to core work tasks in a specific occupational field ("competence area") and the progress of competence development ("step of competence development"). Competence Profiles are formed from individual parts of this Competence Matrix. In the context of ECVET the VQTS project sought to support the transnational mobility of learners. A Competence Matrix can be used for the development of qualifications, training programmes, and job profiles, as well as for human resource planning, the allocation of qualifications to the Qualifications Framework, and for developing higher permeability between vocational education and higher education.

Goals

The main goal of the VQTS model is the development of a systematic process for the comparison of competences and qualifications, and for the transnational transfer of competences acquired abroad (for example between education and working environment, or between vocational and higher education).

Structure

Competence Matrix: A Competence Matrix displays competences in a table according to core work tasks and the progress of competence development.

- The left hand column of the table contains competence areas, based on the various core work tasks.
- The acquisitions of competences, from beginner level to "skilled worker" level, are described for each competence area. Each competence described is a "step of competence development".

The structure and different ranges of Competence Matrices can be shown by these examples:

- Competence Matrix "mechatronics (chart 1)": Developed in VQTS I, this Matrix focuses on the development of competences required from workers at beginner level to skilled worker level.
- Competence Matrix for "electronics/electrical engineering" (chart 2): The VQTS II project intended to develop a Competence Matrix to be used to identify areas of overlap between VET and HE programmes. Therefore, the scope of the Competence Matrix 'electronics/electrical engineering' had to be broadened to include at least some steps of competence development relevant to HE.

A Competence Matrix can be developed via a moderated workshop using experts from the respective areas. Within the VQTS model it is assumed that 5-25 competence areas will be defined per occupational field, and 2-6 steps of the competence development process described for each competence area. It is not easy to describe competences, because they depend on a variety of characteristics and may be localised in different manners. There are no specific determinants for differentiating the steps in the model. Several dimensions could be:

Ability to

- perform independent work tasks
- deal with a certain complexity
- deal with quality standard demands
- deal with dynamic situations
- deal with non-transparency.

Competences in this model refer to cognitive competences (knowledge), functional competences (skills) as well as social competences (behaviour).

Competence Profiles

Competence Profiles are formed from particular parts of a Competence Matrix by identifying competences that are relevant to a certain training programme or qualification (organisational profile) or are reflective the competences acquired so far by a person in training (individual profile). Organisational profiles, developed by the authorities responsible for the respective training programmes or qualification, indicate the relevant competences of the specific training programme or qualification on the Competence Matrix and the corresponding number of Credit Points. Individual profiles, developed by the responsible training provider, asses which stage of competence development and Credit Points the student or apprentice has reached so far. Based on the competence profile of the person in training a Competence Profile Certificate can be issued.

Applications

A Competence Matrix can be used for those purposes where the transparency of competence profiles is very important, such as:

- transferring vocational competences acquired abroad (mobility in VET);
- transferring and recognising competences acquired within the official VET system as well as competences achieved through non-formal or informal learning;
- developing qualifications (for use in the development of the EQF);
- composing job profiles as well as personnel (human resources) planning;
- referencing qualifications to qualifications frameworks;
- enhancing permeability between VET and HE.

Background

Projects: The VQTS models were coordinated by 3s under the "Leonardo da Vinci Programme":

- VQTS I (2003–2006) with partners from Austria, Czech Republic, Denmark, Germany, Hungary, Italy, the Netherlands and the United Kingdom
- VQTS II (2007–2009) with partners from Austria, Czech Republic, Germany, Malta, the Netherlands and Slovenia

Context of Educational Policy

The VQTS project was closely aligned with the aims of the 'Copenhagen Process' wherein the EU countries declared their willingness to foster employability and lifelong learning in Europe by strengthening cooperation and increasing mobility in vocational education and training (VET). According to the 'Copenhagen Process', it should be possible to utilise competences acquired through formal, non-formal and informal learning throughout Europe. The VQTS model is one of the best instruments to implement ECVET and increase the (international) transparency and comparability of qualifications and training offers.

Awards

The VQTS I project received the Helsinki Award 2006 in the 'Recognition of competences and qualifications, ECVET' category, and the gold Lifelong Learning Award 2007 for its contributions to the aims of the 'Copenhagen Process'. The VQTS II project received the "Best Projects 2007" label in ADAM, the project and product portal for Leonardo da Vinci. These projects have strongly contributed to improvements in vocational education and training in Europe in recent years.

Vocational University

A vocational university, sometimes called professional university or applied technological university college of higher vocational studies, is an institution of higher education and sometimes research, which provides both tertiary and sometimes quaternary education and grants academic degrees at all levels (bachelor, master, and sometimes doctorate) in a variety of subjects. In some countries, a vocational university more precisely grants Professional degrees like Professional Bachelor's degree, Professional Master's degree and Professional doctorates). The term is not officially used in many countries and an assignment to a certain type of university in a certain country's educational system is therefore difficult. The UK once had a very extensive vocational university sector with its polytechnic system. Vocational universities are often regulated and funded differently (for example, by the local government rather than the state) from research-focused universities, and the degrees granted are not necessarily interchangeable.

Education

The education which takes place at vocational universities combines teaching of both practical skills and theoretical expertise. Higher vocational education might be contrasted with education in a usually broader scientific field, which might concentrate on theory and abstract conceptual knowledge. This has to do with the fact that, in the Middle Ages, an educational institution was called a university only if a certain classical canon of subjects was taught (typically including philosophy, medicine and theology). In modern times, other subjects, namely natural and engineering sciences, became more important — but still, institutions of tertiary education focusing on these and not offering the classical canon were denied the prestigious denomination "university", so they had to use the general word (High School in English) *Fachhochschule* in German, *Haute Ecole* in French (Belgium and Switzerland), *Hogeschool* in Dutch, *Høyskole* in Norwegian, *Scuola universitaria professionale* in Italian, etc.

There exist vocational universities of applied sciences (also named polytechnics or institutes of technology), vocational universities of liberal arts, etc. In recent years, many vocational universities have received full university status, such as the University of Music and Performing Arts, Vienna, Austria (Universität für Musik und darstellende Kunst Wien, formerly Hochschule für Musik und Darstellende Kunst Wien), or the Örebro University, Sweden (formerly Örebro Högskola). There are also some establishments which now have full university status, but continue to use their former names, such as the Royal Institute of Technology in Stockholm, Sweden.

Vocational Universities in Europe

Austria:

Finland

- Ammattikorkeakoulu (Yrkeshögskola in Swedish, translated *University of Applied Sciences*, literally "vocational high school"). Do not grant licentiate or doctorate degrees.

Notice: certain universities are called *korkeakoulu* because they effectively have only one faculty, e.g. *Teatterikorkeakoulu*, the Theatre Academy, whereas universities with several faculties are called *yliopisto*. The term *ammattikorkeakoulu* (AMK) creates some confusion with *korkeakoulu*, because traditionally AMK's are not considered universities. A graduate of university of applied sciences (*ammattikorkeakoulu*) is generally not eligible for doctoral studies in Finnish universities without formally completing a master's degree from a university (*yliopisto*).

Germany

The term vocational university is not used. In contrast to traditional German universities, a *Fachhochschule* (translated *University of Applied Sciences*) has a more practical profile. Universities of Applied

Sciences grant Bachelor degrees and Master degrees. Some Universities of Applied Sciences run doctoral programmes where the degree itself is awarded by a partner institution. Furthermore, *Berufsakademie* is a college type strongly inspired by the dual education system.

A *Berufsakademie* is called a *university of cooperative education* in English and only grants bachelor's degrees. This type of institution was first created in the German state of Baden-Württemberg and now exists in Hamburg, Hesse, Lower Saxony, Saarland, Saxony, Schleswig-Holstein, and Thuringia, but not in the other German states.

In 2009, Baden-Württemberg transformed its Berufsakademie into a new type of institution, which until now only exists in that state, a "Duale Hochschule". In English, this type of institution is also called *university of cooperative education*, but a Duale Hochschule also offers Master degrees.

Netherlands

As of January 29, 2008, a Dutch *hogeschool* (hbo) is called a university of applied sciences in English.

Hogescholen in the Netherlands have been provided with the right to conduct research by the revised Higher Education and Research Act (WHOO) 2010.

Sweden

The main difference between universities (universitet) and vocational universities (högskola, official translation *university college*) is that only the former ones have the right to award doctorate degrees in all subjects they offer. Some vocational universities have been given such rights within limited areas of research.

Switzerland

Vocational universities in Asia:

China

- Fashion Institute (Ningbo)
- Guangsha College of Applied Construction Technology (Zhejiang)
- Liming Vocational University (Guanzhou)
- Qingdao Vocational and Technical College (Qingdao)
- Vocational Academy of Art (Zhejiang)
- Yuying College of Vocational Technology (Zhejiang)

- Zhejiang Vocational College of Economic & Trade (Zhejiang)
- Zibo College (Shandong)

Hong Kong

Figure: *Hong Kong Institute of Vocational Education*

- College of Higher Vocational Studies of the City University of Hong Kong
- Hong Kong Institute of Vocational Education

India

While the terms vocational university and professional university do not have a clear legal definition in India, the University Grants Commission (UGC), which is the body that recognises universities in India, drawing its power from the *University Grants Commission Act, 1956*, shares power with 15 professional councils. These councils are "responsible for recognition of courses, promotion of professional institutions and providing grants to undergraduate programmes and various awards" in the relevant areas. The bodies relevant for professional education are:

- All India Council of Technical Education (AICTE)
- Medical Council of India (MCI)
- Indian Council for Agricultural Research (ICAR)
- National Council for Teacher Education (NCTE)

- Dental Council of India (DCI)
- Pharmacy Council of India (PCI)
- Indian Nursing Council (INC)
- Bar Council of India (BCI)
- Central Council of Homeopathy (CCH)
- Central Council of Indian Medicine (CCIM)
- Council of Architecture (COA)
- Distance Education Council (DEC)

Malaysia

There are five public vocational universities in Malaysia:

- Universiti Malaysia Pahang (UMP)
- Universiti Malaysia Perlis (UniMAP)
- Universiti Teknikal Malaysia Melaka (UTeM)
- Universiti Tun Hussein Onn Malaysia (UTHM)
- Universiti Malaysia Kelantan (UMK)

Sri Lanka

In 2009, the first University of Vocational Technology was established under the purview of the Ministry of Vocational and Technical Training. There are also nine Technical Colleges in Sri Lanka.

Vocational School

A vocational school (or trade school or career school), providing vocational education, is a school in which students are taught the skills needed to perform a particular job. Traditionally, vocational schools have not existed to further education in the area of liberal arts, but rather to teach only job-specific skills, and as such have been better considered to be institutions devoted to training, and not liberal arts education. That purely vocational focus began changing in the 1990s "toward a broader preparation that develops the academic" and technical skills of students, as well as the vocational. Typically, most career colleges specifically design their curricula for fields that have the best current and future growth potential.

Australia

Vocational schools were called Technical Colleges in Australia and there were more than 20 schools specializing in Vocational Educational Training (VET). But, nowadays only four Technical

Colleges remain and these are now referred to as Trade Colleges. At these colleges, students complete a modified Year 12 certificate and commence a school-based apprenticeship in a trade of their choice. There are two Trade Colleges in Queensland; Brisbane, Australian Trade College and the Gold Coast, Australian Industry Trade College and one in Adelaide, St Patrick's Technical College and another in Perth, Australian Trades College.

In Queensland, students can also undertake Vocational Educational Training at private and public high schools instead of studying for their OP or Overall Position which is a tertiary entrance score. However these students usually undertake more limited vocational education of one day per week whereas in the trade colleges the training is more time intensive.

Canada

Vocational schools are sometimes called colleges in Canada. However, a college may also refer to an institution that offers part of a university degree, or credits that may be transferred to a university.

In Ontario, secondary schools were separated into three streams: Technical Schools, Commercial/Business Schools and Collegiates (the academic schools). Those schools still exist; however, the curriculum has changed that no matter which type of school one attends, they can still attend any post-secondary institution and still study a variety of subjects (either academic or practical).

In Ontario, Ministry of Training, Colleges and Universities have divided postsecondary education into Universities, Community Colleges and Private Career Colleges.

In the province of Quebec, there are some vocational programmes offered at institutions called CEGEP's (*Collège d'enseignement général et professionnel*), but these too may function as an introduction to university. Generally students complete two years at a CEGEP directly out of high school, and then complete three years at a university (rather than the usual four), to earn an undergraduate degree. Alternatively some CEGEP's offer vocational training, but it is more likely that vocational training will be found at institutions separate from the academic institutions, though they may still be called colleges.

Central and Eastern Europe

In Central and Eastern Europe a vocational education is represented in forms of (professional) vocational technical schools often abbreviated as PTU and technical colleges (technikum).

PTU

PTU is usually a preparatory vocational education and is equivalent to the general education of the third degree in the former Soviet education, providing a lower level of vocational education (apprenticeship). It could be compared to a trade high school. In 1920-30s such PTUs were called as schools of factory and plant apprenticeship and later 1940s - vocational schools. Sometime after 1959 the name of PTU was established, however, with the reorganization of the Soviet educational system these vocational schools renamed into lyceums. There were several types of PTUs such as Middle City PTU and Rural PTU.

Technicum

Technical college (technicum) is becoming an obsolete term for a college in different parts of Central and Eastern Europe. Technicums provided a middle level of vocational education. Aside of technicums and PTU there also were vocational schools that also provided a middle level of vocational education. In Ukraine of 1920-30s technicums were a (technical) vocational institutes, however, during the 1930-32s Soviet educational reform they were degraded in their accreditation.

Institute

Institutes were considered a higher level of education, however, unlike universities they were more oriented to a particular trade. With the reorganization of the Soviet education system most institutes have been renamed into technical universities.

Finland

The Finnish system is divided between vocational and academic paths. Currently about 47 percent of Finnish students at age 15 go to vocational school. The vocational school is a secondary school for ages 16–21, and prepares the students for entering the workforce. The curriculum includes little academic general education, while the practical skills of each trade are stressed. The education is divided into eight main categories with a total of about 50 trades. The basic categories of education are

- Humanist and educational branch
- typical trade: youth- and free-time director
- Cultural branch
- typical trade: artisan, media-assistant
- The branch of social sciences, business and merchandise

- typical trade: Vocational Qualification in Business and Administration (Finnish: *merkonomi*)
- Natural Science
- typical trade: IT worker (Finnish: *datanomi*)
- Technology and traffic
- typical trades: machinist, electrician, process worker
- The branch of natural resources and environment
- typical trade: rural entrepreneur, forest worker
- The branch of social work, health care and physical exercise
- typical trade: paramedic (Finnish: *lähihoitaja*)
- The branch of travel, catering and domestic economics
- typical trade: institutional catering worker

In addition to these categories administered by the Ministry of Education, the Ministry of Interior provides vocational education in the security and rescue branch for policemen, prison guards and firefighters.

The vocational schools are usually owned by the municipalities, but in special cases, private or state vocational schools exist. The state grants aid to all vocational schools on the same basis, regardless of the owner. On the other hand, the vocational schools are not allowed to operate for profit. The Ministry of Education issues licences to provide vocational education. In the licence, the municipality or a private entity is given permission to train a yearly quota of students for specific trades. The licence also specifies the area where the school must be located and the languages used in the education.

The vocational school students are selected by the schools on the basis of criteria set by the Ministry of Education. The basic qualification for the study is completed nine-year comprehensive school. Anyone may seek admission in any vocational school regardless of their domicile. In certain trades, bad health or invalidity may be acceptable grounds for refusing admission. The students do not pay tuition and they must be provided with health care and a free daily school lunch. However, the students must pay for the books, although the tools and practice material are provided to the students for free.

In tertiary education, there are higher vocational schools (ammattikorkeakoulu which is translated to *polytechnic* or *university of applied sciences*), which give about 3-4 -year degrees in more involved fields, like engineering or nursing.

In contrast to the vocational school, an academically orientated upper secondary school, or senior high school (Finnish: *lukio*) teaches no vocational skills. It prepares for entering the university or a higher vocational school.

Ireland

A vocational school in Ireland is a type of secondary education school which places a large emphasis on vocational and technical education; this led to some conflict in the 1960s when the Regional Technical College system was in development. Since 2013 the schools have been managed by Education and Training Boards, which replaced Vocational Education Committees which were largely based on city or county boundaries. Establishment of the schools is largely provided by the state; funding is through block grant system providing about 90% of necessary funding requirements.

Vocational schools typically have further education courses in addition to the traditional courses at secondary level. For instance, *Post Leaving Certificate Courses* which are intended for school leavers and pre-third level education students.

Until the 1970s the vocational schools were seen as inferior to the other schools then available in Ireland. This was mainly because traditional courses such as the Leaving Certificate were not available at the schools, however this changed with the *Investment in Education* (1962) report which resulted in an upgrade in their status. Currently about 25% of secondary education students attend these schools.

Japan

In Japan vocational schools are known as *senmon gakkô*. There are part of Japan's higher education system. They are two-year schools that many students study at after finishing high school (although it is not always required that students graduate from high school). Some have a wide range of majors, others only a few majors. Some examples are computer technology, fashion and English.

Netherlands

In the Middle Ages boys learned a vocation through an apprenticeship. They were usually 10 years old when they entered service, and were first called *leerling* (apprentice), then *gezel* (journeyman) and after an exam - sometimes with an example of workmanship called a *meesterproef* (masterpiece) - they were called *meester* (master craftsman). In 1795 all of the guilds in the Netherlands were disbanded by Napoleon, and with them the guild vocational schooling system. After the French occupation, in the 1820s, the need for quality education caused more and more cities to form day and evening schools for various trades. In 1854, the society *Maatschappij tot verbetering van den werkenden stand* (Society to improve the working class) was founded in Amsterdam, that changed its name in 1861 to the *Maatschappij voor de Werkende Stand* (Society for the working class). This society started the first public vocational school (*De Ambachtsschool*) in Amsterdam, and many cities followed. At first only for boys, later the *Huishoudschool* (housekeeping) was introduced as vocational schooling for girls. Housekeeping education began in 1888 with the Haagsche Kookschool in The Hague.

In 1968 the law called the *Mammoetwet* changed all of this, effectively dissolving the Huishoudschool and the Ambachtsschool. The name was changed to *Lagere Technische School* (LTS) (lower technical school) where mainly boys went because of its technical nature. The other option, where most girls went was LBO (Lager Beroepsonderwijsl). In 1992 both LTS and LBO changed to VBO (Voorbereidend Middelbaar Beroepsonderwijs) and since 1999 VBO changed to the current VMBO.

United States

In the United States, there is a very large difference between career college and vocational college. The term *career college* is generally reserved for post-secondary for-profit institutions.

Conversely, vocational schools are Government-owned or at least Government-supported institutions, occupy two full years of study, their credits are by and large accepted elsewhere in the academic world and in some instances such as charter academies or magnet schools may take the place of the final years of high school.

Career colleges on the other hand are generally not government supported in any capacity, occupy periods of study less than a year, their training and certifications are largely if not completely discredited by the larger academic world and are run more as a for-profit business than anything else. In addition, as most career colleges are private schools; this group may be further subdivided into non-profit schools and proprietary schools, operated for the sole economic benefit of their owners.

As a result of this emphasis on the commercialization of education, a widespread and well-deserved for the period poor reputation for quality was retained by a great number of career colleges for over promising what the job prospects for their graduates would actually be in their field of study upon completion of their programme, and for emphasizing the number of careers from which a student could choose. However, although this problem has been largely corrected in modern times due to more stringent regulation. careful research on the career college in question must be performed by the student prior to enrolling in order to get the best value.

Even though career colleges have exploded in recent years, true government-sponsored vocational schools on the other hand have decreased severely in the United States and have largely been replaced by the various alternative trade classes offered at either trade-specific schools or by being merged with their community college cousins, which in addition to offering associate degrees and core university curriculum courses, also offer vocational classes depending on the needs of the local community, all units of which are capable of transferring to four-year institutions.

The Association for Career and Technical Education (ACTE) is the largest American national education association dedicated to the advancement of career and technical education or vocational education that prepares youth and adults for careers, so the wise prospective student may wish to check with them to see if the school is in good standing with this and other trade organizations.

Even though virtually none of the for-profit career colleges have distinguished themselves in any capacity, a great many true vocational schools have gone on to become some of the most prestigious universities in the world. The California Institute of Technology and Carnegie Mellon University are examples.

Reflective Practice

Reflective practice is "the capacity to reflect on action so as to engage in a process of continuous learning", which, according to the originator of the term, is "one of the defining characteristics of professional practice".

According to one definition it involves "paying critical attention to the practical values and theories which inform everyday actions, by examining practice reflectively and reflexively. This leads to developmental insight".

Reflective practice can be an important tool in practice-based professional learning settings where individuals learning from their own professional experiences, rather than from formal teaching or knowledge transfer, may be the most important source of personal professional development and improvement. As such the notion has achieved wide take-up, particularly in professional development for practitioners in the areas of education and healthcare. The question of how best to learn from experience has wider relevance however, to any organizational learning environment. In particular, people in leadership positions have a tremendous development opportunity if they engage in reflective practice.

History and Background

Reflective Practice was introduced by Donald Schön in his book *The Reflective Practitioner* in 1983, however, the concepts underlying reflective practice are much older. John Dewey was among the first to write about Reflective Practice with his exploration of experience, interaction and reflection. Other researchers such as Kurt Lewin, Jean Piaget, William James and Carl Jung were developing theories of human learning and development. Marcus Aurelius' Meditations has also been described as an example of reflective practice.

Dewey's works inspired writers such as Donald Schön and David Boud to explore the boundaries of reflective practice. Central to the development of reflective theory was interest in the integration of theory and practice, the cyclic pattern of experience and the conscious application of that learning experience. For the last 30 years, there has been a growing literature and focus around experiential learning and the development and application of Reflective Practice. Reflective practice also contributes to learning and expressing our own and others' stories (Ivan, 2012).

Donald Schön's 1983 book introduces concepts such as 'reflection on action' and 'reflection in-action' where professionals meet the challenges of their work with a kind of improvisation learned in practice. Reflective Practice has now been widely accepted and used as developmental practices for organisations, networks, and individuals. As Boud *et al* state:

> *"Reflection is an important human activity in which people recapture their experience, think about it, mull it over and evaluate it. It is this working with experience that is important in learning."*

Reflective Practice can be seen and has been recognised in many teaching and learning scenarios, and the emergence in more recent years of blogging has been seen as another form of reflection on experience in a technological age.

Models of Reflective Practice

The concept of Reflective Practice centres around the idea of lifelong learning in which a practitioner analyses experiences in order to learn from them. Reflective Practice is used to promote independent professionals who are continuously engaged in the reflection of situations they encounter in their professional worlds. Several models of reflection exist and are used to draw lessons out of experiences.

Argyris and Schön 1978

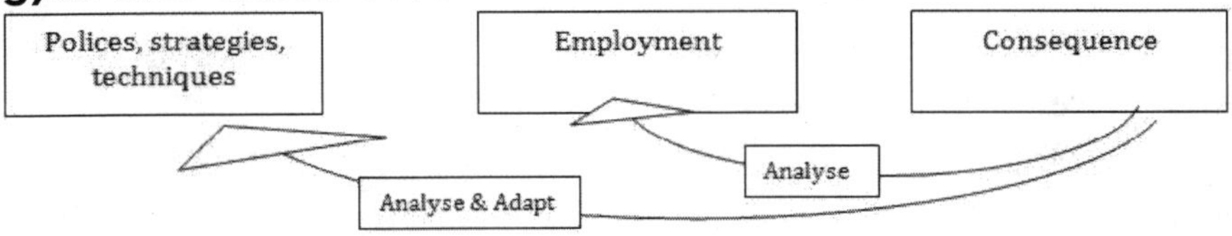

Figure: *Adaptation of the single and double loop learning model by Argyris and Schön*

Figure: *Adaptation of the reflective model by Schön*

Argyris and Schön pioneered the idea of single loop and double loop learning in 1978.

The theory was built around the recognition and amendment of a perceived fault or error. Single loop learning is when a practitioner or organisation, even after an error has occurred and a correction is made, continues to rely on current strategies, techniques or policies when a situation again comes to light. Double loop learning involves the modification of personal objectives, strategies or policies so that when a similar situation arises a new framing system is employed.

Schön himself introduced some years later the concept of Reflection-in-action and Reflection-on-action. Reflection-in-action can be described as the ability of a practitioner to 'think on their feet', otherwise known as 'felt-knowing'.

It revolves around the idea that within any given moment, when faced with a professional issue, a practitioner usually connects with their feelings, emotions and prior experiences to attend to the situation directly. Reflection-on-action on the other hand is the idea that after the experience a practitioner analyses their reaction to the situation and explores the reasons around, and the consequences of, their actions. This is usually conducted through a documented reflection of the situation.

Kolb 1975

Kolb was highly influenced by the research conducted by Dewey and Piaget in the 1970s. Kolb's reflective model highlights the concept of experiential learning and is centred around the transformation of information into knowledge. This takes place after the situation has occurred and entails a practitioner reflecting on the experience, gaining a general understanding of the concepts encountered during the experience and then testing these general understandings on a new situation. In this way the knowledge that is gained from a situation is continuously applied and reapplied building on a practitioners prior experiences and knowledge.

Gibbs 1988

Graham Gibbs discussed the use of structured debriefing to facilitate the reflection involved in Kolb's "experiential learning cycle". He presents the stages of a full structured debriefing as follows:

- (Initial experience)
- Description:

"What happened? Don't make judgements yet or try to draw conclusions; simply describe."

- Feelings:

"What were your reactions and feelings? Again don't move on to analysing these yet."

- Evaluation:

"What was good or bad about the experience? Make value judgements."

- Analysis:

"What sense can you make of the situation? Bring in ideas from outside the experience to help you."

"What was really going on?"

"Were different people's experiences similar or different in important ways?"

- Conclusions (general):

"What can be concluded, in a general sense, from these experiences and the analyses you have undertaken?"

- Conclusions (specific):

"What can be concluded about your own specific, unique, personal situation or way of working?"

- Personal action plans:

"What are you going to do differently in this type of situation next time?"

"What steps are you going to take on the basis of what you have learnt?"

Gibbs' suggestions are often cited as Gibbs' reflective cycle or Gibbs' model of reflection (1988), and simplified into the following six distinct stages:

- Description
- Feelings
- Evaluation
- Analysis
- Conclusions
- Action plan.

Johns 1995

Johns' model is a structured mode of reflection that provides a practitioner with a guide to gain greater understanding. It is designed to be carried out through the act of sharing with a colleague or mentor, which enables the experience to become learnt knowledge at a faster rate than reflection alone. Johns highlights the importance of experienced knowledge and the ability of a practitioner to access, understand and put into practice information that has been acquired through empirical means. In order for this to be achieved reflection occurs though 'looking in' on ones thoughts and emotions and 'looking out' at the situation experienced. Johns draws on the work of Carper (1978) to expand on the notion of 'looking out' at an experience. Five patterns of knowing are incorporated into the guided reflection, having a practitioner analyse the aesthetic, personal, ethical, empirical and the reflexive elements experienced through the situation. Johns' model is comprehensive and allows for reflection that touches on many important elements.

Brookfield 1998

Critically reflective practitioners constantly research their assumptions by seeing practice through four complementary lenses: the lens of their autobiography of learners of reflective practice, the lens of learners eyes, the lens of colleagues' perception and the lens of theoretical, philosophical and research literature. Reviewing practice through these lens makes us more aware of the power dynamics that infuse all practice settings

It also helps us detect hegemonic assumptions-assumptions that we think are in our own best interests but actually work against us in the long run (BROOKFIELD 1998) To become critically reflective Brookfield thinks that the four lenses stated above will reflect back to us stark and differently highlighted picture of who we are and what we do. Lens 1 Our autobiography as a learner is an important source of insight into practice. As we talk to each other about critical events in our practice, we start to realize that individual crises are usually collectively experienced dilemmas.

Analysing our autobiographies allows us to draw insight and meanings for practice on a deep visceral emotional level Lens 2 Our learners Eyes. seeing ourselves through learners eyes we discover that learners are interpreting our actions in the way that we mean them. But often we are surprised by the diversity of meanings people read into our words and actions.

A cardinal principle of seeing ourselves through learners eyes is that ensuring the anonymity of their critical opinions. You have to make students feel safe. Seeing our practice through learners eyes help us teach more responsively Lens 3 Our colleagues' Experiences. our colleagues serve as critical mirrors reflecting back to us images of our actions. Talking to colleagues about problems and gaining their perspective increases our chance finding some information that can help our situation lens 4 Theoretical Literature. Theory can help us "name"our practice by illuminating the general elements of what we think are idiosyncratic experiences

Rolfe 2001

Rolfe's reflective model is based around Borton's 1970 developmental model. A simplistic cycle composed of 3 questions which asks the practitioner, What, So What and Now What. Through this analysis a description of the situation is given which then leads into the scrutiny of the situation and the construction of knowledge that has been learnt through the experience. Subsequent to this, ways in which to personally improve and the consequence of ones response to the experience are reflected on.

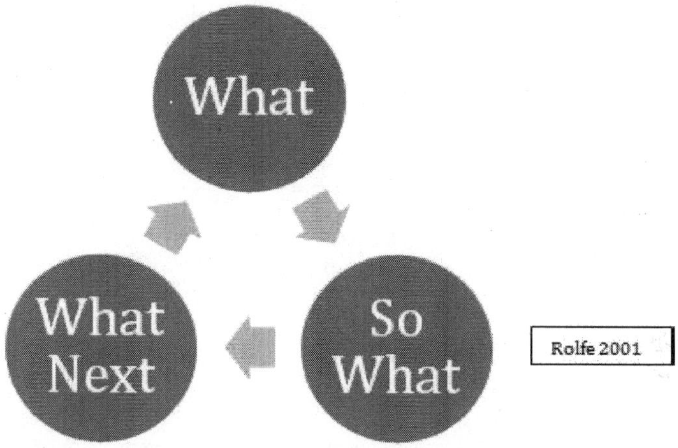

Figure: *Adaptation of the Rolfe Reflective Model*

Application

Reflective Practice has been described as an unstructured approach directing understanding and learning, a self regulated process, commonly used in health and teaching professions, though applicable to all professions. Reflective practice is a learning process taught to professionals from a variety of disciplines by practitioners, with the aim of enhancing abilities to communicate and making informed/ balanced decisions.

The practice has historically been applied most in the educational and medical field. When reflection in action and reflection on action described by Donald Schon are utilized in practice and when practitioners are able to identify these actions they become better at reflective practice. Professional Colleges such as the College of Nurses and College of Dental Hygienists are recognizing the importance of reflective practice and require practitioners to prepare reflective portfolios as a requirement to be licensed, and for yearly quality assurance purposes.

Education

In education, reflective practice refers to the process of the educator studying his or her own teaching methods and determining what works best for the students. It involves the consideration of the ethical consequences of classroom procedures on students.

The appeal of the use of reflective practice for teachers is that as teaching and learning are complex, and there is not one right approach, reflecting on different versions of teaching, and reshaping past and current experiences will lead to improvement in teaching practices. Schön's reflection-in-action assists teachers in making the professional knowledge that they will gain from their experience in the classroom an explicit part of their decision-making.

As Larrivee argues, Reflective Practice moves teachers from their knowledge base of distinct skills to a stage in their careers where they are able to modify their skills to suit specific contexts and situations, and eventually to invent new strategies. In implementing a process of Reflective Practice teachers will be able to move themselves, and their schools, beyond existing theories in practice. Larrivee concludes that teachers should "resist establishing a classroom culture of control and become a reflective practitioner, continuously engaging in a critical reflection, consequently remaining fluid in the dynamic environment of the classroom".

Health Professionals

Reflective Practice is associated with learning from experience, and is viewed as an important strategy for health professionals who embrace lifelong learning. Due to the ever changing context of healthcare and the continual growth of medical knowledge, there is a high level of demand on healthcare professionals' expertise. Due to this complex and continually changing environment, healthcare professionals could benefit from a programme of reflective practice.

Price (2004) recognizes that there are several reasons why a healthcare practitioner would engage in reflective practice: To further understand yourself, motives, perceptions, attitudes, values and feelings associated with client care; To provide a fresh outlook to practice situations and challenge existing thoughts, feelings as well as actions; To explore how the practice situation may be approached differently.

In the field of nursing there is concern that actions may run the risk of habitualisation, thus dehumanising patients and their needs. In utilising Reflective Practice, nurses are able to plan their actions and consciously monitor the action to ensure it is beneficial to their patient.

The act of reflection is seen as a way of promoting the development of autonomous, qualified and self-directed professionals. Engaging in

Reflective Practice is associated with the improvement of the quality of care, stimulating personal and professional growth and closing the gap between theory and practice. Activities to promote reflection are now being incorporated into undergraduate, postgrduate and continuing medical education across a variety of health professions Mann (2009) found through her research that in practising professionals the process of reflection appears to be multifactorial and to include different aspects. In addition to reflection both on and during experiences that the anticipation of a challenging situation also stimulated reflection. Practicing professionals vary in their tendency and ability to reflect.

Davies (2012) identifies that there are both benefits as well as limitations to reflective practice:

Benefits to Reflective Practice

- Increased learning from an experience for situation
- Promotion of deep learning
- Identification of personal and professional strengths and areas for improvement
- Identification of educational needs
- Acquisition of new knowledge and skills
- Further understanding of own beliefs, attitudes and values
- Encouragement of self-motivation and self-directed learning
- Could act as a source of feedback
- Possible improvements of personal and clinical confidence

Limitations of Reflective Practice

- Not all practitioners may understand the reflective process
- May feel uncomfortable challenging and evaluating own practice
- Could be time consuming
- May have confusion as to which situations/experiences to reflect upon
- May not be adequate to resolve clinical problems

Environmental Management and Sustainability

There is some criticism that traditional environmental management which simply focuses on the problem at hand, fails to integrate the wider context in which the environment sits into the decision making. While research and science must inform the process of environmental management, it is up to the practitioner to integrate those results within this wider context. In order to deal with this and to reaffirm the utility of environmental management Bryant and Wilson propose that a "more reflective approach is required that seeks to rethink the basic premises of environmental management as a process". This style of approach has been found to be successful in sustainable development projects where participants appreciated and enjoyed the educational aspect of utilising reflective practice throughout, however the authors noted the challenges with melding the "circularity" of reflective practice theory with the "doing" of sustainability.

Leadership Positions

Reflective Practice provides a tremendous development opportunity for those in leadership positions. Managing a team of people requires a delicate balance between people skills and technical expertise, and success in this type of role does not come easily. Reflective Practice provides leaders with an opportunity to critically review what has been successful in the past and where improvement can be made.

To support reflective learning organizations have invested in coaching programmes for their emerging and established leaders. Coaching is defined by the International Coaching Federation as partnering with clients in a thought provoking and creative process that inspires them to maximize their personal and professional potential. Leaders frequently engage in self-limiting behaviours because of their over reliance on their preferred ways of reacting and responding. To help support the establishment of new behaviours, coaching is extremely useful as it encourages reflection, critical thinking and transformative learning.

Adults have acquired a body of experience throughout their life or frames of reference that define their world. Coaching programmes support the process of questioning and potentially rebuilding these pre-determined frames of reference. The goal is for a leader to maximize their professional potential and in order to do this, there must be a process of critical reflection on current assumptions.

Other Professions

Reflective Practice can help an individual to develop personally, and is useful for professions other than those discussed above. It allows professionals to continually update their skills and knowledge and consider ways to interact with their colleagues.

Suggested ways for professionals to practice reflective management include:

- Coaching;
- Keeping a journal;
- Seeking feedback;
- View experiences objectively; and
- Taking time at the end of each day, meeting, experience etc. to reflect-on-actions.
- Anecdotal Notes
- Group discussion

Experiential Learning

Experiential learning is the process of making meaning from direct experience, i.e., "learning from experience".

The experience can be staged or left open. Aristotle once said, "For the things we have to learn before we can do them, we learn by doing them". David A. Kolb helped to popularize the idea of experiential learning drawing heavily on the work of John Dewey, Kurt Lewin, and Jean Piaget. His work on experiential learning has contributed greatly to expanding the philosophy of experiential education.

Contents

Overview: Experiential learning is learning through reflection on doing, which is often contrasted with rote or didactic learning. Experiential learning is related to, but not synonymous with, experiential education, action learning, adventure learning, free choice learning, cooperative learning, and service learning. While there are relationships and connections between all these theories of education, importantly they are also separate terms with separate meanings.

Experiential learning focuses on the learning process for the individual. It is often used synonymously with the phrase experiential education, however, while experiential learning considers the individual learning process, experiential education should be considered a broader philosophy of education. As such, it is concerned with issues such as the relationship of teacher and student, as well as broader issues of educational structure and objectives. An example of experiential learning is going to the zoo and learning through observation and interaction with the zoo environment, as opposed to reading about animals from a book.

Thus, one makes discoveries and experiments with knowledge firsthand, instead of hearing or reading about others' experiences. In business school, internship, and job-shadowing opportunities in a student's field of interest are elevated as examples of valuable experiential learning which contribute significantly to the student's overall understanding of the real-time environment.

A third example of experiential learning is learning how to ride a bike, a process which can illustrate the widely known four-step experiential learning model (ELM) as purported by Kolb and outlined in Figure below. Following this example, in the "concrete experience" stage, the learner physically experiences the bike in the "here-and-now".

This experience forms "the basis for observation and reflection" and he or she has the opportunity to consider what is working or failing (reflective observation), and think about ways to improve on the next attempt made at riding it (abstract conceptualization). Every new attempt to ride is informed by a cyclical pattern of previous experience, thought and reflection (active experimentation).

Table: *David Kolb's Experiential Learning Model (ELM)*

	→	Concrete Experience	↓	
Active Experimentation				Reflective Observation
	↑	Abstract Conceptualization	←	

Experiential learning can exist without a teacher and relates solely to the meaning making process of the individual's direct experience. However, though the gaining of knowledge is an inherent process that occurs naturally, for a genuine learning experience to occur, there must exist certain elements.

According to David A. Kolb, an American educational theorist, knowledge is continuously gained through both personal and environmental experiences. He states that in order to gain genuine knowledge from an experience, certain abilities are required:

- The learner must be willing to be actively involved in the experience;
- The learner must be able to reflect on the experience;
- The learner must possess and use analytical skills to conceptualize the experience; and
- The learner must possess decision making and problem solving skills in order to use the new ideas gained from the experience.

Implementation

Experiential activities are among the most powerful teaching and learning tools available. Experiential learning requires self-initiative, an "intention to learn" and an "active phase of learning". Kolb's cycle of experiential learning can be used as a framework for considering the different stages involved. Jennifer A. Moon has elaborated on this cycle to argue that experiential learning is most effective when it involves: 1) a "reflective learning phase" 2) a phase of learning resulting from the actions inherent to experiential learning, and 3) "a further phase of learning from feedback". This process of learning can result in "changes in judgement, feeling or skills" for the individual and can provide direction for the "making of judgements as a guide to choice and action".

Most educators understand the important role experience plays in the learning process. The role of emotion and feelings in learning from experience has been recognised as an important part of experiential learning. While those factors may improve the likelihood of experiential learning occurring, it can occur without them. Rather, what is vital in experiential learning is that the individual is encouraged to directly involve themselves in the experience, and then to reflect on their experiences using analytic skills, in order that they gain a better understanding of the new knowledge and retain the information for a longer time.

Reflection is a crucial part of the experiential learning process, and like experiential learning itself, it can be facilitated or independent. Dewey wrote that "successive portions of reflective thought grow out of one another and support one another", creating a scaffold for further learning, and allowing for further experiences and reflection. This reinforces the fact that experiential learning and reflective learning are iterative processes, and the learning builds and develops with further reflection and experience.

Facilitation of experiential learning and reflection is challenging, but "a skilled facilitator, asking the right questions and guiding reflective conversation before, during, and after an experience, can help open a gateway to powerful new thinking and learning". Jacobson and Ruddy, building on Kolb's four-stage Experiential Learning Model and Pfeiffer and Jones's five stage Experiential Learning Cycle, took these theoretical frameworks and created a simple, practical questioning model for facilitators to use in promoting critical reflection in experiential learning. Their "5 Questions" model is as follows:

- Did you notice...?
- Why did that happen?
- Does that happen in life?
- Why does that happen?
- How can you use that?

These questions are posed by the facilitator after an experience, and gradually lead the group towards a critical reflection on their experience, and an understanding of how they can apply the learning to their own life. Although the questions are simple, they allow a relatively inexperienced facilitator to apply the theories of Kolb, Pfeiffer, and Jones, and deepen the learning of the group.

While it is the learner's experience that is most important to the learning process, it is also important not to forget the wealth of experience a good facilitator also brings to the situation. However, while a "facilitator", traditionally called a "teacher", may improve the likelihood of experiential learning occurring, a "facilitator" is not essential to experiential learning.

Rather, the mechanism of experiential learning is the learner's reflection on experiences using analytic skills. This can occur without the presence of a facilitator, meaning that experiential learning is not defined by the presence of a facilitator. Yet, by considering experiential learning in developing course or programme content, it provides an opportunity to develop a framework for adapting varying teaching/ learning techniques into the classroom.

Experiential Learning in Schools

- Think Global School is a four-year travelling high school that holds classes in a new country each term. Students engage in experiential learning through activities such as workshops, cultural exchanges, museum tours, and nature expeditions.
- The Dawson School in Boulder, Colorado, devotes two weeks of each school year to experiential learning, with students visiting surrounding states to engage in community service, visit museums and scientific institutions, and engage in activities such as mountain biking, backpacking, and canoeing.

Experiential Learning in Business Education

As higher education continues to adapt to new expectations from students, experiential learning in business and accounting programmes has become more important. For example, Clark & White (2010) point out that "a quality university business education programme must include an experiential learning component". With reference to this study, employers note that graduating students need to build skills in "professionalism" – which can be taught via experiential learning. Students also value this learning as much as industry.

Learning styles also impact business education in the classroom. Kolb transposes four learning styles, *Diverger, Assimilator, Accommodator* and *Converger*, atop the Experiential Learning Model, using the four experiential learning stages to carve out "four quadrants", one for each learning style. An individual's dominant learning style can be identified by taking Kolb's Learning Style Inventory (LSI). Robert Loo (2002) undertook a meta-analysis of 8 studies which revealed that Kolb's learning styles were not equally distributed among business majors in the sample.

More specifically, results indicated that there appears to be a high proportion of assimilators and a lower proportion of accommodators than expected for business majors. Not surprisingly, within the accounting sub-sample there was a higher proportion of convergers and a lower proportion of accommodators. Similarly, in the finance sub-sample, a higher proportion of assimilators and lower proportion of divergers was apparent.

Within the marketing sub-sample there was an equal distribution of styles. This would provide some evidence to suggest that while it is useful for educators to be aware of common learning styles within business and accounting programmes, they should be encouraging students to use all four learning styles appropriately and students should use a wide range of learning methods.

Comparisons

Experiential learning is most easily compared with academic learning, the process of acquiring information through the study of a subject without the necessity for direct experience. While the dimensions of experiential learning are analysis, initiative, and immersion, the dimensions of academic learning are constructive learning and reproductive learning.

Though both methods aim at instilling new knowledge in the learner, academic learning does so through more abstract, classroom-based techniques, whereas experiential learning actively involves the learner in a concrete experience.

Information Literacy in Vocational Education: A Course Model

With the development of information technology, vocational education has gone through major changes in recent years. Computers are now available in almost every office. And information is exploding regardless of the field of study. Consequently, vocational education is high in demand and more specialized. However, how this type of education should be conducted to offer students necessary skills and knowledge remains in question.

The library literature presents little scholarship on the issue of information literary and vocational education. As a result, practice of integrating information literacy into vocational schools is little known to the outside world. While scholarship on incorporating information literacy into the classroom is widely available at the college and university level, the need to examine how the issue of information literacy is dealt with in vocational education seems to be urgent to certain degree, given the nature of the mission of this particular type of educational institution.

The Katharine Gibbs School in Melville, New York, is one of the vocational schools which have experimented with incorporating information literacy into the vocational education, and in the authors' opinions, has successfully done so. A course model of teaching information literacy skills at the Katharine Gibbs School will be introduced. And the guidelines in place for incorporating information literacy into the curriculum will be described as well as their implementation, the course design, and the evaluation process.

Vocational Education

Vocational education is a relatively modern educational development. Until the 19th century, such education was provided only through apprenticeship. With the growth of industrialization during the 19th century, however, several European countries began introducing vocational education in elementary and secondary schools, and it was established in Great Britain in the 20th century.

By the late 19th century, public school vocational education in the United States consisted of manual training and practical arts. These programmes were gradually expanded until 1917 when Federal aid was provided to public schools for trade and industrial, agricultural, and homemaking courses. After World War II, the demand for trained paraprofessionals in the relatively new fields of computer science, electronics, and medical services led to an increased interest in short-term postsecondary specialized training programmes in these areas as an alternative to a traditional college education. Michael E. Wonacott, a research scholar at the Centre on Education and Training Career and Vocational Education at Ohio State University, describes:

...In the last hundred years, vocational education has evolved from its original inception in response to changes in society, technology, education and education philosophy, and the workplace. At the dawn of the 21th century, vocational, or career and technical, education goes far beyond the specific technical knowledge and skills required for a particular occupation; today, vocational education encompasses not only technical preparation but also sound academic foundations, higher-order thinking skills, and personal qualities needed for success in the workplace.

In more recent years, there is a steady increase of interest among high school students in taking courses in vocational education. The data from the National Centre for Education Statistics indicate that almost all public high school students take at least one vocational education course, that 16 percent of all public high school credits are earned in vocational education, and that 49 percent of all students seeking subbaccalaureate degrees major in vocational fields.

In the past decade in particular, with the Internet and online resources becoming increasingly available, vocational education faced challenges in more specialized fields. For example, about one out of every five public high school graduates who take a concentrated vocational programme also completes a rigorous "college prep" programme; and over half (55 percent) of the public high school graduates who take concentrated vocational coursework enroll in a postsecondary institution within 2 years of graduation. About half (49 percent) of all subbaccalaureate students major in a vocational field. Among subbaccalaureate students, those pursuing a vocational major are more likely than those pursuing an academic major to have a previous postsecondary credential; and as the education level of their parents increases, subbaccalaureate students are less likely to major in vocational fields and more likely to major in academic fields.

Information Literacy

Library associations in the United States have attempted to define the concept of information literacy. And efforts have been made to incorporate information literacy into the curriculum on various levels. The National Forum on Information Literacy (NFIL), created in 1989 as a response to the recommendations of the American Library

Association's Presidential Committee on Information Literacy, describes information literacy as: "the ability to know when there is a need for information, to be able to identify, locate, evaluate, and effectively use that information for the issue or problem at hand."

The Middle States Association of Colleges and Schools, a degree-granting agency for colleges and universities in the Middle States region, has further defined information literacy and requires it to be incorporated in the regional accreditation standards. In Standard 11, the section on educational offerings, it defines information literacy and sets the framework in which information literacy is an important part of the general education:

Information literacy is an intellectual framework for identifying, finding, understanding, evaluating, and using information .... Information literacy is vital to all disciplines and to effective teaching and learning in any institution. Institutions of higher education need to provide students and instructors with the knowledge, skills, and tools to obtain information in many formats and media in order to identify, retrieve, and apply relevant and valid knowledge and information resources to their study, teaching, or research.

The Middle States Association of Colleges and Schools further requires that "upon degree completion, students are proficient in oral and written communication, scientific and quantitative reasoning, technological capabilities appropriate to the discipline, and information literacy, which includes critical analysis and reasoning..." Consequently, an effective mechanism is built in the process of education that is necessary for students to be equipped with lifelong learning skills.

Information Literacy and the Vocational School Curriculum

With the shifted focus in vocational education in recent decades and the support and recommendations from organizations such as degree-granting agencies and professional associations, efforts in incorporating information literacy into the vocational education curriculum have taken serious and substantial steps. These efforts have focused on active learning, lifelong learning, critical thinking, problem solving, career preparation, undergraduate research, and assessment of learning outcomes. The confluence of the changes in information technology, information explosion, and educational reform, makes "the time ripe for a traditional mission for teaching 'library skills' into a broader mandate for teaching 'information literacy.' "

These efforts have been met by the support from legal organizations and government agencies, which provide policy guidelines for vocational education. Stevenson pointed out that "It is ... not surprising that the importance of information literacy skills has been associated with the employment and education policy of national governments throughout the world during the last decade. Many of these policies conceive of information literacy as being a functional competence necessary for the modern workplace." Such policies have lent a great deal of support to establishing guidelines regarding the role of information literacy in vocational education.

The Katharine Gibbs School

The Katharine Gibbs School at Melville, located on the Long Island of New York, 30 miles from New York City, is one of the 82 private, for-profit vocational institutes of Career Education Corporation (CEC). The Katharine Gibbs School offers associate degree programmes in Business, Medical and Legal Office Administration, Computer Network Operations, Criminal Justice, Graphic Design, Health Care Administration – Long Term Care, as well as many certificate programmes with the goal of preparing students for professional careers.

The school currently has 838 enrolled students at Melville, including both traditional and non-traditional students. A typical student seeking associate degrees takes four courses, about 12 credits, in each quarter, which lasts eleven weeks. The Katharine Gibbs School, like most of the community colleges, serves students from a wide range of socioeconomic backgrounds, ages, levels of academic preparation, educational aspirations, work and family responsibilities, and levels of English competency. Incorporating information literacy into the curriculum needs to take all these into consideration.

Information Literacy Course Implementation

Information Literacy, as a full 3-credit course, has been implemented across the curriculum as one of the fundamental courses since January 2003 with the hiring of a full-time Information Literacy Librarian and other adjunct professors. This was the result of persistent effort of the head librarian who took over the library in 1996 and had been working as a solo librarian till the year of 2003.

As discussed earlier, the Katharine Gibbs School as one of the higher education institutions under the Middle States Association for Colleges and Universities, is required to have information literacy integrated into the school's curriculum. The Information Literacy course was first developed to provide information literacy skills to three programmes in the school's curriculum, and was expanded to seven programmes in less a year.

The course had been well received by faculty, administrators and students. It proved that Information Literacy is desirable for all students on the Katharine Gibbs School campus and plays an important role in the preparation for the professional workforce.

The Information Literacy course is mainly taught by librarians at the Katharine Gibbs School. Librarians and faculty members collaborate to have information literacy incorporated into a subject course as part of an assignment to address information literacy issues tailored to that course. The fact that librarians have already established strong relationships with a number of faculty members provides a favourable environment.

Course Design

Based on the recommendation from the American Library Association's (ALA) mission statement for the global information society in the 21st century, and as required by the Middle States Association of Colleges and Schools, the Katharine Gibbs School incorporates the concept of lifelong learning into the school's mission statement. To accomplish that goal, the Katharine Gibbs School Library has developed the following objectives to address information literacy. An information literate person is able to:

- understand the steps of the research process;
- determine the extent of information needed;
- access the needed information effectively and efficiently;
- understand the basic sources of information – both print and electronic;
- evaluate information and its sources according to credibility and relevance;
- understand key terms used in library research such as author, title, call #, subject heading, and citation;
- incorporate selected information into a person's knowledge base;
- develop appropriate strategies for selecting search terms;
- use information effectively to accomplish a specific purpose;
- combine search terms effectively;

- communicate using a variety of information technologies;
- understand library services.

With the goal of developing a curriculum that would motivate students to become information literacy competent, the course was designed with student active learning in mind and ways to incorporate information literacy, based on the objectives developed. Each session consists of a combination of lecture and demonstration, followed by a hands-on exercise, designed to reinforce skills or concepts taught earlier. Homework assignments expand on in-class instruction and exercises.

These instructional methods are appropriate because information competence is best learned and/or enhanced by "doing". Hands-on exercises in collaborative groups give students an opportunity to try out techniques which have been demonstrated by the lecturer in a non-threatening environment with help readily available. The course is taught with a focus on life-learning skills that are transferable from one occupation or profession to another.

It should be noted that students at the Katharine Gibbs School share much the same characteristics with those at most community colleges. According to Schuetz, about half of all students entering community colleges need to be assigned to some remedial course, mainly in Math and English. This is also true with students entering the Katharine Gibbs School. Compared with their counterparts at four-year institutions, students at Gibbs may benefit more when provided with the opportunity to learn fundamental and systematic knowledge about information.

Course Development

According to Hunt and Birks, "To achieve information literacy goals successfully, instructors must first break down the skills and concepts into their basic components. These components should then be presented sequentially and in increasing levels of complexity allowing time for practice and repetition." Accordingly, the Information Literacy course at the Katharine Gibbs School has been developed for an eleven-week long term with the following objectives and measures:

Week One

Objectives:

- define information and the modern dilemma of information overload;

- recognize the different ways of information organization;
- discuss characteristics and formats of information;
- develop a searchable topic.

This session gears towards discussion on general issues surrounding information. Information is ideas, facts and imaginative works of the mind that can be communicated, recorded or published formally or informally in any formats. Despite the realization that information is organized generally by subject terms, few students have knowledge of schemes of such organization. This session discusses popular existing classification systems, with an emphasis on the Dewey Decimal Classification System and the Library of Congress Classification System. It also introduces the information characteristics, including factual vs. analytical, subjective vs. objective, and primary vs. secondary.

Students are required to establish a research topic that would motivate them to undertake a "formal information research" project throughout the whole semester. The topics can either be issues that interest them or an assignment from another class. It would be a perfect match if students use what has been discussed from the Information Literacy class for their writing assignment of another class. Needless to say, when students see its immediate benefit to their course work or to an assignment that they need to accomplish, they will be most receptive to learn.

Each student needs to keep a research log to contain all details in the process of information searching. The log should include specific citations retrieved, steps, errors made, tools used, skills or strategies applied, and any thoughts for information evaluation. The research log serves several functions:

- Students perform research in an attentive manner, and it helps them to interact with the information world.
- The research log will assist students to organize their work, which will facilitate all pieces of information to fall in place at the end. At the end of the project, each of the students needs to submit an annotated bibliography and present an oral report to share their research experience. The annotated bibliography requires students to select a number of sources on their topics in various formats. Specifically, each student will compile a list of sources containing: one primary source, one secondary source, two reference entries, one book entry, one or two scholarly

articles, one or two popular articles, and two websites. All of the sources should be provided with annotation – a descriptive and evaluative paragraph of the source.

Week Two

Objectives:

- focuses on refining research topics;
- discuss facets of a topic and relationships between subject fields and disciplines;
- create subject terms or keywords.

It is generally a difficult task for students to know what to write about, and even more difficult when they need to narrow down a topic. Prior to addressing this issue, librarians discuss facets of a topic and the relationship between disciplines, subject fields and topics. Facets of a topic, according to List, refer to aspects or angle of a topic, and discipline refers to the three major divisions of knowledge: the Sciences, the Social Sciences and the Humanities. Each discipline contains an expandable number of subjects which are not equivalent to topics. List continues to say that: "a topic is the idea you're researching and its subject field is the field of knowledge or study into which your idea (topic) fits." It is important to teach these conceptual differences to students.

Clarification of the relationship between topics, subject fields, and disciplines provides tremendous help in the process of broadening and narrowing a research topic. Consequently, students find it easier to work out focused research questions. In order to help students understand research process or steps, as defined in the course objectives, students are required to select a research topic, explore the research questions from any possible angles for a better understanding and mold it into a searchable topic, write research statement paragraphs, and construct the research outline.

Students are guided to brainstorm concepts or terms associated with their topics. Once the research topic is narrowed down to a manageable level, a set of search terms will be created to provide means of access into the literature. The most important, and sometimes frustrating, part of finding information is to identify key words, as pointed out by Larkin and Pines. Once again, students find it beneficial to have done analysis and discussions about the relationship of disciplines, subjects and facets of topics, as one needs to understand the topic well enough to come up with the right set of terms or concepts for information searching.

The hands-on section focuses on familiarizing students with selected reference materials for further understanding of concepts at different levels. Students are asked to construct a conceptual taxonomy, in which a search term or keyword can be positioned in a framework of "superordinate (broader), subordinate (narrower) and co-ordinate (synonymous)" Students were instructed to use the Subject Heading's list from the Library of Congress, thesauri, dictionaries, and encyclopedias to facilitate this task.

Week Three

Objectives:

- discuss information access, including access tools and access points;
- use the library catalogue;
- develop search strategies;
- introduce search skills such as Boolean logic, truncation, wild cards, etc.;
- formulate a research question.

Information is organized with the purpose of being accessed so it can be utilized. Apparently, means of access is the key. Although students are comfortable accessing the Web via popular search engines, few of them have the knowledge of looking for various types of information through other tools available.

The library's online catalogue is an ideal tool for manipulating search terms and "unlocking a library's resource". Oftentimes, it is not surprising to see one retrieve hundreds or even thousands of hits when searching library databases or the Internet with one term. However, the library catalogue may return nothing due to incorrect search terms used. For instance, a student will not get any relevant results by typing in "ecstasy" into the School's online catalogue until he or she tries "drug abuse".

The library catalogue as a search tool is an excellent starting point to provide students with a relatively controlled environment for understanding the concepts of access points: author, title, subject, or keyword. In other words, students will find it easier to apply those skills as to other databases or the Web. For the hands-on part, students are expected to do the following:

1. Complete an exercise on using School's Online Public Access Catalogue (OPAC);

2. Use both School's and other networked OPAC to locate books, and then select one book source and two reference sources relevant to their topics to enter into their research logs;
3. Write an annotation for each source, and record their searching experience;
4. Finish a well designed exercise on using reference works;
5. Write a research question.

Week Four

Objectives:

- continue to instruct on information search tools with emphasis on library databases;
- discuss scholarly communication (peer-reviewed, scientific) and types of periodicals;
- cover the topic of research statement.

Concepts such as scholarly communication, peer-reviewed and scholarly journals, and scientific communities are fairly foreign to the student population. Before discussing these issues, students are divided into groups, with 4-5 students in each, and provided with a set of periodicals comprising popular, professional or trade, and scholarly journals. They follow instructions to identify similarities and differences of selected articles on features, contents, structure or format, length, availability of commercials, authorship, etc.

Discussions ensue on concepts of peer review, scholarly communications, and scientific communities after students have had first-hand experience with the publications provided. Based on the knowledge gained on different types of periodicals in print version, it will be natural to introduce the concept of electronic publications, especially scholarly journal articles which could be found in subscribed electronic databases.

According to the pre-testing results done during the first session, the majority of students may not be aware of the availability of electronic databases. In fact, the Katharine Gibbs School makes available a range of electronic databases mainly through Career Education Corporation – the Cyber Library, which functions as a comprehensive virtual library, supplementing to the School's physical library. It provides access to full-text databases, electronic books, links to relevant websites, and guides for research through a group of database providers such as EBSCOhost, ProQuest, Thomson Gale, and Wilson Web. These vendors provide both general and discipline-specific databases, including Academic Search Premier, CINAHL, Business Source Elite, Art Full-text, Criminal Justice Periodicals and National Newspaper.

After being instructed on how to use the above databases, students will be given an assignment to locate two scholarly and two popular articles on their topics, recording entries to the research log and completing a 3-page exercise as a reinforcement on using electronic databases. Questions from the exercise intend to familiarize students with the various database interface structures.

Week Five

Objectives:

- instruction on information evaluation for relevance, currency, reliability, coverage/completeness, and accuracy.

The ability to evaluate retrieved sources is even more desirable in today's rich information environment. Students are expected to be critical thinkers who possess the ability to assess the authenticity or accuracy of information claims or arguments to successfully meet information needs within this setting.

Students again work in groups with distributed sample books, articles, pamphlets and audio-visual materials. They follow given guidelines, which help them to evaluate any given source in aspects of authoritativeness, timeliness, credibility, objectivity, and intended audience. The detailed evaluative content should be presented in the form of questions within each category.

For instance, in category of "Credibility", students should answer the following questions: Is the information based on facts? Are the facts supported by authors in other sources? Is the information trustworthy? Then the class will get together to have a focused discussion on the results from each group, where students are given an opportunity to elaborate on their choices and opinions, through which critical thinking skills are exercised.

Week Six

Midterm Objective:

- test students on what has been learned thus far.

The test is administered in the form of multiple choices, true/false questions, and short essays. It is designed for students to apply previously learned knowledge and skills in locating required information and evaluating that information.

It is important and necessary to test on previously learned knowledge, something that is often missing in information literacy instruction. Instructors are often pressed by time and tend to present a tremendous amount of information, skills or concepts to a group of learners with little learning experience. Julien and Boon ask the right question:

"How can one know whether anything has been learned if students are not tested on the content of that learning?" This exercise will prove that learning needs to be reinforced.

Week Seven

Objectives:

- continue to work on information search tools;
- focus on Web searching;
- cover topic of writing research paper outline.

Issues surrounding information technology will be addressed here. Basic Internet concepts, including search engines, relationship between the subscribed databases and the Web, portal and nonlinear feature of the web are discussed in class. Type of information the Web provides, and special features coming with the information presentation will also be investigated. Website content evaluation is the primary theme in this session.

Use of clues from website addresses such as .com for commercial, .gov for government, etc. for making initial filtering is recommended. Students may find it hard to locate author(s) or responsible body of the site, to distinguish from title of the whole site and title for a specific piece of information on a page, and to search for credential information of the site's creator.

These types of information tend to be hard to locate and are not presented in an organized manner. Based on the findings, students will realize that information from the open Web may have issues of credibility and reliability. They will also learn that being critical is the key in Web searching.

The assignment for this session is to locate and evaluate two websites on chosen topics, to make entries to the log, to complete a search exercise on comparing the Internet and other electronic databases, and to construct an outline for the research paper using guidelines from the textbook.

Week Eight and Week Nine

Objective:

- cite sources in standard style;
- instruct on promoting awareness of the ethical, legal and socio-political issues surrounding information and technology.

Instruction on citing sources using a specific style is seldom provided in regular two-year colleges. And quite a number of students experience difficulties in this area. The Modern Language Association (MLA) style is adopted at the Katharine Gibbs School. How to cite books and print journal articles in the MLA style is demonstrated and discussed in detail so that students will understand essential elements of a citation and therefore be able to create citations. Students are instructed to use the title page, front and verso, for needed elements of a book citation. They are provided with a photocopy of a book title page (both sides) with notes added. In the case of a journal, by the same token, a copied page with necessary information is provided. Students have a writing manual to follow. But the instruction and discussion will be of great help. Issues on plagiarism will be addressed extensively, which clarifies concepts between a direct and an indirect quotation, paraphrase, and summary. In-text citation will also be addressed.

By now, students should be able to compile their annotated bibliographies containing the following sources: one primary source, one secondary source, two reference entries, one book source, one or two scholarly articles, one or two popular articles, and two websites. They are also prepared, at this point, for the upcoming presentations based on research logs.

The last two sessions are used for students presenting their accomplishments, experiences, successes and failures in the information searching process. Each student is required to give a presentation in front of the whole class on what they have found and how they have done it. They are encouraged to create and communicate information using various media.

Course Evaluation

Instructors shall observe students' progress in learning information literacy concepts and skills through interactions and consultation with students throughout the course. A pretest and a posttest will be given to students to collect information on the level of their knowledge in information literacy, based on Stevenson's theory of "initial assessment and summative assessment." Students' final presentations are served as an important means for them to communicate and present to the class what they have leaned in terms of information literacy competence, based on the objectives set forth during the course implementation process. A quantitative evaluative study of this course model to determine the value placed in the programme will be highly desirable.

Conclusion

Many lessons are learned during the course implementation process. First of all, it is important to have information literacy standards as guidelines to determine the goals to be achieved. Objectives should follow, designed to accomplish each specific goal. It is also important to know your students for whom these goals and objectives are designed and implemented, particularly in the vocational educational environment.

As discussed in this study, the world of information is changing, and so is vocational education. Vocational education must meet the needs of the students who are changing with the environments they are in. The Katherine Gibbs School is facing these changes and meeting these challenges. The case at the Katherine Gibbs School may serve as a model for other educational institutions in their endeavour to meet the challenge of providing a broader education that develops the academic, vocational, and technical skills of students for more competitive careers or advanced studies.

Adult Education

Adult education is the practice of teaching and educating adults. Adult education takes place in the workplace, through "extension" school (e.g. Harvard Extension) or "school of continuing education" (Columbia School of Continuing Education). Other learning places include community colleges, folk high schools, colleges and universities, libraries, and lifelong learning centres. The practice is also often referred to as "Training and Development" and is often associated with workforce or professional development. It has also been referred to as *andragogy* (to distinguish it from *pedagogy*). Adult education is different from vocational education, which is mostly workplace-based for skill improvement; and also from non-formal adult education, including learning skills or learning for personal development.

In 1926, the American Library Association study *Libraries and Adult Education* was published and the association established the

Board on Library and Adult Education (later the Adult Education Board) with reports in the *ALA Bulletin*. The concept of the library as an agency of ongoing education for adults became firmly established in US society. In her historical review of libraries and adult education, Margaret E. Monroe (1963: 6) identified a variety of library services provided by libraries to adults during the first half of the twentieth century that incorporated aspects of adult education.

Many libraries have a literacy centre, either within their community or in the building; others offer on-site tutoring for adults, or at least space for tutors to meet with students. Family literacy programmes are also quite popular within libraries and schools. The US Institute of Museum and Library Services helps create vibrant, energized learning communities recognizing that "Our achievement as individuals and our success as a democratic society depends on learning continually, adapting to change readily, and evaluating information critically."

Characteristics

Programmes provide one-to-one tutoring and small group sessions for adults at the 6th grade level or below. Public libraries, nonprofit organizations and school systems administer these programmes across the country. Many adult education centres from community colleges receive grants from Welfare and Unemployment departments to offer training to welfare and unemployment recipients to help these individuals gain life and work skills to facilitate their return to the mainstream. They also provide programmes for ex-offenders to reintegrate to society.

Educating adults differs from educating children in several ways. One of the most important differences is that adults have accumulated knowledge, work experience or military service that can add to the learning experience. Another difference is that most adult education is voluntary, therefore, the participants are generally better motivated. So researcher André Lemieux (Université du Québec à Montréal) pointed out that the learning of wisdom should be the focus of future university programmes to educate the elderly in one of his research.

Adults frequently apply their knowledge in a practical fashion to learn effectively. They must have a reasonable expectation that the knowledge recently gained will help them further their goals. One example, common in the 1990s, was the proliferation of computer training courses in which adults (not children or adolescents), most of whom were office workers, could enroll. These courses would teach basic use of the operating system or specific application software. Because the abstractions governing the user's interactions with a PC were so new, many people who had been working white-collar jobs for ten years or more eventually took such training courses, either at their own whim (to gain computer skills and thus earn higher pay) or at the behest of their managers.

In the United States, a more general example, and stereotypical, is that of the high-school dropout who returns to school to complete general education requirements. Most upwardly mobile positions require at the very least a high school diploma or equivalent. A working adult is unlikely to have the freedom to simply quit his or her job and go "back to school" full-time. Public school systems and community colleges usually offer evening or weekend classes for this reason. In Europe this is often referred to as "second-chance", and many schools offer tailor-made courses and learning programmes for these returning learners.

Those adults who read at the very lowest level get help from volunteer literacy programmes. These national organizations provide training, tutor certification, and accreditation for local volunteer programmes. States often have state organizations such as Literacy Florida!Inc., which provide field services for volunteer literacy programmes.

In the USA, the equivalent of the high-school diploma earned by an adult through these programmes is to pass the General Education Development (GED) exam.

Another fast-growing sector of adult education is English for Speakers of Other Languages (ESOL), also referred to as English as a Second Language (ESL) or English Language Learners (ELL). These courses are key in assisting immigrants with not only the acquisition of the English language, but the acclimation process to the culture of the United States.

A common problem in adult education in the US is the lack of professional development opportunities for adult educators. Most adult educators come from other professions and are not well trained to deal with adult learning issues. Most of the positions available in this field are only part-time without any benefits or stability since they are usually funded by government grants that might last for only a couple of years.

Cooperative Education

Cooperative education is a structured method of combining classroom-based education with practical work experience. A cooperative education experience, commonly known as a "co-op", provides academic credit for structured job experience. Cooperative education is taking on new importance in helping young people to make the school-to-work transition, service learning, and experiential learning initiatives. Co-operative Education is also the use of active participation methods in which students learn how to work together to solve problems, this is normally founded on the principles of children's rights, equality, equity and participation in decision-making. Its methods include game playing, expressing opinions, democratic participation, sharing, ensuring students all have an equal opportunity to take part, and conflict resolution.

History of Cooperative Education

Robert Owen's New Lanark: In Great Britain at the beginning of the 19th century co-operative living and learning were promoted by the successful cotton industrialist, Robert Owen. In 1817 he founded a school in his cotton mill community of New Lanark in Scotland. This was based on the principles of co-operation, that children should be at school and not labouring in the mills, that the rules of the playground should be to be happy and help others to be happy. He employed adults who loved children, not teachers, and saw children as naturally inquisitive. He saw geography and comparative religion as ways that children might learn that who they were to become was defined by the culture and religion they were brought-up in. He believed that we could create co-operative based communities through learning and reason. His work was so important that New Lanark is a UNESCO heritage site, and at the time people from around the world would visit it to see how it worked.

Schneider's Foundations

While at Lehigh University at the beginning of the 20th Century, Herman Schneider (1872–1939), engineer, architect, and educator, concluded that the traditional classroom was insufficient for technical students (Smollins 1999). Schneider observed that several of the more successful Lehigh graduates had worked to earn money before graduation. Gathering data through interviews of employers and graduates, he devised the framework for cooperative education (1901). About that time, CarnegiTechnical School, now Carnegie Mellon

University, opened and thereby minimized the need for Schneider's co-op plan in the region around Lehigh University. However, in 1903 the University of Cincinnati appointed Schneider to their faculty. In 1905 the UC Board of Trustees allowed Schneider to "try this cooperative idea of education for one year only, for the failure of which they would not be held responsible." The cooperative education programme was launched in 1906, and became an immediate success. The University of Cincinnati returned to the matter in its September 2005 board meeting, declaring the 100 year trial period of one hundred years of Cooperative Education officially ended, for the success of which the Board resumed full responsibility.

Schneider, beginning from the rank of Assistant Professor, would rise through the rank of Dean of Engineering (1906–1928) to become Interim President (1929–32) of the University of Cincinnati, based largely upon the strength of the co-op programme. Throughout his career, he was an advocate for the co-op framework. His thirty years of service to the University of Cincinnati are partly credited for that institution's worldwide fame. In 2006 the University of Cincinnati unveiled a statue of dean Schneider outside the window of his office in Baldwin Hall.

In 1965, The Cooperative Education and Internship Association (CEIA) created "The Dean Herman Schneider Award" in honour of the contributions made by Dean Schneider in cooperative education. The award is given annually to an outstanding educator from faculty or administration. In 2006 The University of Cincinnati established the Cooperative Education Hall of Honour "to give a permanent place of honour to individuals and organizations that have made a significant qualitative difference in the advancement of Cooperative Education for the benefit of students".

Post-Cincinnati Evolutions

In 1909, seeing the possibility of co-op education, Northeastern University began using co-op in their engineering programme, becoming only the second institution to do so in this country. By 1921, Antioch College had adapted the co-op practices to their liberal arts curricula, for which reason many called co-op the "Antioch Plan." In 1919 the General Motors Institute (GMI) was opened following this model to train new General Motors hires. This school was later renamed Kettering University.

In 1922, Northeastern University emphasized its commitment to co-op by extending it to the College of Business Administration. As new colleges opened at Northeastern, such as the College of Liberal Arts (1935) and College of Education (1953), they became co-op schools as well. By the 1980s, Northeastern was the acknowledged leader in co-op education across the world. (Smollins 1999)

In 1926, Dean Schneider invited those interested in forming an Association of Co-operative Colleges (ACC) to the University of Cincinnati for the first convention. The idea took hold, and was followed by three more annual conventions. In 1929, the Society for the Promotion of Engineering Education, now called American Society for Engineering Education (ASEE), formed the Division of Cooperative Engineering Education, incorporating the membership of the ACC (Auld 1972).

In 1961, the Ford and Edison Foundations commissioned a study of co-operative education, published as *Work-study college programmes; appraisal and report of the study of cooperative education,* (James Warner Wilson and Edward H Lyons, New York: Harper). That study resulted in the formation of the National Commission for Cooperative Education (NCCE). NCCE remains today to promote and lobby for co-operative education in the United States. Its membership comprises sponsoring corporations and organizations (not individuals) from academia and business.

By 1962, about 150 academic institutions used co-op education, in one form or another. Many were outside of engineering. The need for professional support of non-engineering programmes became obvious, and the membership of ASEE, in 1963, began the Cooperative Education Association. To reflect its membership more accurately, it was eventually (sometime in the 1990s or early 2000s) named the Cooperative Education and Internship Association, it remains today as the professional association for co-operative education outside of ASEE.

Much of those early efforts of NCCE focused on lobbying and promotiing co-operative education. In 1965, the federal Higher Education Act provided support specifically for co-operative education. Funding continued from the federal government through 1992, when Congress ended its support of co-operative education. In all, a total of over $220 million was appropriated by the federal government toward co-operative education (Carlson 1999)

In 1979, educators from Australia, Britain, Canada, and the United States (Northeastern's President, Kenneth Ryder), met to discuss work-related programmes in their respective countries. In

1981 and 1982, this group, headed by President Ryder, convened an international conference on cooperative education. In 1983, several college and university presidents, educational specialists, and employers from around the world (including Australia, Canada, Hong Kong, the Netherlands, the Philippines, the United States and the United Kingdom) formed the World Council and Assembly on Cooperative Education to foster co-operative education around the world. In 1991, it renamed itself the World Association for Cooperative Education (WACE). By 2005, that Association boasted a membership of over 1,000 individuals from 43 different countries.

Co-op Models

From its beginnings in Cincinnati in 1906, cooperative education has evolved into a programme offered at the secondary and post-secondary levels in two predominant models (Grubb & Villeneuve 1995). In one model, students alternate a semester of academic coursework with an equal amount of time in paid employment, repeating this cycle several times until graduation. The parallel method splits the day between school and work, typically structured to accommodate the student's class schedule. Thus, like school-to-work (STW), the co-op model includes school-based and work-based learning and, in the best programmes, "connecting activities" such as seminars and teacher-coordinator work site visits. These activities help students explicitly connect work and learning.

Co-op's proponents identify benefits for students (including motivation, career clarity, enhanced employability, vocational maturity) and employers (labour force flexibility, recruitment/retention of trained workers, input into curricula) as well as educational institutions and society (ibid.). Beyond informal and anecdotal evidence, however, a familiar refrain in the literature is the lack of well-done research that empirically demonstrates these benefits (Barton 1996; Wilson, Stull & Vinsonhaler 1996). Barton (1996) identifies some of the research problems for secondary co-op as follows: federal data collection on high school co-op enrollments and completions ceased in the 1980s; some studies use data in which co-op was not isolated from other work experience programmes. Ricks et al. (1993) describe other problems: due to lack of a clear or consistent definition of cooperative education, researchers cannot accurately identify variables and findings cannot be compared; theory is not well developed; theory, research, and practice are not integrated; and co-op research does not adhere to established standards.

Another set of problems involves perceptions of the field and its marginalization. Because of its "vocational" association, co-op is not regarded as academically legitimate; rather, it is viewed as taking time away from the classroom (Crow 1997). Experiential activities are necessarily rewarded in post-secondary promotion and tenure systems (except in certain extenuating situations), and co-op faculty may be isolated from other faculty (Crow 1997; Schaafsma 1996). Despite the current emphasis on contextual learning, work is not recognized as a vehicle for learning (Ricks et al. 1993). Schaafsma (1996) and Van Gyn (1996) agree that the field places too much emphasis on placements rather than learning. Wilson, Stull & Vinsonhaler (1996) also decry the focus on administration, logistics, placements, and procedures.

Some institutions are fully dedicated to the co-op ideal (such as Georgia Institute of Technology, RIT, Kettering University, LaGuardia Community College and Purdue University). In others, the co-op programme may be viewed as an add-on and therefore is vulnerable to cost cutting (Wilson, Stull & Vinsonhaler 1996). Even where co-op programmes are strong they can be threatened, as at Cincinnati Technical College when it became a comprehensive community college (Grubb & Villeneuve 1995) or LaGuardia during a budget crisis (Grubb & Badway 1998). For students, costs and time to degree completion may be deterrents to co-op participation (Grubb & Villeneuve 1995).

New Approaches

Despite these problems, there is optimism about the future of co-op education; "Social, economic, and historic forces are making cooperative education more relevant than ever" (Grubb & Villeneuve 1995, p. 17), including emphasis on university-industry-government cooperation, a fluid and demanding workplace, new technology, the need for continuous on-the-job learning, globalization, and demands for accountability (John, Doherty & Nichols 1998). Federal investments in school-to-work and community service have resulted in a number of initiatives designed to provide "learning opportunities beyond the classroom walls" (Furco 1996, p. 9). Because this has always been a principle of co-op, the field is in a position to capitalize on its strengths and the ways it complements other experiential methods in the effort to provide meaningful learning opportunities for students. To do this, however, cooperative education must be redesigned.

For Wilson, Stull & Vinsonhaler (1996), a new vision involves conceiving, defining, and presenting co-op "as a curriculum model that links work and academics - a model that is based on sound learning theory" (p. 158). Ricks (1996) suggests affirming the work-based learning principles upon which co-op is based. These principles assert that cooperative education fosters self-directed learning, reflective practice, and transformative learning; and integrates school and work learning experiences that are grounded in adult learning theories.

Schaafsma (1996) also focuses on learning, seeing a need for a paradigm shift from content learning to greater understanding of learning processes, including reflection and critical thinking. Co-op is an experiential method, but learning from experience is not automatic. Therefore, Van Gyn (1996) recommends strengthening the reflective component that is already a part of some co-op models. "If co-op is only a vehicle for experience to gain information about the workplace and to link technical knowledge with workplace application, then its effectiveness is not fully developed" (Van Gyn 1996, p. 125).

The Bergen County Academies, a public magnet high school, utilizes co-op education in a programme called Senior Experience. This programme allows all 12th grade students to participate in cooperative education or an internship opportunity for the full business day each Wednesday. Students explore a wide range of career possibilities. This new approach was recognized as an educational best practice and has been adopted as a state educational initiative for 12th grade students.

Integrating Experiential Methods

School-to-work and service learning have also been promoted as ways to link theory and practice through meaningful experiential learning experiences. Furco (1996) outlines the similarities between school-to-work and service learning. Although school-to-work, service learning, and co-op have different goals, each of his points also applies to cooperative education:

- Based on the philosophy that learners learn best through active engagement in meaningful activities
- View of students as active learners and producers of knowledge
- Use of such instructional strategies as contextual learning and application of knowledge to real situations
- Requirement for schools to establish formal partnerships with outside entities
- Concern for integrating school experiences and external experiences

The Community Service Scholarship Programme at California State University-Fresno combines cooperative education with service learning. Students receive co-op/internship credit and scholarships for completing a placement at a community service site (Derousi & Sherwood 1997). As in traditional co-op work placements, students get real-world training, opportunities to explore career options, and enhanced employability skills such as communication, problem solving, and leadership as well as awareness of community and social problems. Combining co-op and service learning thus prepares students for roles as workers and citizens.

Research on highly successful co-op programmes in Cincinnati (Grubb & Villeneuve 1995) and at LaGuardia Community College (Grubb & Badway 1998) shows that they share the basic philosophy and fundamental characteristics of the educational strategy of school-to-work. The reconceptualization of co-op should recognize and build upon this connection. At the same time, lessons from successful co-op programmes can benefit the broader STW movement.

There is a need for broader definition of acceptable models for integrating work and learning. Barton (1996) and Wilson, Stull & Vinsonhaler (1996) identify a variety of work-based learning activities taking different names: co-op, internships, externships, apprenticeship, career academies, etc. Work-based learning programmes should look for connections and develop collaborative relationships. The alternating and parallel co-op models may not meet the needs of returning adult students and dislocated workers needing retraining (Varty 1994). Alternatives such as extended-day programmes emphasizing mentoring should be considered.

Connecting activities to integrate school- and work-based learning are an essential part of STW. At LaGuardia, the required co-op seminar helps students make connections by giving them a structure within which to reinforce employability skills, examine larger issues about work and society, and undertake the crucial activities of critical reflection (Grubb & Badway 1998).

Grubb & Badway (1998) and Grubb & Villeneuve (1995) found that the value of cooperative education is embedded in the culture of the institution (LaGuardia) and the region (Cincinnati). In this supportive culture, employer support does not have to be repeatedly obtained and there are clearly understood long-term expectations on all sides (schools, employers, students). This "informal culture of expectations around work-based learning may be more powerful in the long run than a complex set of regulations and bureaucratic requirements" (Grubb & Villeneuve 1995, p. 27).

However, even LaGuardia has found it difficult to sustain co-op culture over time (Grubb & Badway 1998). "The only way in which STW programmes can find a permanent place in schools and colleges is for the work-based component to become so central to the educational purposes of the institutions that it becomes as unthinkable to give it up as it would be to abandon math, English, or science" (Grubb & Badway 1998, p. 28).

Finn (1997) believes that the answer lies in going beyond reconceiving co-op as an "educational strategy, pedagogy, model, methodology, or curriculum" (Finn 1997, p. 41). She asserts that it is time for cooperative education to develop and define its body of knowledge, investigate its unique phenomena-e.g., the concept of learning from experience, and clarify and strengthen the qualifications of co-op practitioners. For Ricks (1996), cooperative education is inherently committed to improving the economy, people's working lives, and lifelong learning abilities. It can thus position itself to serve the experiential learning needs of students into the 21st century.

Cates and Cedercreutz (2008) demonstrate that the assessment of student work performance as pursued by co-op employers, can be used for continuous improvement of curricula. The methodology, funded by the Fund for Postsecondary Education (FIPSE) has been developed to a level allowing institutionalization. The methodology could, when implemented over a larger front, provide a substantial competitive advantage for the entire field.

Examples

- The University of Waterloo in Waterloo, Ontario, Canada has the largest co-operative education programme in the world, with more than 14,000 students enrolled in co-op programmes and more than 3,500 active co-op employers. It offers fully automated Web-based job submission (for employers) and job application/resume posting (for students). Waterloo's engineering programme is one of the few co-op only engineering programmes in Canada. Waterloo's 5-year co-op programme includes 24 months of work experience, the longest undergraduate co-op experience in Canada. Enrolling in the a co-op programme at the University of Waterloo does not guarantee co-op employment. The school requires students to have a minimum of 16 months of valid work experience (depending on the programme of study) to successfully complete their academic programme. Despite a high percentage of employment via the coop programme, many students obtain employment by other methods, including a student's personal networks and unpaid full-time volunteering positions.

- Also in Waterloo is Wilfrid Laurier University and the Laurier School of Business & Economics, which provides a co-op business programme. It has a competitive entry limited to about one-third of the students who start the BBA programme in their first-year, offers three four-month work terms, and uses web-based tools for job application. It is the first programme of its kind in Canada. Additionally, the school offers a co-op MBA programme for high calibre students with less than 2 years of work experience.
- Located in Vancouver, Canada, the University of British Columbia's co-operative education programme includes over 3000 students from the faculties of Arts, Commerce, Engineering, Forestry, Kinesiology, and Science. Since its inception over 30 years ago, UBC Co-op has grown to become the largest programme offered by post-secondary institutions in British Columbia, Canada.
- All Antioch College students participate in the college's Co-Op Programme as part of their academic requirements for graduation. Under the programme, students spend a total of four 12-week terms, distributed throughout their undergraduate years, working as paid, full-time employees in local, national, or international settings. The programme at Antioch, which is located in Yellow Springs, Ohio, began in 1921.
- The Florida Institute of Technology has the most condensed cooperative education programme allowing students to graduate in four years with 3-semester work terms. This programme is only followed by engineering students and requires students to take online coursework while they are working full-time as a cooperative education student.This programme's formal title is "ProTrack".
- Drexel University in Philadelphia, Pennsylvania has one of the largest co-operative education programmes in the United States, branded as "The Ultimate Internship". Drexel has a fully Internet-based job database, where users can submit resumes and request interviews with any of the hundreds of companies that are offering positions. A student graduating

from Drexel with a 5-year degree typically has a total of 18 months of internship with up to three different companies.

- Northeastern University in Boston, MA has the largest, and second-oldest, co-operative education programme in the United States- A student graduating from Northeastern with a 5-year bachelor's degree has a total of 18 months of internship experience with up to three different companies.
- Rochester Institute of Technology was among the first universities to begin cooperative education back in 1912. Today RIT's programme is the fourth-oldest and one of the largest in the world.
- Georgia Institute of Technology was one of the first universities to offer cooperative education in 1912. It is the fourth-oldest and the largest optional co-op programme in the United States. Georgia Tech, Drexel, Northeastern, and RIT have perennially been listed in U.S. News & World Report as one of the "Top Ten" co-op programmes in America.
- Kettering University in Flint, Michigan enrolls students in co-operative education from their first year on campus, specializing in engineering, science, and management degree programmes.
- Steinbeis Centre of Management and Technology of Steinbeis University Berlin offers an international masters programme (Master of Business Engineering, MBE)for graduates and young professionals which integrates practical and theoretical learning, along with on the job training by managing projects for a sponsoring company.
- Wentworth Institute of Technology has a 2 semester co-operative education programme with an optional 3rd semester in the students sophomore summer. Every student in the Institute is required to do 2 co-ops. Co-operative education has been active since 1975 with over 1 thousand students in a co-op each year.
- EPUSP - Escola Politecnica da Universidade de Sao Paulo in Sao Paulo, Brazil was the first university to offer cooperative education in Brazil.
- TOBB University of Economics and Technology in Ankara, Turkey was the first university to offer cooperative education in Turkey.

6

Service-learning

Service learning is a method of teaching that combines classroom instruction with meaningful community service. This form of learning emphasizes critical thinking and personal reflection while encouraging a heightened sense of community, civic engagement, and personal responsibility. The Community Service Act of 1990, which authorized the Learn and Serve America grant programme, defines service learning as:

> *"a method under which students or participants learn and develop through active participation in thoughtfully organized service that is conducted in and meets the needs of a community; is coordinated with an elementary school, secondary school, institution of higher education, or community service programme, and with the community; and helps foster civic responsibility; and that is integrated into and enhances the academic curriculum of the students, or the educational components of the community service programme in which the participants are enrolled; and provides structured time for the students or participants to reflect on the service experience."*

Service learning offers students immediate opportunities to apply classroom learning to support or enhance the work of local agencies that often exist to effect positive change in the community. The National Youth Leadership Council defines service learning as

> *"a philosophy, pedagogy, and model for community development that is used as an instructional strategy to meet learning goals and/or content standards."*

"Service learning is a method of instruction in which classroom learning is enriched and applied through service to others" (Florida Department of Education).

Key Components

Service learning combines experiential learning and community service. It can be distinguished in the following ways:

- *Curricular connections-* Integrating learning into a service project is key to successful service learning. Academic relations should be clear and build upon existing disciplinary skills.
- *Student voice* - Beyond being actively engaged in the project itself, students have the opportunity to select, design, implement, and evaluate their service activity, encouraging relevancy and sustained interest. In community settings, this is alternatively called youth voice.
- Students discussion - Students discuss their learning experience during in-class discussions.
- *Reflection* - Structured opportunities are created to think, talk, and write about the service experience. The balance of reflection and action allows a student to be constantly aware of the impact of their work.
- *Community partnerships* - Partnerships with community agencies are used to identify genuine needs, provide mentors, and to work towards completing a project. In a successful partnership, both sides will give to and benefit from the project. In order for this partnership to be successful, clear guide lines must be implemented as to how often a student engages in service to a particular community agency.
- *Authentic community needs* – Local community members or service recipients are involved in determining the significance and depth of the service activities involved.
- *Assessment* - Well structured assessment instruments with constructive feedback through reflection provide valuable information regarding the positive 'reciprocal learning' and serving outcomes for sustainability and replication.

In 2008, the National Youth Leadership Council released the K–12 Service-Learning Standards for Quality Practice that used research in the field to determine eight standards of quality service-learning practice. The standards are:

- Meaningful Service
- Link to Curriculum
- Reflection
- Diversity
- Investigation
- Partnerships
- Progress Monitoring
- Project Design
- Action
- Demonstration
- Recognition

Further, to distinguish high quality from low quality service-learning experiences, Youth Service California has published the "Seven Elements of High Quality Service Learning" that include:

- Integrated Learning
- High Quality Service
- Collaboration
- Student Voice
- Civic Responsibility
- Reflection
- Evaluation

Origins of Service-Learning

Two philosophies have been instrumental in the formation of Service-Learning; progressivism and pragmatism. John Dewey and William James popularized these ideas with influence from Socrates, John Locke, Confucius, and many others. Using these philosophies, Service-Learning becomes a practice combined with learning; or learning while practicing.

Progressivism

Progressivism is a philosophy that can be brought into education, politics, etc..., however, this section deals with this philosophy in relation to education. Progressivism in education encourages the students to learn in a hands-on manner. John Dewey observed that most students tend to learn and retain information more effectively when learning this way. He also saw that students became more productive and efficient through this method. Progressivism moves the focus off the subject matter and onto the student.

Pragmatism

The word 'pragmatism' is originated from the Greek word, 'pragma,' which means 'action.' Pragmatism connects thoughts or ideas with action. For example, instead of a student merely thinking, "I should go volunteer at the humane society," pragmatism encourages that student to go out and do it.

Combining these philosophies, Service-Learning becomes a practice. It also encourages students to use their talents, ideas, and gifts to serve, and while performing the service, to learn.

Various Types of Service-Learning Plans

The Florida Department of Education. Florida Campus Compact. has published Standards for Service-Learning in Florida: A Guide for Creating and Sustaining Quality Practice. which states the four following types of service learning

Direct Service Learning: Person-to-person, face-to-face projects in which service impacts individuals who receive direct help from students (tutoring, work with elderly, oral histories, peer mediation, etc.).

Indirect Service Learning: Projects with benefits to a community as opposed to specific individuals (i.e., environmental, construction, restoration, town histories, food and clothing drives).

Advocacy Service Learning: Working, acting, speaking, writing, teaching, presenting, informing, etc., on projects that encourage action or create awareness on issues of public interest (i.e., promoting reading, safety, care for the environment, local history, violence and drug prevention, disaster preparedness).

Research Service Learning: Surveys, studies, evaluations, experiments, data gathering, interviewing, etc., to find, compile, and report information on topics in the public interest (i.e., energy audits of homes or public buildings, water testing, flora and fauna studies, surveys).

Comprehensive Action Plan for Service Learning (CAPSL)

- CAPSL Identifies four constituencies on which a programme for service learning needs to focus its principle activities: institution, faculty, students, and community.

- CAPSL also identifies a sequence of activities (Planning; awareness; prototype; resources; expansion; recognition; monitoring; evaluation; research; institutionalization)to be pursed for each of the four constituencies(institution, faculty, students, and community).
- CAPSL provide a heuristic for guiding the development of a service learning programme in higher education.
- Advantages of CAPSL : it is general enough that the execution of each cell can be tailored to local conditions.
- Disadvantages of CAPSL: it is not possible to detail how each step can be successfully accomplished to take the sequence of activities from the whole CAPSL model and apply it to any cell in the matrix.

Typology

As Defined by Robert Sigmon, 1994:

- Service-LEARNING: Learning goals primary; service outcomes secondary.
- SERVICE-Learning: Service outcomes primary; learning goals secondary.
- service learning: Service and learning goals completely separate.
- SERVICE-LEARNING: Service and learning goals of equal weight and each enhances the other for all participants.

In this comparative form, the typology is helpful not only in establishing criteria for distinguishing service-learning from other types of service programmes but also in providing a basis for clarifying distinctions among different types of service-oriented experiential education programmes (e.g., school volunteer, community service, field education, and internship programmes)

Objections to Service Learning

Although service learning has broad support among contemporary academics, there have been some objections to this approach to education. Towson University Professor John Egger, writing in the Spring 2008 issue of the journal "Academic Questions", argued that service learning does not really teach useful skills or develop cultural knowledge. Instead, Egger maintained, service learning mainly involves the inculcation of communitarian political ideologies. Tulane Professor Carl L. Bankston III has described his own university's policy of mandating service learning as the imposition of intellectual conformity by the university administration on both students and faculty. According to Bankston, by identifying specific types of civic engagement as worthy community service, the university was prescribing social and political perspectives. He argued that this was inconsistent with the idea that individuals in a pluralistic society should choose their own civic commitments and that it was contrary to the ideal of the university as a site for the pursuit of truth through the free exchange of ideas.

Learning in Service-learning

Experiential and hands-on learning is a major factor of service-learning. As well as the academic benefits, service-learning aims to furnish students with knowledge that will help them better understand the world. Janet Eyler, in the book "Where's the Learning in Service-Learning?", outlines the different ways student learn through service-learning. First there is interpersonal learning, in which students reevaluate personal values and motivations by channelling a passionate interest to service-learning projects, as well as build a connection and commitment to the community. The second form is academic material that is taught through practical application and reflective instruction, so that it may be practiced outside classrooms and test-taking. On pg 16, Janet Eyler explains, "it is the product of continuous challenge to old conceptions and reflection on new ways to organize information and use the new material." Thirdly is cognitive development where students are challenged to use critical thinking and problem solving skills in a context that provides additional information and experience for student evaluation, because service-learning deals with numerous problems in complex situations. The fourth form is transformation within the students, which "is about thinking about things in a new way and moving in new direction—creating a new picture without relying on the old lines." Finally, service-learning focuses on effective citizenship and behavioural issues, and this helps the students better understand social issues relevant to their own community. Learning in all these ways makes service-learning effective to those serving as well as those being served, and "learning begins with the impact service-learning on the personal and interpersonal development of the students."

What is Service Learning?

Service learning is a programme that must have a perfect balance between traditional learning and real life serving experience for it to be effective. The goal of this course is to equip you with knowledge that must be used for the required service hours. Unlike other courses, service learning does not just supply you with knowledge that might never be used, it prepares you and shows to you how this knowledge can be used effectively to solve different types of social problems. The importance of service learning is immense as it combines traditional learning and physical action, adding value to each experience while transforming our views of academics and life, in terms of thinking how to apply what is learned in class to real life and enjoy that rather than just studying to pass a test.

When this becomes our mindset we develop a new understanding of the learning experience and view it as not a necessary roadblock but as a building block for how it can all be applied. According to the book, 'where's the learning in service learning?','. The popularity of service learning has skyrocketed since 1994 and now has many schools teaching these courses to actively involved students. The outcome and effect of this project is not only for the transformation and good of the student, but the transformation and good of the community that is being served. Transformation in a student is necessary for the actual learning process to take place, and that only happens when you learn to connect your personal, social, and educational lives all together into one learning, changing, and serving life to benefit yourself and others.

Community-engaged Writing

Community-engaged writing is a method of getting students to write toward and about public problems and issues. A variety of approaches are used by instructors, depending on age group of students and theoretical approach. Two illustrative/related summaries follow.

In "Literacy as Violence Prevention," Ena Rosen, Associate Director of Need in Deed, describes a specific example of the teaching methods of Need in Deed, a Philadelphia-based education agency. This newsletter article is based on an anecdotal set of reports on an eighth grade teacher's work with one classroom in 2005. Rosen's purpose is to promote the effectiveness and work of Need in Deed, and Rosen ultimately shows that this method of working with urban youth is an effective teaching method and social intervention: "Meaningful service that addresses a root cause and meets an authentic community need: the best of service-learning and civic engagement" (Rosen).

In "Rogue Cops and Health Care: What Do We Want from Public Writing?" Susan Wells argues that writing teachers should not merely have students write within classrooms on socially relevant issues, such as gun control. She uses Habermas's definition of the public sphere to analyze an example of a "citizen" attempting to enter the public sphere through discourse—President Clinton's speech on health care reform—and ultimately demonstrates the failure of that effort. However, Wells contrasts Clinton's failed strategies to get health care reform passed with a more local example of a Temple student who successfully entered the public sphere by writing a citizen's complaint about his arrest and subsequent beating by a Philadelphia police officers. Wells concludes by suggesting four alternatives for writing teachers interested in helping students move their rhetoric into the public sphere: classroom as one type of public sphere itself, analysis of public and academic discourses, writing with and for public/community needs, and analysis of academic discourses as they intervene in the public sphere.

The Effects of Service Learning

Based upon various studies, students who participate in Service Learning Courses or Projects seem to encounter a multitude of benefits. The book *Where's the Learning in Service-Learning?* discusses the effects of Service Learning upon students, as well service learning in general. A study by students from Bates College also reports on the positive outcomes of Service Learning in Education. It should be mentioned that the effects of service learning upon the participants vary based on their participation and their job within the project.

The actual service in service learning obviously impacts the community, but right now, our focus will be the student. According to *Where's the Learning in Service-Learning?*, most college students who participated in service learning, or "service learners", said that it helped them understand themselves better. These service learners also stated that it contributed to personal development and change. Almost half of them considered spiritual formation an important part of their service learning experience and said that the course helped them satisfy religious convictions. The majority of service learners received self-satisfaction from the act of assisting others in their community. In general, service learners felt more confident in their abilities such as management.

Service Learners retained more of the information they learned in their studies and were provided a sense of engagement not usually found in most classes. Beyond the classroom, service learners felt more attached to and involved in their communities. Because service learning promoted teamwork, participants developed better communication, decision making, and coordinated effort. Service Learning also fostered people's leadership abilities. Most service learners gained practical skills based upon the tasks they had in the course. For example, someone might become a talented carpenter since they built tables in a service learning project. Finally, service learners gained tolerance of people from different backgrounds and better appreciated other cultures.

Service Learning in Language Education

Service learning can be used in all standard disciplines and recently has been explored for use in improving language instruction. A recent study found that integrating environmental issues with foreign language study provides significant opportunities for students to increase their language proficiency, develop their understanding of concepts related to the environment, and become more involved in a global community through a virtual service learning project. Similar work has found that students can contribute to sustainable development while improving their language skills.

Effect on Engineering Education

Many engineering educators see service learning as the solution to several prevalent problems in engineering education today. In the past, engineering curriculum has fluctuated between emphasizing engineering science to focusing more on practical aspects of engineering. Today, many engineering educators are concerned their students do not receive enough practical knowledge of engineering and its context. Some speculate that adding context to engineering help to motivate engineering students' studies and thus improve retention and diversity in engineering schools. Others feel that the teaching styles do not match the learning styles of engineering students.

Many engineering faculty members believe the educational solution lies in taking a more constructivist approach, where students construct knowledge and connections between nodes of knowledge as opposed to passively absorbing knowledge. Educators see service learning as a way to both implement a constructivism in engineering education as well as match the teaching styles to the learning styles of typical engineering students. As a result, many engineering schools have begun to integrate service learning into their curricula and there is now a journal dedicated to service learning in engineering. Recent work has also proposed that the use of open-source appropriate technology could be useful for integrating service learning into the engineering curricula.

Supporting Programmes

There are a number of substantial national efforts in the United States that promote service learning in its myriad forms. They include the following organizations:

The State Education Agency K–12 Service-Learning Network (SEANet) is a national network of professionals committed to advancing school-based service-learning initiatives in K–12 schools and school districts all across the country (seanetonline.org). Our members are directors, coordinators, specialists, or other staff working in a State Education Agency (SEA), or in an organization designated by a State Education Agency, who provide leadership in their respective states for the advancement of school-based service learning. They promote, develop, and expand school-based service learning to K–12 schools and school districts; they provide direct assistance in the form of technical support and professional development opportunities to local school-community partnerships; and they administer and disseminate the annual K–12 school-based state formula grants from Learn and Serve America, the primary federal funding source for service learning.

Learn and Serve America's National Service-Learning Clearinghouse (NSLC) provides the world's largest database of Service-learning materials, electronic resources, and job listings. It supports and encourages service learning throughout the United States, and enables over one million students to contribute to their community while building their academic and civic skills. This organization instills an ethic of lifelong community service; supports and encourages service learning throughout the United States, and enables over one million students to contribute to their community while building their academic and civic skills. By engaging our nation's young people in service learning, Learn and Serve America instills an ethic of lifelong community service.

National Service-Learning Partnership is a national network of members dedicated to advancing service learning as a core part of every young person's education. Service learning is a teaching method that engages young people in solving problems within their schools and communities as part of their academic studies or other type of intentional learning activity. The Partnership concentrates on strengthening the impact of service-learning on young people's learning and development, especially their academic and civic preparation.

The Jimmy and Rosalynn Carter Partnership Foundation fosters academic service learning in higher education with awards and grants to students/faculty and their 501(c)(3) community partners who demonstrate best practices or innovative approaches in the field. These programmes can be found at The Carter Academic Service Entrepreneur grant programme seeks to motivate students to develop innovative service-learning projects by providing $1,000 grants to the community organization partner of the student with the most innovative proposal in a state-wide or school-wide competition. ServiceBook sponsored and maintained by JRCPF, is the online community for academic service learning. JRCPF programmes have been held in 16 U.S. states, India and the United Kingdom.

The Leadership, Ethics, and Social Action Minor at Indiana University-Bloomington focuses on civic participation, community decision-making, and citizenship skills: how to communicate and organize and lead while serving as a citizen. The LESA programme is a chance to develop your own voice and interests while you research, serve, and take action in the community. A student who enjoys thinking and working independently and who would like to develop his or her professional presentation through serving the needs of the community will find opportunities to do so with LESA. Pre-professional students who wish to be involved in a community setting are attracted to the programme. Pre-law and pre-med, as well as pre-business, students find opportunities to develop their professional presentation.

A partnership between Youth Service America, America's Promise Alliance, and State Farm Companies Foundation launched GoToServiceLearning. It is recognized as a resource for teachers seeking to learn how to incorporate service-learning into their lessons. GoToServiceLearning.org is an interactive Web site housing a database of quality service-learning lesson plans from across the country, all tied to state academic standards.

Service-learning in Engineering Education

Many engineering educators see service-learning as the solution to several prevalent problems in engineering education today. In the past, engineering curriculum has fluctuated between emphasizing engineering science to focusing more on practical aspects of engineering. Today, many engineering educators are concerned their students do not receive enough practical knowledge of engineering and its context. Some speculate that adding context to engineering help to motivate engineering students' studies and thus improve retention and diversity in engineering schools. Others feel that the teaching styles do not match the learning styles of engineering students.

Many engineering faculty members believe the educational solution lies in taking a more constructivist approach, where students construct knowledge and connections between nodes of knowledge as opposed to passively absorbing knowledge. Educators see service-learning as a way to both implement a constructivism in engineering education as well as match the teaching styles to the learning styles of typical engineering students. As a result, many engineering schools have begun to integrate service-learning into their curricula.

History

The end of World War II marked the beginning of a movement toward increased emphasis on engineering science in engineering education. Initially, this movement enhanced the quality of engineering education. However, after decades of rising focus on science engineering, undergraduate engineering education began to lack instruction on practical engineering applications. Concurrently, the undergraduate engineering experience became increasingly fragmented. As one author described it, "Schools break knowledge and experience into subjects, relentlessly turning wholes into parts, flowers into petals, history into events, without ever restoring continuity."

In the 1980s, many different organizations, including both research institutions and professional associations, conducted studies in attempts to resolve the educational problems in the engineering field. Though they conducted their research independently, they arrived at several common conclusions. Researchers agreed that the engineering schools should continue to provide solid basic theory knowledge. However, they also called for added emphasis on synthesis and design understanding as well as increased exposure to societal context and interdisciplinary teamwork. Later reports reiterated the need for more exposure to engineering's context as well as a need to make engineering more attractive and relevant to students. Papers also reported the need for engineering students to develop professional and interpersonal skills.

Engineering Education Today

Today, requirements for engineering programmes reflect a movement to resolve the engineering education problems found in past studies. Many engineering educators see service-learning as a way to enhance their programmes by exposing students to engineering context while also giving them a chance to develop professional and interpersonal skills. These values are reflected in the Accreditation

Board for Engineering and Technology (ABET) standards for engineering schools. For an engineering programme to maintain accreditation, ABET requires that they "demonstrate that their students attain the broad education necessary to understand the impact of engineering solutions in a global, economic, environmental, and societal context".

Pedagogical Implications

The service-learning method ties in well with a teaching philosophy known as constructivism. Constructivism is an educational theory rooted in psychology and sociology. It asserts that learners construct knowledge from previous knowledge rather than passively absorbing knowledge from outside sources. Furthermore, learning includes both creation of new factual knowledge and understanding the connections between different nodes of knowledge. Service-learning provides an environment where students can actively construct knowledge while engaging in actual projects. The reflection portion of service-learning gives students time to create connections between old and new knowledge.

While accepted by many, some educators have criticized constructivism both epistemologically and pedagogically. Pedagogically, critics claim that a constructivist approach gives students in-depth knowledge but not breadth of knowledge. Since in a constructivist approach takes a significant amount of time to allow students to create new knowledge and relate it to previous knowledge through reflection, instructors usually cannot cover a large amount of material. However, while this may become a real concern for many courses, the specific role of service-learning plays in engineering school courses mitigates these concerns. Service-learning typically appears in introductory or optional courses in the engineering school. The goals of these courses is not to much to gain a detailed and broad understand of a field, but rather to have a real world engineering experience. This is notably different from courses where students must obtain vast amounts of accurate knowledge for precise calculations.

Critics also worry that a constructivist approach to education leaves the learner too disconnected from reality since it constantly focuses on building new knowledge based on pre-existing knowledge. Thus, theoretically, as they continue building knowledge off of their pre-existing knowledge in isolation, their view of the world could slowly become skewed from reality. While this may be a weakness for many courses, in service-learning, students work to create real solutions for a real customer. Thus their ideas must be resolved, not only with fellow engineering team members, but also with reality.

Learning Styles

In past years, studies on engineering education revealed the learning styles of most engineering students and the teaching styles of many engineering professors were incompatible. The five well known learning style dimensions include: sensing/intuitive, visual/auditory, inductive/deductive, active/reflective, and global/sequential.

According to Richard Felder from North Carolina State University and Linda Silverman from the Institute for the study of Advanced Development, most engineering students are visual, sensing, inductive, and active learners. Also, many of the creative students are global learners. However, most engineering education is auditory, intuitive, deductive, passive and sequential.

However, such conclusions are not well-supported by research. There is no evidence that identifying a student's learning style produces better outcomes, and there is significant evidence that the widespread "meshing hypothesis" (that a student will learn best if taught in a method deemed appropriate for the student's learning style) is invalid. Well-designed studies "flatly contradict the popular meshing hypothesis".

Online Service Learning

Though the interest in service learning at educational institutions has increased, these projects are often very costly to students and universities. However, there have been some examples of successful service learning projects facilitated over the Internet.

At Clarion University of Pennsylvania, a course in Physics of Energy and Environment included a service learning project which involved students studying the impact of switching the bulbs in stoplights around eastern Pennsylvania from standard incandescent bulbs to LEDs, which was facilitated completely online through the Appropriate Technology website Appropedia Other work in Canada has shown positive outcomes with engineering service learning used in hybrid assignments, where some work is done online while still maintaining a field component. With the transition of the open source paradigm to appropriate technology there has also been work at MIT and elsewhere calling for the development of open source appropriate technology to bolster engineering education.

Engineering Programmes with Service-learning

Many different universities have incorporated service-learning into their curricula to address the contextual, motivational, and multi-disciplinary team needs. Purdue University created the Engineering Projects in Community Service (EPICS) programme in 1995. Under this programme, freshman to senior undergraduate engineering students form multi-disciplinary teams to meet community needs. Students earn a variable number of credit hours based on their year in school and related contribution to the project. At Purdue, the service projects are long-term and students earn up to seven semesters worth of credit working on the service project. The programme began with 40 students on 5 teams but has quickly grown to 400 students on 24 teams.

The EPICS programme at Purdue as well as service-learning programmes at other universities, have succeeded in offering students practical experience, context, and motivation for engineering. Seventy seven percent of the students who were able to come back to the EPICS programme stayed for additional semesters. On student evaluations, 70% of students indicated that the programme positively impacted their decision to stay in engineering; of the 30% that responded differently, several indicated they had previously decided to stay in the engineering before the programme and thus, the programme did not affect their decision to stay in engineering. Student responses also returned favourable results for the educational objectives.

On evaluation comments, students also expressed that EPICS had completely changed their view of engineering, giving them both meaning and direction in all of their engineering studies.

Penn State University has created a certificate programme entitled 'Humanitarian Engineering'. The emphasis of the programme is on relationship building - and are not simply project-driven exercises. Long-term, sustainable, collaborative partnerships are formed with host universities and marginalized communities. This enables development of outreach programmes at the universities reaching into local communities. The Penn State programme is vertically integrated across the four-year engineering programme allowing students to form these long-term relationships with the host communities. This method allows for greater understanding of the cultural aspects of engineering design and its impact, as well as development of technical proficiency. There is also a very strong emphasis on entrepreneurship in the programme. Engineering design solutions are developed and students are encouraged to develop business plans and implement them in the host community.

Social and Ethical Implications

The ACM Code of Ethics lists contributing to society and human well-being as well as improving public understanding of an engineer's practice area. Through service-learning provides engineers with the opportunity to both contribute to society and educate the public.

Along with fostering a good community-university relationship, educators hope incorporating service-learning will increase diversity and retention in the engineering school. Diversifying the engineering population will allow engineering teams to maintain a better understanding of the needs in a society. So diversifying engineering teams will allow engineers to both meet real needs as well as provide interfaces to their solutions which the public can understand. Likewise, a society needs a vast population of engineers to meet the needs of a vast society.

Outdoor Education

Outdoor education usually refers to organized learning that takes place in the outdoors. Outdoor education programmes sometimes involve residential or journey-based experiences in which students participate in a variety of adventurous challenges in the form of outdoor activities such as hiking, climbing, canoeing, ropes courses and group games. Forest Schools and the John Muir Award are amongst organizations which encourage and provide opportunities for outdoor learning. Outdoor education draws upon the philosophy, theory, and practices of experiential education and environmental education.

Scope

Definitions: Outdoor education can be simply defined as *experiential learning in, for, or about the outdoors*. The term 'outdoor education', however, is used broadly to refer to a range of organized activities that take place in a variety of ways in predominantly outdoor environments. Common definitions of outdoor education are difficult to achieve because interpretations vary according to culture, philosophy, and local conditions.

Outdoor education is often referred to as synonymous with adventure education, adventure programming, and outdoor learning, outdoor school, adventure therapy, adventure recreation, adventure tourism, expeditionary learning, challenge education, experiential education, environmental education, Forest schools and wilderness education. Consensus about the meaning of these terms is also difficult to achieve. However, outdoor education often uses or draws upon these related elements and/or informs these areas. The hallmark of outdoor education is its focus on the "outdoor" side of this education; whereas adventure education would focus on the adventure side and environmental education would focus on environmental. Wilderness education involves expeditions into wilderness "where man is but a visitor."

Education Outside the Classroom

"Education outside the classroom" describes school curriculum learning, other than with a class of students sitting in a room with a teacher and books. It encompasses biology field trips and searching for insects in the school garden, as well as indoor activities like observing stock control in a local shop, or visiting a museum. It is a concept currently enjoying a revival because of the recognition of benefits from the more active style. The Education and Skills Committee of the House of Commons of the United Kingdom has reported that it brings history and art to life, develops social skills, and clearly enhances geography and science., while DfES has prepared practical guidelines for outdoor activities.

Despite the evidence supporting an extension of outdoor learning for children, there are a number of obstacles in the way. One of these obstacles is risk aversion amongst teachers, parents and others, raising reluctance to such diverse and physical tasks. The journalist Tim Gill has written about parental and institutional risk aversion affecting many activities with children in his book "No Fear". Another obstacle is the perceived high cost of facilitating outdoor learning. Creating an outdoor learning environment needn't cost a great deal, however. The UK Early Years Framework Stage, which outlines best practice in Early Years teaching, asserts that: "Outdoor learning is more effective when adults focus on what children need to be able to do rather than what children need to have. An approach that considers experiences rather than equipment places children at the centre of learning and ensures that individual children's learning and developmental needs are taken account of and met effectively"

Linda Tallent, a UK-based educational consultant who has worked extensively with schools to develop their outdoor spaces into learning environments, agrees. She believes that by focussing on activities and skill development, it is possible to develop an outdoor learning curriculum on a 'shoe string'. She cites a comment by Will Nixon, who reminds readers that 'Using the real world is the way learning has happened for 99.9% of human existence.

Only in the last hundred years have we put it into a little box called a classroom.'. Tallent also refers to evidence from a number of studies that the most effective way of learning is through participation, and calls on educators to make a special effort to create opportunities for children to participate in their learning.

Aims

Some typical aims of outdoor education are to:

- learn how to overcome adversity
- enhance personal and social development
- develop a deeper relationship with nature.

Outdoor education spans the three domains of self, others, and the natural world. The relative emphasis of these three domains varies from one programme to another. An outdoor education programme can, for example, emphasize one (or more) of these aims to:

- teach outdoor survival skills
- improve problem solving skills
- reduce recidivism
- enhance teamwork
- develop leadership skills
- understand natural environments
- promote spirituality

History

Modern outdoor education owes its beginnings to a number of separate initiatives. Organized camping was evident in the late nineteenth century and early twentieth century in Europe, the UK, the USA, Australia, and New Zealand. The Scouting movement, established in 1907 by Robert Baden-Powell, employs non-formal education with an emphasis on practical outdoor activities. The first Outward Bound centre at Aberdovey in Wales was established during the Second World War. The Forest schools of Denmark are examples of European programmes with similar aims and objectives.

A key outdoor education pioneer was Kurt Hahn, a German educator who founded schools such as the Schule Schloss Salem in Germany, Gordonstoun School in Scotland, Atlantic College in Wales, the United World Colleges movement, the Duke of Edinburgh Award scheme (which emphasizes community service, craftsmanship skills, physical skill, and outdoor expeditions), and the Outward Bound movement.

The second half of the twentieth century saw rapid growth of outdoor education in all sectors (state, voluntary, and commercial) with an ever-widening range of client groups and applications. In this period Outward Bound spread to over 40 countries around the world, including the USA in the 1960s. Other US based outdoor education programmes include Project Adventure and the National Outdoor Leadership School (NOLS). Project Adventure focuses on day use of ropes courses. NOLS uses the outdoor setting to train leaders for outdoor programmes and for other settings including training every new US astronaut and 10% of the US Naval Academy. The Association for Experiential Education is a professional association for "experiential" educators. The Wilderness Education Association (WEA) is a consortium of college outdoor education programmes with a standard curriculum based on an academic model.

A history of outdoor education in the UK has been documented by Lyn Cook (1999) . and a history of outdoor education in New Zealand has been published in Pip Lynch's 'Camping in the Curriculum' (2007).

Philosophy and Theory

Philosophy and theory about outdoor education tends to emphasise the effect of natural environments on human beings, the educative role of stress and challenge, and experiential learning.

One view is that participants are at their "rawest" level when outdoors because they are "stripped" of many of the conveniences of modern life. Participants can become more aware that they are part of a greater ecosystem and are not as bound by social customs and norms. In essence participants can be true to themselves and more able to see others as people regardless of race, class, religion etc. Outdoor education also helps instill the basic elements of teamwork because participants often need to work together and rely on others. For many people a high ropes course or an outdoor activity may stretch their comfort zone and cause them to challenge themselves physically which in turn can lead to challenging oneself mentally.

The roots of modern outdoor education can be found in the philosophical work of:

- Comenius
- John Dewey
- William James
- Aldo Leopold
- John Locke
- John Muir
- Jean-Jacques Rousseau
- Henry David Thoreau
- Pestalozzi

Foundational work on the philosophy of outdoor education includes work by:

- Kurt Hahn
- Willi Unsoeld

A wide range of social science and specific outdoor education theories and models have been applied in an effort to better understand outdoor education. Amongst the key theoretical models or concepts are:

- Experiential education theories
- Group development theories
- the Outward Bound Process Model
- Stress, optimal arousal, comfort zone, and psychological flow theories
- Psychoevolutionary theory and the Biophilia hypothesis

Around the World

Outdoor education occurs, in one form or another, in most if not all countries of the world. However, it can be implemented very differently, depending on the cultural context. Some countries, for example, view outdoor education as synonymous with environmental education, whilst other countries treat outdoor education and environmental education as distinct. Modern forms of outdoor education are most prevalent in UK, USA, Australia, New Zealand, Europe and to some extent Asia and Africa.

The UK: The UK has established an English Outdoor Council where they have defined outdoor education as a way for students and teachers to be fully engaged in a lesson, all the while embracing the outdoors. The UK deems outdoor education as "providing depth to the curriculum and makes an important contribution to students' physical, personal and social education."

The English Outdoor Council has developed 11 outcomes of outdoor education for educators to look towards when developing curriculum documents. They are as follows: enjoyment, confidence, social awareness, environmental awareness, activity skills, personal qualities, key skills, health & fitness, increased motivation & appetite for learning and broadened horizons. They seek to encourage all schools in The UK to participate in outdoor education, as the council believes it is a way for students to expand their minds and ability to grow with nature.

Outdoor Education in The UK:

- Institute For Outdoor Learning:
- Outdoor Education Centres:
- Ardroy Outdoor Education Centre:
- Scottish Outdoor Education Centres:

The USA: The USA's founding fathers of outdoor education are two mountaineers who have a passion for teaching others about the environment. Paul Petzoldt and Willi Unsoeld believed in educating students and adults through nature, and incorporated outdoor education in The USA over the years. There are many ways that outdoor education is present in The USA, due largely in part to the national parks, shorelines, and tight-knit communities who are proud to call their backyard a wilderness oasis. Within The USA, outdoor educators teach such things as being 'one with nature', scientific excursions, and team building courses. From The Colorado Mountains, to the sandy shores of Florida, outdoor education is present within the many organizations and companies who work towards developing sound outdoor education sanctuary for all to embrace.

Outdoor Education in The USA:

- Outdoor Education Employment:
- California Association for Environmental & Outdoor Education:
- Association for Experiential Education:

Australia & New Zealand: Australia & New Zealand are home to a plethora of outdoor education certificate programmes within each country. With such pristine coastlines, and mountainous areas, there is much to explore through the art of outdoor education. Once teachers have completed there schooling, many have opportunities to work at various outdoor education centres in either country. The Australian outdoor council has developed curriculum documents to ensure schools are partaking in outdoor education throughout the country.

Outdoor Education in Australia & New Zealand:

- Outdoor Education Australia:
- Australia Journal of Outdoor Education:
- The Outdoor Education Group:
- Outdoor Education New Zealand:
- Outward Bound New Zealand:

Canada: Canada is well known for its outdoor education experiences. With Ontario's Algonquin Park, to the beautiful Rocky Mountains in British Columbia, there is much to boast about in terms of outdoor education. Environmental education, most notably outdoor education in Canada is seen through outdoor camp and residential programmes, school-based programmes and commercial travel operations. Outdoor education in Canada is based around ""hard" technical skills—often travel and camping skills - and the "soft" - group skills and personal growth qualities—are blended with, one might say, the "green" and "warm" skills of a complementary eco-adventure focus." Adventures are found whether one is partaking in environmental awareness or team-building workshops throughout Canada. Many schools and after-school programmes such as The YMCA camps lean towards outdoor education, especially during the summer months.

Outdoor Education in Canada:

- Norval Outdoor Education:
- Sea To Sky Outdoor Education:
- Outdoor Education:

Research and critical views

There is much anecdotal evidence about benefits of outdoor education experiences; teachers, for example, often speak of the improvement they have in relationships with students following a trip. However, hard evidence showing that outdoor education has a demonstrable long-term effect on behaviour or educational achievement is harder to identify; this may be in part because of the difficulty involved in conducting studies which separate out the effects of outdoor education on meaningful outcomes.

A major meta-analysis of 97 empirical studies indicated a positive overall effect of adventure education programmes on outcomes such as self-concept, leadership, and communication skills. This study also indicated that there appeared to be ongoing positive effects. The largest empirical study of the effects of outdoor education programmes (mostly Outward Bound programmes) found small-moderate short-term positive impacts on a diverse range of generic life skills, with the strongest outcomes for longer, expedition-based programmes with motivated young adults, and partial long-term retention of these gains.

In "Adventure in a Bun", Chris Loynes has suggested that outdoor education is increasingly an entertainment park consumption experience. In a paper entitled "The Generative Paradigm", Loynes has also called for an increase in "creativity, spontaneity and vitality". These dialogues indicate a need for those working in outdoor education to examine assumptions to ensure that their work is educational (Hovelynck & Peeters, 2003).

Outdoor education has been found more beneficial to those students who find classroom learning more challenging. This may be due to a non-academic family background, a personal psychological trait such as attention deficit hyperactivity disorder, or because they are boys.

When German children from forest kindergartens went to primary school, teachers observed a significant improvement in reading, writing, mathematics, social interactions and many other areas.

Using the Environment as an Integrating Context for learning (EIC) is the foundation of a substantial report which found benefits in learning outside the classroom on standardized measures of academic achievement in reading, writing, math, science, and social studies; reduced discipline problems; and increased enthusiasm for learning and pride in accomplishments.

Practice-based Professional Learning

Practice-based professional learning (pbpl) is best understood in contrast to 'classroom-' or 'theory-based' learning. It is kindred to terms such as 'work-based', 'workplace' or 'work-centred' learning. Distinctive, though, are a concern for *professional* learning, and the preference for 'practice' rather than 'work'. While it does not disdain propositional knowledge and what is sometimes called 'theory', its prime interest is in the formation of self-renewing and effective professional practices—a distinct theoretical position in its own right.

The range of concerns may be seen, for example, in the UK Open University's practice-based professional learning centre, one of the Higher Education Funding Council for England's centres for excellence in teaching and learning. Its interests cover the inter-relation of various forms of professional knowledge, ways of fostering them and their co-ordination, workplaces as sites of learning, the assessment of practice-based learning achievements, and the use of modern technologies to support distributed learning.

Other centres for excellence occupy some or all of the territory, notably the Professional Development Unit at the University of Chester, SCEPTrE in the University of Surrey, CEPLW in the University of Westminster and NCWBLP in Middlesex University.

Interest in this territory is not confined to the UK, with some of the most respected work associated with David Boud at the University of Technology, Sydney, NSW.

Cooperative Learning

Cooperative learning is an approach to organize classroom activities into academic and social learning experiences. It differs from group work, and it has been described as "structuring positive interdependence." Students must work in groups to complete tasks collectively toward academic goals. Unlike individual learning, which can be competitive in nature, students learning cooperatively capitalize on one another's resources and skills (asking one another for information, evaluating one another's ideas, monitoring one another's work, etc.). Furthermore, the teacher's role changes from giving information to facilitating students' learning. Everyone succeeds when the group succeeds. Ross and Smyth (1995) describe successful cooperative learning tasks as intellectually demanding, creative, open-ended, and involve higher order thinking tasks. Five essential elements are identified for the successful incorporation of cooperative learning in the classroom.

History

Prior to World War II, social theorists such as Allport, Watson, Shaw, and Mead began establishing cooperative learning theory after finding that group work was more effective and efficient in quantity, quality, and overall productivity when compared to working alone. However, it wasn't until 1937 when researchers May and Doob found that people who cooperate and work together to achieve shared goals, were more successful in attaining outcomes, than those who strived independently to complete the same goals. Furthermore, they found that independent achievers had a greater likelihood of displaying competitive behaviours.

Philosophers and psychologists in the 1930s and 40's such as John Dewey, Kurt Lewin, and Morton Deutsh also influenced the cooperative learning theory practiced today. Dewey believed it was important that students develop knowledge and social skills that could be used outside of the classroom, and in the democratic society. This theory portrayed students as active recipients of knowledge by discussing information and answers in groups, engaging in the learning process together rather than being passive receivers of information (e.g., teacher talking, students listening). Lewin's contributions to cooperative learning were based on the ideas of establishing relationships between group members in order to successfully carry out and achieve the learning goal. Deutsh's contribution to cooperative learning was positive social interdependence, the idea that the student is responsible for contributing to group knowledge.

Since then, David and Roger Johnson have been actively contributing to the cooperative learning theory. In 1975, they identified that cooperative learning promoted mutual liking, better communication, high acceptance and support, as well as demonstrated an increase in a variety of thinking strategies among individuals in the group. Students who showed to be more competitive lacked in their interaction and trust with others, as well as in their emotional involvement with other students.

In 1994 Johnson and Johnson published the 5 elements (positive interdependence, individual accountability, face-to-face interaction, social skills, and processing) essential for effective group learning, achievement, and higher-order social, personal and cognitive skills (e.g., problem solving, reasoning, decision-making, planning, organizing, and reflecting).

Types

Formal cooperative learning is structured, facilitated, and monitored by the educator over time and is used to achieve group goals in task work (e.g. completing a unit). Any course material or assignment can be adapted to this type of learning, and groups can vary from 2-6 people with discussions lasting from a few minutes up to an entire period. Types of formal cooperative learning strategies include:

1. The jigsaw technique
2. Assignments that involve group problem solving and decision making
3. Laboratory or experiment assignments
4. Peer review work (e.g. editing writing assignments).

Having experience and developing skill with this type of learning often facilitates informal and base learning. Jigsaw activities are wonderful because the student assumes the role of the teacher on a given topic and is in charge of teaching the topic to a classmate. The idea is that if students can teach something, they have already learned the material.

Informal cooperative learning incorporates group learning with passive teaching by drawing attention to material through small groups throughout the lesson or by discussion at the end of a lesson, and typically involves groups of two (e.g. turn-to-your-partner discussions). These groups are often temporary and can change from lesson to lesson (very much unlike formal learning where 2 students may be lab partners throughout the entire semester contributing to one another's knowledge of science).

Discussions typically have four components that include formulating a response to questions asked by the educator, sharing responses to the questions asked with a partner, listening to a partner's responses to the same question, and creating a new well-developed answer. This type of learning enables the student to process, consolidate, and retain more information.

In group-based cooperative learning, these peer groups gather together over the long term (e.g. over the course of a year, or several years such as in high school or post-secondary studies) to develop and contribute to one another's knowledge mastery on a topic by regularly discussing material, encouraging one another, and supporting the academic and personal success of group members.

Base group learning (e.g., a long term study group) is effective for learning complex subject matter over the course or semester and establishes caring, supportive peer relationships, which in turn motivates and strengthens the student's commitment to the group's education while increasing self-esteem and self-worth. Base group approaches also make the students accountable to educating their peer group in the event that a member was absent for a lesson. This is effective both for individual learning, as well as social support.

Elements

Brown & Ciuffetelli Parker (2009) and Siltala (2010) discuss the *5 basic and essential elements* to cooperative learning:

- Positive interdependence
- Students must fully participate and put forth effort within their group
- Each group member has a task/role/responsibility therefore must believe that they are responsible for their learning and that of their group
- Face-to-face promotive interaction
- Members promote each other's success
- Students explain to one another what they have or are learning and assist one another with understanding and completion of assignments
- Individual and group accountability
- Each student must demonstrate mastery of the content being studied
- Each student is accountable for their learning and work, therefore eliminating "social loafing"
- Social skills
- Social skills that must be taught in order for successful cooperative learning to occur
- Skills include effective communication, interpersonal and group skills
- Leadership
- Decision-making
- Trust-building
- Communication
- Conflict-management skills
- Group processing
- Every so often groups must assess their effectiveness and decide how it can be improved

In order for student achievement to improve considerably, two characteristics must be present:

1. When designing cooperative learning tasks and reward structures, individual responsibility and accountability must

be identified. Individuals must know exactly what their responsibilities are and that they are accountable to the group in order to reach their goal.

2. All group members must be involved in order for the group to complete the task. In order for this to occur each member must have a task that they are responsible for which cannot be completed by any other group member.

Cooperative Learning Techniques

There are a great number of cooperative learning techniques available. Some cooperative learning techniques utilize student pairing, while others utilize small groups of four or five students. Hundreds of techniques have been created into structures to use in any content area. Among the easy to implement structures are Think-Pair-Share, Think-Pair-Write, variations of Round Robin, and the Reciprocal Teaching Technique. A well known cooperative learning technique is the Jigsaw, Jigsaw II and Reverse Jigsaw.

Think Pair Share

Originally developed by Frank T. Lyman (1981), Think-Pair-Share allows for students to contemplate a posed question or problem silently. The student may write down thoughts or simply just brainstorm in his or her head. When prompted, the student pairs up with a peer and discusses his or her idea(s) and then listens to the ideas of his or her partner. Following pair dialogue, the teacher solicits responses from the whole group.

Jigsaw

Students are members of two groups: home group and expert group. In the heterogeneous home group, students are each assigned a different topic. Once a topic has been identified, students leave the home group and group with the other students with their assigned topic. In the new group, students learn the material together before returning to their home group. Once back in their home group, each student is accountable for teaching his or her assigned topic.

Jigsaw II

Jigsaw II is Robert Slavin's (1980) variation of Jigsaw in which members of the home group are assigned the same material, but focus on separate portions of the material. Each member must become an "expert" on his or her assigned portion and teach the other members of the home group.

Reverse Jigsaw

This variation was created by Timothy Hedeen (2003) It differs from the original Jigsaw during the teaching portion of the activity. In the Reverse Jigsaw technique, students in the expert groups teach the whole class rather than return to their home groups to teach the content.

Reciprocal Teaching

Brown & Paliscar (1982) developed reciprocal teaching. It is a cooperative technique that allows for student pairs to participate in a dialogue about text. Partners take turns reading and asking questions of each other, receiving immediate feedback. Such a model allows for students to use important metacognitive techniques such as clarifying, questioning, predicting, and summarizing. It embraces the idea that students can effectively learn from each other.

The Williams

Students collaborate to answer a big question that is the learning objective. Each group has differentiated questions that increases in cognitive ability to allow students to progress and meet the learning objective.

STAD (or Student-Teams-Achievement Divisions)

Students are placed in small groups (or teams). The class in its entirety is presented with a lesson and the students are subsequently tested. Individuals are graded on the team's performance. Although the tests are taken individually, students are encouraged to work together to improve the overall performance of the group.

Research Supporting Cooperative Learning

Research on cooperative learning demonstrated "overwhelmingly positive" results and confirmed that cooperative modes are cross-curricular. Cooperative learning requires students to engage in group activities that increase learning and adds other important dimensions.

The positive outcomes include academic gains, improved race relations and increased personal and social development. Students who fully participate in group activities, exhibit collaborative behaviours, provide constructive feedback, and cooperate with their groups have a higher likelihood of receiving higher test scores and course grades at the end of the semester. Cooperative learning is an active pedagogy that fosters higher academic achievement. Cooperative learning has also been found to increase attendance, time on task, enjoyment of school and classes, motivation, and independence.

Benefits and applicability of cooperative learning:

- Students demonstrate academic achievement
- Cooperative learning methods are usually equally effective for all ability levels
- Cooperative learning is effective for all ethnic groups
- Student perceptions of one another are enhanced when given the opportunity to work with one another
- Cooperative learning increases self-esteem and self-concept
- Ethnic and physically/mentally handicapped barriers are broken down allowing for positive interactions and friendships to occur

Cooperative learning results in:

- Increased higher level reasoning
- Increased generation of new ideas and solutions
- Greater transfer of learning between situations

Cooperative learning is significant in business:

- Cooperative learning can be seen as a characteristic of innovative businesses
- The five stage division on cooperative learning creates a useful method of analyzing learning in innovative businesses
- Innovativity connected to cooperative learning seems to make the creation of innovations possible

Limitations

Cooperative Learning has many limitations that could cause the process to be more complicated than first perceived. Sharan (2010) describes the constant evolution of cooperative learning as a threat. Because cooperative learning is constantly changing, there is a possibility that teachers may become confused and lack complete understanding of the method. Teachers implementing cooperative learning may also be challenged with resistance and hostility from students who believe that they are being held back by their slower teammates or by students who are less confident and feel that they are being ignored or demeaned by their team.

Students often provide feedback in the success of the teamwork experienced during cooperative learning experiences. Peer review and evaluations may not reflect true experiences due to perceived competition among peers. A confidential evaluation process may help to increase evaluation strength.

7

Collaborative Learning

Collaborative learning is a situation in which two or more people learn or attempt to learn something together. Unlike individual learning, people engaged in collaborative learning capitalize on one another's resources and skills (asking one another for information, evaluating one another's ideas, monitoring one another's work, etc.). More specifically, collaborative learning is based on the model that knowledge can be created within a population where members actively interact by sharing experiences and take on asymmetry roles. Put differently, collaborative learning refers to methodologies and environments in which learners engage in a common task where each individual depends on and is accountable to each other. These include both face-to-face conversations and computer discussions (online forums, chat rooms, etc.). Methods for examining collaborative learning processes include conversation analysis and statistical discourse analysis.

Collaborative learning is heavily rooted in Vygotsky's views that there exists an inherent social nature of learning which is shown through his theory of zone of proximal development. Often, collaborative learning is used as an umbrella term for a variety of approaches in education that involve joint intellectual effort by students or students and teachers. Thus, collaborative learning is commonly illustrated when groups of students work together to search for understanding, meaning, or solutions or to create an artifact or product of their learning. Further, collaborative learning redefines traditional student-teacher relationship in the classroom which results in controversy over whether this paradigm is more beneficial than harmful. Collaborative learning activities can include collaborative writing, group projects, joint problem solving, debates, study teams, and other activities. The approach is closely related to cooperative learning.

Alternatively, collaborative learning occurs when individuals are actively engaged in a community in which learning takes place through explicit or implicit collaborative efforts. Collaborative learning has often been portrayed as solely a cognitive process by which adults participate as facilitators of knowledge and children as receivers.

However, Indigenous communities of the Americas illustrate that collaborative learning occurs because individual participation in learning occurs on a horizontal plane where children and adults are equal. Thus collaborative learning also occurs when children and adults in engage play, work, and other activities together.

Examples of Collaborative Learning

- Collaborative Networked Learning According to Findley (1987) "Collaborative Networked Learning (CNL) is that learning which occurs via electronic dialogue between self-directed co-learners and learners and experts. Learners share a common purpose, depend upon each other and are accountable to each other for their success. CNL occurs in interactive groups in which participants actively communicate and negotiation meaning with one another within a contextual framework which may be facilitated by an online coach, mentor or group leader."
- Computer-supported collaborative learning (CSCL) is a relatively new educational paradigm within collaborative learning which uses technology in a learning environment to help mediate and support group interactions in a collaborative learning context. CSCL systems use technology to control and monitor interactions, to regulate tasks, rules, and roles, and to mediate the acquisition of new knowledge.
- Learning Management System In this context, collaborative learning refers to a collection of tools which learners can use to assist, or be assisted by others. Such tools include Virtual Classrooms (i.e. geographically distributed classrooms linked by audio-visual network connections), chat, discussion threads, application sharing (e.g. a colleague projects spreadsheet on another colleague's screen across a network link for the purpose of collaboration), among many others.

- Collaborative Learning Development Enables developers of learning systems to work as a network. Specifically relevant to e-learning where developers can share and build knowledge into courses in a collaborative environment. Knowledge of a single subject can be pulled together from remote locations using software systems.
- Collaborative Learning in Virtual Worlds Virtual Worlds by their nature provide an excellent opportunity for collaborative learning. At first learning in virtual worlds was restricted to classroom meetings and lectures, similar to their counterparts in real life. Now collaborative learning is evolving as companies starting to take advantage of unique features offered by virtual world spaces - such as ability to record and map the flow of ideas, use 3D models and virtual worlds mind mapping tools.
- Collaborative learning in thesis circles in higher education is another example of people learning together. In a thesis circle, a number of students work together with at least one professor or lecturer, to collaboratively coach and supervise individual work on final (e.g. undergraduate or MSc) projects. Students switch frequently between their role as co-supervisor of other students and their own thesis work (incl. receiving feedback from other students).
- Collaborative Learning can lead to student success by deepening the understanding of a given topic. An example highlighted in Edutopia's Schools That Work series is The College Preparatory School in Oakland, CA. In this setting students utilized daily class worksheets and periodic group tests designed to be more challenging than individual homework or exams, and students quickly learn how they are able to solve problems as a group that they might not have struggled with on their own. Essentially, Collaborative Learning at The College Preparatory School aims to actively engage students with material and each other to maximize knowledge retention.

Research

When compared to more traditional methods where students non-interactively receive information from a teacher, cooperative, problem-based learning demonstrated improvement of student engagement and retention of classroom material. More than 1200 studies comparing cooperative, competitive, and individualistic efforts have found that cooperative learning methods improve students' time on tasks and motivation to learn, as well as students' interpersonal relationships and expectations for personal success. A meta-analysis comparing small-group work to individual work in K-12 and college classrooms also found that students working in small groups achieved significantly more than students working individually, and optimal groups for learning tended to be three- to four-member teams with lower-ability students working best in mixed groups and medium-ability students doing best in homogeneous groups. For higher-ability students, group ability levels made no difference. In more than 40 studies of elementary, middle, and high school English classrooms, discussion-based practices improved comprehension of the text and critical-thinking skills for students across ethnic and socioeconomic backgrounds. Even discussions lasting as briefly as ten minutes with three participants improved perceived understanding of key story events and characters.

Cultural Examples of Collaborative Learning

Cultural Variations: There also exists cultural variations in ways of collaborative learning. Research in this area has mainly focused on children in Indigenous Mayan communities of the Americas or in San Pedro, Guatemala and European American middle-class communities.

Generally, researchers have found that children in Indigenous Mayan communities such as San Pedro typically learn through keenly observing and actively contributing to the mature activities of their community. This type of learning is characterized by the learner's collaborative participation through multi-modal communication verbal and non-verbal and observations. They are highly engaged within their community through focused observation. Mayan parents believe that children learn best by observing and so an attentive child is seen as one who is trying to learn. It has also been found that these children are extremely competent and independent in self-maintenance at an early age and tend to receive little pressure from their parents.

Research has found that even when Indigenous Mayan children are in a classroom setting, the cultural orientation of indigenous learners shows that observation is a preferred strategy of learning. Thus children and adults in a classroom setting adopt cultural practice and organize learning collaboratively. This is in contrast to the European-American classroom model, which allocates control to teachers/adults allowing them to control classroom activities.

Within the European American middle-class communities, children typically do not learn through collaborative learning methods. In the classroom, these children generally learn by engaging in initiation-reply-evaluation sequences. This sequence starts with the teacher iniatiating an exchange, usually by asking a question. The student then replies, with the teacher evaluating the student's answer. This way of learning fits with European-American middle-class cultural goals of autonomy and independence that are dominant in parenting styles within European-American middle-class culture.

An article featured on Edutopia suggests reforming this educational practice in favour of facilitating collaborative learning. To start, teachers configure K-12 classroom geography to encourage face-to-face communication and eye contact, where students are allowed to take equally distributed initiative, with teachers acting as guides. In the process, students lead discussions and work independently with teacher oversight and help when asked, rather than explicit direction.

Examples from Indigenous Communities in the Americas

Although learning happens in a variety of ways in indigenous communities, collaborative learning is one of the main methods used in indigenous learning styles instead of using European-American approaches to learning. These methods include learning in a horizontal plane where children and adults share contribution in ideas and activities.

For example, Mayan people of San Pedro use collaboration in order to build upon one another's ideas and activities. Mayan mothers do not act as teachers when completing a task with their children, but instead collaborate with children through play and other activities. People of this Mayan community use the shared endeavours method more than European-Americans who tend to use the transmit-and-test model more often. The shared endeavours model is when people go off of others ideas and learn from them, while the transmit-and-test model is what is used in most American schools when a teacher gives students information and then tests the students on the information. The shared endeavours model is a form of collaborative learning because everyone learns from one another and get to hear and share others ideas.

Indigenous people of the Americas utilize collaborative learning through their emphasis on role sharing and responsibility sharing within their communities. The Mayan community of San Pedro, Guatemala utilize flexible leadership that allow children to take a more active role in their learning. Children and adults work as cohesive groups when tackling new projects. Collaborative learning is prevalent in Indigenous communities due to the integration of children in the daily lives of the adults. This is unique in that age is not a determining factor in whether or not individuals are incorporated into collaborative efforts and learning that occurs in Indigenous communities.

Participation of learner is a key component to collaborative learning as it functions as the method by which the learning process occurs. Thus collaborative learning occurs when children and adults in communities switch between "knowledge performers" and "observing helpers".

For example, when parents in an indigenous Mazahua community where assigned the task of organizing children to build a roof over a market stand in such a way that they would learn to do it themselves, parents and children both collaborated on a horizontal structure. Switching between knowledge performer and observing helper, adults and children completed the task peacefully, without assigned roles of educator/student and illustrated that children still took initiative even when adults were still performing.

Adults and children in Indigenous communities of the Americas participate in a horizontal organizational structure; therefore when they work together with one another they are reciprocals of each other. This horizontal structure allows for flexible leadership, which is one of the key aspects of collaborative learning. The Indigenous communities of the Americas are unique in their collaborative learning because they do not discriminate upon age, instead Indigenous communities of the Americas encourage active participation and flexible leadership roles regardless of age. Children and adults regularly interchange their roles within their community. In addition, Indigenous communities consider observation to be a part of the collaborative learning process.

Collaborative Scripts

Collaborative scripts structure collaborative learning by creating roles and mediating interactions while allowing for flexibility in dialogue and activities. Collaborative scripts are used in nearly all cases of collaborative learning some of which are more suited for face-to-face collaborative learning—usually, more flexible—and others for computer-supported collaborative learning—typically, more constraining. Additionally, there are two broad types of scripts: macro-scripts and micro-scripts. Macro-scripts aim at creating situations within which desired interactions will occur. Micro-scripts emphasize activities of individual learners.

Alternative Education

Alternative education, also known as non-traditional education or educational alternative, includes a number of approaches to teaching and learning separate from what is offered by mainstream or traditional education. Educational alternatives are often rooted in various philosophies that are fundamentally different from those of mainstream or traditional education. While some alternatives have strong political, scholarly, or philosophical orientations, others are started by informal associations of teachers and students dissatisfied with some aspects of mainstream or traditional education. Educational alternatives, which include charter schools, alternative schools, independent schools, and home-based learning vary widely, but often emphasize the values of small class sizes, close relationships between students and teachers and a strong sense of community.

Terminology

Alternative education refers to any type of education which does not match the conventional standard. The public school system frequently sets this standard, although public schools use alternative approaches in some cases, as well. Other words used in place of "alternative" include "non-traditional," "non-conventional," or "non-standardized," although these terms are used less frequently and may have negative connotations or multiple meanings. Those involved in forms of education which differ in their educational philosophy (as opposed to their intended pupil base) often use words such as "authentic," "holistic," and "progressive." However, these words have different meanings which are either more specific or more ambiguous than the term "alternative."

Origins

"Alternative education" presupposes a kind of tradition to which the "alternative" is opposed. In general, this limits the term to the last two or three centuries, with the rise of standardized and, later, compulsory education at the primary and secondary levels. Many critics during this period suggested that the education of young people should be undertaken in radically different ways than the one in practice. In the 19th century, the Swiss humanitarian Johann Heinrich Pestalozzi; the American transcendentalists Amos Bronson Alcott, Ralph Waldo Emerson, and Henry David Thoreau; the founders of progressive education, John Dewey and Francis Parker; and educational pioneers, such as Friedrich Fröbel, Maria Montessori and Rudolf

Steiner (founder of the Waldorf schools); among others, all insisted that education should be understood as the art of cultivating the moral, emotional, physical, psychological, and spiritual aspects of the developing child. Anarchists such as Leo Tolstoy and Francisco Ferrer Guardia emphasized education as a force for political liberation, secularism, and elimination of class distinctions. After World War II alternative approaches to early childhood education were developed in Reggio Emilia, Italy; this is known as the Reggio Emilia approach.It was started by Loris Malaguzzi.

More recently, social critics such as John Caldwell Holt, Paul Goodman, Frederick Mayer, George Dennison and Ivan Illich have examined education from more individualist, anarchist, and libertarian perspectives, that is, critiques of the ways that they feel conventional education subverts democracy by molding young people's understandings. Other writers, from the revolutionary Paulo Freire to American educators like Herbert Kohl and Jonathan Kozol, have criticized mainstream Western education from the viewpoint of their varied left-liberal and radical politics. The argument for an approach that caters more to the personal interest and learning style of each individual is supported by recent research that suggest that learner-responsible models prove to be more effective than the traditional teacher-responsible models. Ron Miller has identified five core elements common to many contemporary educational alternatives:

1. Respect for every person
2. Balance
3. Decentralization of authority
4. Noninterference between political, economic, and cultural spheres of society
5. A holistic worldview

Modern Forms

A wide variety of educational alternatives exist at the elementary, secondary, and tertiary levels of education. These generally fall into four major categories: school choice, alternative school, independent school, and home-based education. These general categories can be further broken down into more specific practices and methodologies.

School Choice

Public school alternatives include entirely separate schools in their own settings, as well as classes, programmes, and even semiautonomous "schools within schools." Public school choice options are open to all students in their communities, though some have waiting lists. Among these are charter schools, combining private initiatives and state funding; and magnet schools, which attract students to particular themes, such as performing arts.

Alternative School

The term alternative school is used to describe a wide variety of educational approaches employing nontraditional philosophies, curricula and/or methods. Some alternative schools have strong philosophical, political, or practical orientations, while others are more *ad-hoc* assemblies of teachers and students seeking to explore possibilities not available within mainstream or traditional education.

Alternative Education of At-Risk Students and Drop Out Prevention

Advocates of programmes designed to prevent, or discourage, students from dropping out before they graduate (usually from high school) believe that leaving school without a diploma negatively impacts an individual's professional and personal life. Collectively, this negatively impacts society.

Drop Out Prevention Methods

Individual schools in the U.S. have tried to tackle the problem through their own programme initiatives. Three that have been used and studied for success are: the Check & Connect programme; the Career Academies initiative; and the Talent Development High School model. These programmes are designed to work with high risk students before they drop out of school.

The Check & Connect Programme This alternative is a dropout prevention model that was developed in Minnesota through a partnership with the University of Minnesota, the local public schools and community service organizations. It was used in the Minneapolis public schools, specifically focusing in on students with learning, emotional and behavioural disabilities. The "Check" portion pairs each student with a mentor, deemed a "monitor". This mentor figure assesses attendance, academics and overall performance with regular discussions about twice a month. The "Connect" aspect utilizes this individualized attention to connect this student with school personnel, family and community service providers that can intervene to keep the student on track.

Effectiveness: A 1998 study conducted by Sinclair and colleagues shows overall positive effects on 94 high school students from

Minneapolis public schools in the Check & Connect programme. The study found that students enrolled in the programme were significantly less likely to have dropped out of school after the end of freshman year (9% compared with 30%). This positive outcome remained after the final check-up at the end of senior year—39% of students enrolled dropped out of high school compared to 58% of those not enrolled.

In addition to actually staying in school, the study also found the students' progress in school to be positive as well; Check & Connect students earned more course credits in their night-grade year than non-intervention students.

Cost Efficiency: According to the Dakota County schools in Minnesota, the cost of implementing the Check & Connect programme is around $1,400 per student in 2001-2002. This model is very cost-inefficient, and now in 2011, the total may even be costlier.

The Career Academies Initiative

This alternative intervenes to target the most at-risk students. The Career Academies is a school-within-a-school model with a career-themed approach to learning. Developed 35 years ago, this alternative has evolved and around 2,500 academies are operated nationwide. It tends to be found in larger high schools and helps create a smaller community by keeping students with the same teachers for three or fours years of high school. The programme requires students to take the career-related courses with the "Academy" in subjects such as finance or technology and even partners with local employers to offer internship opportunities.

Effectiveness: A 2000 study conducted by Kemple and Snipes shows overall positive effects for 1,700 high school students in nine different Career Academies. The study found that the most at-risk students participating in the programme produced significantly fewer dropouts (21% compared with 32%). When assessing progress in school, the high-risk students earned more credits by their senior year and 40% had earned enough credits to graduate, as opposed to only 25% of non-intervention students, posting positive results for the programme.

Cost Efficiency: According to the California Partnership Academies, average cost estimates for the Career Academies intervention are $600 more per pupil than the average cost for a non-Academy student in 2004. This figure does not include additional costs of intensive services for high-risk students.

The Talent Development High School Model

This alternative was developed in 1994 by The Centre for Research on the Education of Students Placed at Risk and initiated at Patterson High School in Baltimore, Maryland. The Talent Development High School (TDHS) approach is an entire reform intervention, with dropout prevention as one component. It includes breaking the larger high school into smaller learning communities, like Career Academies, but is more extensive. There is a separate ninth grade academy, a career academy for the upper grades and an additional "Twilight School" after school programme for those with chronic discipline and attendance issues. This model homes in on reforming students' low expectations and schools' poor academic preparation through a college-preparatory sequence in ninth and tenth grade as well as increased focus on English and Math courses.

***Effectiveness*:** A 2005 study conducted by Kemple, Herlihy, and Smith, which followed 30 cohorts of participants for four years in Philadelphia, Pennsylvania, shows positive effects of the Talent Development High School (TDHS) model, primarily on academic progress. The study found that students using this model earned more course credits over the first two years of high school than those not in the programme (9.5 credits compared with 8.6 credits). These students were also more likely to move onto the tenth grade (68% compared with 60%).

Cost Efficiency: According to Johns Hopkins University 's Centre for the Social Organization of Schools (CSOS), the developer of the initiative, average costs for a student participating in the Talent Development High School model run an additional $350 a year per student. This estimate includes the cost of materials and ongoing technical assistance.

These are just three of many possible alternative education models to help at-risk students.

The matter has also gained national attention. On March 1, 2010, President Barack Obama called on states to identify and focus on schools with graduation rates below 60 percent. Those districts could be eligible for federal aid as his budget proposal includes $900 million in "school turnaround grants" on top of $3.5 billion in federal dollars the administration has committed to persistently low-performing schools. With respect to keeping students engaged and on-track to graduation specifically, he committed $50 million to the Graduation Promise Fund.

Popular Education

Popular education was related in the 19th century to the workers' movement. Such experiences have been continued throughout the 20th century, such as the folk high schools in Scandinavian countries, or the "popular universities" in France.

Independent School

Independent, or private, schools have more flexibility in staff selection and educational approach. The most plentiful of these are Montessori schools, Waldorf schools (the latter are also called Steiner schools after their founder), and Friends schools. Other independent schools include democratic, or free schools such as Sands School, Summerhill School and Sudbury Valley School, Krishnamurti schools, open classroom schools, those based on experiential education, as well as schools which teach using international curriculum such as the International Baccalaureate and Round Square schools.

An increasing number of traditionally independent school forms now also exist within state-run, public education; this is especially true of the Waldorf and Montessori schools. The majority of independent schools offer at least partial scholarships.

Homeschooling

Families who seek alternatives based on educational, philosophical, or religious reasons, or if there appears to be no nearby educational alternative can decide to have home-based education. One branch is termed unschooling, an approach based on interest rather than a set curriculum. Others enroll in umbrella schools which provide a curriculum to follow. Many choose this alternative for religious-based reasons, but practitioners of home-based education are of all backgrounds and philosophies.

Higher Education

Alternative teaching methodologies in the realm of higher education may include various forms of on-line and computer-based education, various forms of classroom education other than the traditional lecture or discussion format, or alternative curricula (such as interdisciplinarity).

Alternative forms of higher education are often employed by more traditional institutions alongside their regular curriculum, as the primary focus of an alternative educational institution, or as a means of self-education.

Self-education

Self-directed enquiry as an educational process is recognized at all levels of education, from the unschooling of young children to the autodidacticism of adults, and may occur either separately from or concurrently with more traditional forms of education.

Other

There are also some interesting grey areas with defining alternative education. For instance, home-educators have combined to create resource centres where they meet as often as five or more days a week, but their members all consider themselves home-educated. In some states publicly run school districts have set up programmes for homeschoolers whereby they are considered enrolled, and have access to school resources and facilities.

Also, many traditional schools have incorporated methods originally found only in alternative education into their general approach, so the line between alternative and mainstream education is continually becoming more blurred.

Alternative Schooling in Different Countries

India: In India, from the early 20th century, some educational theorists discussed and implemented radically different forms of education. Rabindranath Tagore's Visva-Bharati University, and Sri Aurobindo's Sri Aurobindo International Centre of Education are prime examples. In recent years many new alternative schools have formed.

The traditional system of learning in India was for students to stay in Gurukulas, where they received free food, shelter, and education from a "guru" ("teacher" in Sanskrit). Progress was not based on examinations and marks; tests were given by the gurus but not ranks. This system aimed to nurture the students' natural creativity and all-round personality development.

While the mainstream education system in India is still based on that introduced by Lord Macaulay, a few projects aim to rejuvenate the early system, Some students in these and similar projects take up research work in the field of Sanskrit studies, Vedic studies, Vedic science, Yoga and Ayurveda.

Others after completing their education in a Gurukula continue into regular mainstream education such as Bachelor degrees in Commerce, Science, Engineering etc.

Japan

Japanese education has been run as a nation-wide standardized system under the full control of the Ministry of Education. The only alternative option has been accredited private schools that have more freedom to offer different curriculum including the choice of textbooks (public schools can use only the government approved textbooks) and foreign languages, teaching methods, hiring guidelines. However, almost all of these private schools require competitive entrance examination and tuition with very few scholarships available.

An interest in alternative education was stimulated first by problems of student violence against people and property, since the 1980s by problems of bullying by peers, frequently leading to school refusal, acute social withdrawal and in the worst case, suicide. A desire to enable young people to keep in an increasingly globalized economy provided an independent impetus for alternative educational possibilities.

Ijime and Free Schools

Free school is the term used in Japan to describe a non-profit group or independent school which specialized in the care and education of children who refused to go to school. The first school based on democratic schools was founded in 1985, starting as a shelter for children who avoided the school environment; a number of other schools working on this basis, as well as other schools for school refusers, have since been established. In 1987, the first of what are now seven Waldorf schools in Japan was founded. Other alternatives include a growing homeschooling movement.

In 2003, Japan introduced Special Zones for Structural Reform (Ëi □9ei—yr%R:SßW), based on China's Special Economic Zone policy, which enable the opening of government-accredited schools providing alternative education. In 2005, the first school was founded under the new law.

Globalization and International Schools

Increasingly, parents are interested in sending their children to International schools to acquire a fluent command of a foreign language, usually English. Although international schools are not legally certified by the Japanese government, many of them are approved by their native country such as the US, Canada, Germany, France, Korea and China, and some offer the International Baccalaureate programme.

For the past two decades, international schools, especially American or English-based schools, have been very popular in spite of their costly tuition. A new trend in the early 21st century has been attending Chinese schools.

United Kingdom

In 2003 there were approximately 70 alternative schools in the United Kingdom. Summerhill School was established by A.S. Neill in 1921 as the first of what are now a number of democratic schools. There are a number of Steiner-Waldorf schools in the UK. Homeschooling is also a popular alternative. Though alternative schools were until recently fee-paying, the introduction of state-funded Academies in the last year has been changing the educational landscape.

United States

There are many Montessori and Waldorf schools in the USA; some of these are fee-paying, while others are public or charter schools. There are also many home school programmes.

There are many public and private educational provisions available in the USA for children with autism, attention deficit hyperactivity disorder, Asperger's syndrome, obsessive-compulsive disorder, nonverbal learning disorder, etc.

At the level of higher education several alternative practices have arisen, especially since the late 20th century. St. John's College, for example, is a Great Books school with a standard curriculum culminating in a singular degree for all students, primary source readings, and gently moderated classroom discussions. Other colleges use narrative evaluations rather than standardized grades for assessment or do not have traditional academic departments and are instead organized around interdisciplinary units.

The Netherlands

At the level of higher education there is Intercultural Open University, an alternative education provider for person-centred graduate education. In keeping with the philosophy of alternative education, the university does not issue grades; narrative evaluations are used for assessment. There are no traditional academic departments or paid faculty and staff; its faculty and staff are volunteers. Learners develop a self-directed individualized curriculum under the guidance of a faculty advisor.

Teaching for Social Justice

Teaching for social justice is a philosophy of education centred on the promotion of social justice, and the instillation of such values in students. Educators may employ social justice instruction to promote unity on campus, as well as mitigate boundaries to the general curriculum. These boundaries often include race, class, ability, language, appearance, sexuality, and gender.

While enjoying some popularity in teacher training programmes, teaching for social justice has also provoked criticism. Critics' arguments are twofold: there is a lack of evidence supporting the philosophy's effectiveness as either a behavioural or instructional strategy, and secondly, values cannot be explicitly taught, nor should they.

About

Herbert Kohl argues that teachers may be inclined to teach against their conscience, limit their methodology, and focus heavily on being good teachers without placing similar emphasis on being good citizens. Overcoming these inclinations is the crux of what he and many other educators call "teaching for social justice".

Other popular educators who have explored the practice of teaching for social justice include John Dewey, who may have been the first advocate for teaching for social justice when he developed the first theories about technical education and student engagement in the classroom in *Democracy and Education.*

Following him were George Counts, who focused on a democratically-inclusive, socialistic educational model, while Charles A. Beard and Myles Horton both provided more individualistic lenses which emphasized teaching for social justice. A variety of social and political theories and backgrounds inform the practice of teaching for social justice. Starting as early as the work of W. E. B. Du Bois in the early 1900s, social activists and educators have called for the realignment of educative practices towards a conscious, deliberative practice of engaging society in fostering justice for all.

After the publication of *Pedagogy of the Oppressed* in 1971, Brazilian educator Paulo Freire became closely associated with teaching for social justice. Freire expounded the belief that teaching is a political act that is never neutral. Over the course of dozens of books, Freire proposed that educators focus on creating equity and changing systems of oppression within public schools and society.

The main goal of engaging in social justice through education is to fight oppression by giving all groups the opportunity to receive resources more equally. Esposito and Swain studied urban teachers that promote social justice in their teaching by using culturally relevant pedagogy. Esposito and Swain found that these teachers that engage in social justice through their teaching have to ensure that their students not only thrive academically, but also socially, which can create a burden on educators (). By promoting social justice pedagogy, students can increase a sociopolitical consciousness, have a sense of agency, and help students develop a positive social and cultural identity ().

Recently teaching for social justice has been built on ethnographic and discourse research on the complex work of educators, including works by bell hooks, who pioneered a culturally-relevant, critical classroom theory strongly informing teaching for social justice. Ira Shor, Peter McLaren, Henry Giroux, Joe L. Kincheloe, and Stanley Aronowitz have each built upon the contributions of Freire to develop uniquely American critical examinations of culture and society. Michael Apple is remarkable for his democracy-focused project which reinforces the tenets of teaching for social justice. Jonathan Kozol, Alfie Kohn, Susan Searls Giroux, Khen Lampert, Michelle Rosser, and Lisa Delpit are among the growing body of modern educational theorists who have also contributed greatly to this practice.

Attention to social justice issues incorporates a broad range of sociological dimensions in teaching, and education more generally, including attention to fairness and equity with regard to gender, race, class, disability, sexual orientation, etc.

Teaching for social justice has a common goal of preparing teachers to recognize, name, and combat inequality in schools and society through culturally relevant pedagogy, anti-racist pedagogy, and intercultural teaching among others (). A number of subject specific fields of practice and enquiry in education, including science education and mathematics education have sub-communities of teachers and scholars working on social justice issues. For example the 2007 special issue no. 20 of Philosophy of Mathematics Education Journal is devoted to social justice issues in mathematics education.

Peer Relationships

Peer relationships among learners are largely determinant of the outcomes of schools. Methods including cooperative group work, and diverse group interactions. In the modern educational realm of teaching and learning, students are now seen as active participants in the learning process. Lev Vygotsky's (1978) social development theory requires students to play untraditional roles as they collaborate with one another. The physical environment of the classroom also plays a role in peer relationships. Based on Vygotsky's (1978) theory, clustered desks would enable peer collaboration as well as small group instruction. Therefore, the instructional design of material being learned would encourage peer-to-peer interaction. To that effect, the classroom serves as a community of learning.

Teacher Relationships

The relationships teachers have with students also affect teaching for social justice. If the student does not like the teacher, a student will not want to listen to what they have to say. In this sense, parent/ teacher relationships are central, as is access to information and resources for every student appointing at a desk, understanding the role of youth-adult partnerships in the classroom, and teachers literally learning about their students.

A teacher should not only teach, they should learn. Helping students understand how they learn helps students identify their strengths and weaknesses as learners. It is also important for students to note equity issues in their classrooms. The purpose of the teacher is to propose learning through facilitation, which can aid in the production of knowledge. Through this metacognitive approach to learning, students can also develop new ways to use their strengths in order to improve their weaknesses.

Classrooms

The number of specific classroom issues that affect teaching for social justice are almost countless. Understanding the effects of teachers on student learning is vital, and a teacher cannot teach under the assumption that "equal means the same." Students come from numerous cultures, languages, lifestyles and values and a monocultural framework will not suit all student needs.

Additionally, teachers need to be critically conscious and offer students well-planned units and lessons that develop knowledge of a wide range of groups. Curriculum building on acknowledgment rather than neglect the experiences of students. Educators can also match students' cultures to the curriculum and instructional practices

In essence, monocultural education creates a context in which schools do not embrace minority students' cultural knowledge, which includes historical, social, and cultural background experiences. Often, there is also cultural and linguistic bias factors in the education of minority students. To allude, insufficient teacher awareness of culturally diverse students can create a few misunderstandings in the area of teaching minority students. For example, whenever a mainstream teacher thinks minority student's behaviour is bizarre, rude, or unexpected, it can be a sign of cultural misunderstanding. According to Harper de Jong, "Students who speak a language other than English at home and whose proficiency in English is limited are the fastest growing group of k-12 students in the United States.

Unfortunately, well-intentioned efforts to include diverse learners in general education reforms are often based on misconceptions about effective instruction for ELLs. The misconceptions stem from two basic assumptions that guide much current teacher preparation for diversity." As a result, a teacher may be unaware of the background knowledge of minority students. To this effect, the teacher is unable to help minority students solve daily learning tasks, which can cause any lesson to become meaningless.

Many school districts call for teachers to become critically conscious of diversity in education by offering students well-planned units and lessons that develop knowledge of a wide range of groups. It is also hopeful for teachers' to understand that culture is a significant driving force in the lives of their student's learning the English language. Educators can also match students' cultures to the curriculum and instructional practices. Culturally responsive teaching is a very important element in regards to embracing a diverse students background.

The ethnic background of culturally diverse students should not be dishonoured in the classroom. Instead, it should be embraced and recognized as an important aspect of ones ethnic identity. There are a variety of learning materials that would aid in the assistance of educating other students to appreciate various ethnic perspectives (i.e. multicultural literature, diverse learning styles and techniques of other cultures, etc.).

Geneva Gay draws on the importance that "literature in the classroom would reflect multiple ethnic perspectives and literary genres. Math instruction would incorporate everyday-life concepts, such as economics, employment, and consumer habits of various ethnic groups. In order to teach to the different learning styles of students, activities would reflect a variety of sensory opportunities-visual, auditory, tactile." With this in mind, it is important for teachers encourage the use of multicultural materials that will not only enhance the learning capacity of minority learners but also mainstream learners.

In actuality, the importance of the nature and role of culture and cultural groups in students' language and literacy development will help increase student self-esteem. Therefore, it is imperative that teachers incorporate the culture of a student and relate it to the class work. If culture is not incorporated, then minority students will ultimately feel apprehensive and subjugated to a dull educational atmosphere.

For example, teachers should dedicate a day out of each month to celebrate the culture of a particular minority student's heritage. Not only will learning occur, but also a time where heritage speakers can explore communicative activities such as experience sharing from his or her own native country. In essence, this celebration and storytelling will encourage communication, which is a key element to the process of teaching and learning.

Also, the use of multicultural literature books can be used as an essential component to each student's heritage, which can also be implemented into the curriculum. This is a fascinating method to educate others in the class about their peer's native background. There are various multicultural trade books on the market that not only educate students, but also strengthen their ability to read and comprehend each student's heritage background.

With a greater appreciation, teachers could design lesson plans for students to understand a traditional custom or event through the use of the following strategies: timelines, dioramas, creative costumes, story reenactment, poster boards, pictures depicting an event, or re-write an ending to a story. Any of these interactive approaches to learning about one's culture will make the lesson more interesting for minority learners. Some children's literature, such as historical fiction or stories related to social issues can also be used effectively with older or advanced proficient learners.

According to H. Douglas Brown, "Your own language classroom is an excellent place to begin the quest for a more humane world. Our classroom can themselves become models of mutual respect across cultural, political, and religious boundaries." Therefore, it is noted that educators should not teach based on mistaken belief systems in the teaching of minority learners, but on student ability, needs, and cultural values that will foster a lasting educational foundation .

Relevant Organizations

Many universities and colleges have programmes focused on teaching for social justice, including the University of Massachusetts, Amherst, The University of South Carolina, the University of Regina, The Evergreen State College, State University of New York at Oswego, Pennsylvania State University, Swarthmore College, the University of California, Los Angeles and the University of Washington. A number of nonprofit organizations also support the practice in schools, including Mosaic, the Institute for Community Leadership and the Freechild Project.

Criticism

Sudbury model of democratic education schools maintain that values, social justice included, must be learned through experience as Aristotle said: *"For the things we have to learn before we can do them, we learn by doing them."* They adduce that for this reason schools must relatively encourage ethical behaviour and personal responsibility. In order to achieve this ambition, schools must profound students the three great freedoms—freedom of choice, freedom of action, freedom to bear the results of action. That constitutes personal responsibility.

In reference, critics contour that the political and ideological practices of the Teaching for Social Justice movement have little or nothing to do with the actual problems that struggling students face and in spirit harms the quality of the teacher that knows proper etiquette and grammar.

Special Education

Special education or special needs education is the education of students with special needs in a way that addresses the students' individual differences and needs. Ideally, this process involves the individually planned and systematically monitored arrangement of teaching procedures, adapted equipment and materials, accessible settings, and other interventions designed to help learners with special needs achieve a higher level of personal self-sufficiency and success in school and community than would be available if the student were only given access to a typical classroom education.

Common special needs include challenges with learning, communication challenges, emotional and behavioural disorders, physical disabilities, and developmental disorders. Students with these kinds of special needs are likely to benefit from additional educational services such as different approaches to teaching, use of technology, a specifically adapted teaching area, or resource room.

Intellectual giftedness is a difference in learning and can also benefit from specialized teaching techniques or different educational programmes, but the term "special education" is generally used to specifically indicate instruction of students whose special needs reduce their ability to learn independently or in an ordinary classroom, and gifted education is handled separately.

In most developed countries, educators are modifying teaching methods and environments so that the maximum number of students are served in general education environments. Special education in developed countries is often regarded less as a "place" and more as "a range of services, available in every school." Integration can reduce social stigmas and improve academic achievement for many students.

The opposite of *special education* is *general education*. General education is the standard curriculum presented with standard teaching methods and without additional supports.

Identifying Students with Special Needs

Some children are easily identified as candidates for special needs from their medical history. They may have been diagnosed with a genetic condition that is associated with mental retardation, may have various forms of brain damage, may have a developmental disorder, may have visual or hearing disabilities, or other disabilities.

Among students whose identification is less obvious, such as students with learning difficulties, two primary methods have been used for identifying them: the discrepancy model and the response to intervention model. The discrepancy model depends on the teacher noticing that the students' achievements are noticeably below what is expected. The response to intervention model advocates earlier intervention.

In the discrepancy model, a student receives special educational services for a specific learning difficulty (SLD) if and only if the student has at least normal intelligence and the student's academic achievement is below what is expected of a student with his or her IQ. Although the discrepancy model has dominated the school system for many years, there has been substantial criticism of this approach (e.g., Aaron, 1995, Flanagan and Mascolo, 2005) among researchers. One reason for criticism is that diagnosing SLDs on the basis of the discrepancy between achievement and IQ does not predict the effectiveness of treatment. Low academic achievers who also have low IQ appear to benefit from treatment just as much as low academic achievers who have normal or high intelligence.

The alternative approach, response to intervention, identifies children who are having difficulties in school in their first or second year after starting school. They then receive additional assistance such as participating in a reading remediation programme. The response of the children to this intervention then determines whether they are designated as having a learning disability. Those few who still have trouble may then receive designation and further assistance. Sternberg (1999) has argued that early remediation can greatly reduce the number of children meeting diagnostic criteria for learning disabilities. He has also suggested that the focus on learning disabilities and the provision of accommodations in school fails to acknowledge that people have a range of strengths and weaknesses and places undue emphasis on academics by insisting that people should be propped up in this arena and not in music or sports.

Individual Needs

A special education programme should be customized to address each individual student's unique needs. Special educators provide a continuum of services, in which students with special needs receive services in varying degrees based on their individual needs. Special education programmes need to be individualized so that they address the unique combination of needs in a given student.

In the United States, Canada, and the UK, educational professionals used the initialism IEP when referring to a student's individualized education plan.

Students with special needs are assessed to determine their specific strengths and weaknesses. Placement, resources, and goals are determined on the basis of the student's needs. Accommodations and Modifications to the regular programme may include changes in curriculum, supplementary aides or equipment, and the provision of specialized physical adaptations that allow students to participate in the educational environment to the fullest extent possible. Students may need this help to access subject matter, to physically gain access to the school, or to meet their emotional needs. For example, if the assessment determines that the student cannot write by hand because of a physical disability, then the school might provide a computer for typing assignments, or allow the student to answer questions orally instead. If the school determines that the student is severely distracted by the normal activities in a large, busy classroom, then the student might be placed in a smaller classroom such as a resource room.

Methods of Provision

Figure: *PS 721, a special school in Brooklyn, New York exclusively for the education of students with special needs.*

Schools use different approaches to providing special education services to identified students. These can be broadly grouped into four categories, according to whether and how much contact the student with special needs has with non-disabled students (using North American terminology):

- Inclusion: In this approach, students with special educational needs spend all, or at least more than half, of the school day with students who do not have special educational needs. Because inclusion can require substantial modification of the general curriculum, most schools use it only for selected students with mild to moderate special needs, for which is accepted as a best practice. Specialized services may be provided inside or outside the regular classroom, depending on the type of service. Students may occasionally leave the regular classroom to attend smaller, more intensive instructional sessions in a resource room, or to receive other related services that might require specialized equipment or might be disruptive to the rest of the class, such as speech and language therapy, occupational therapy, physical therapy, rehabilitation counselling, or might require greater privacy, such as counselling sessions with a social worker.

- Mainstreaming refers to the practice of educating students with special needs in classes with non-disabled students during specific time periods based on their skills. Students with special needs are segregated in separate classes exclusively for students with special needs for the rest of the school day.
- Segregation in a separate classroom or special school exclusively for students with special needs: In this model, students with special needs spend no time in classes with non-disabled students. Segregated students may attend the same school where regular classes are provided, but spend all instructional time exclusively in a separate classroom for students with special needs. If their special class is located in an ordinary school, they may be provided opportunities for social integration outside the classroom, e.g., by eating meals with non-disabled students. Alternatively, these students may attend a special school.
- Exclusion: A student who does not receive instruction in any school is excluded from school. Historically, most students with special needs have been excluded from school. Such exclusion still affects about 23 million disabled children worldwide, particularly in poor, rural areas of developing countries. It may also occur when a student is in hospital, housebound, or detained by the criminal justice system. These students may receive one-on-one instruction or group instruction. Students who have been suspended or expelled are not considered excluded in this sense.

Effective Instruction for students with disabilities: 1.) Goal Directed- Each child must have an Individualized Education Programme (IEP) that distinguishes his or her particular needs. The child must get the services that are designed for him. These services will allow him to reach his annual goals which will be assessed at the end of each term along with short term goals that will be assessed at the end of every few months. 2.) Research-Based Methods- There has been a lot of research done about students with disabilities and the best way to teach them. Testing, IQs, interviews, the discrepancy model, etc. should all be used to determine where to place the child.

Once that is determined, the next step is the best way for the child to learn. There are plenty of different programmes such as the Wilson Reading Programme and Direct Instruction 3.) Guided by student performance- While the IEP goals may be assessed every few months to a year, constant informal assessments must take place. These assessments will guide instruction for the teacher. The teacher will be able to determine if the material is too difficult or to easy.

Special Schools

A *special school* is a school catering for students who have special educational needs due to severe learning difficulties, physical disabilities or behavioural problems. Special schools may be specifically designed, staffed and resourced to provide the appropriate special education for children with additional needs. Students attending special schools generally do not attend any classes in mainstream schools.

Special schools provide individualised education, addressing specific needs. Student:teacher ratios are kept low, often 6:1 or lower depending upon the needs of the children. Special schools will also have other facilities for the development of children with special needs, such as soft play areas, sensory rooms, or swimming pools, which are vital for the therapy of certain conditions.

In recent times, places available in special schools are declining as more children with special needs are educated in mainstream schools. There will always be some children, however, whose learning needs are not appropriately met in a regular classroom setting and will require specialised education and resources to provide the level of support they require. An example of a special need that may require the intensive services a special school provides is mental retardation. However this practice is often frowned upon by school districts in the USA in the light of Least Restrictive Environment as mandated in the Individuals with Disabilities Education Act.

An alternative is a special unit or special classroom, also called a self-contained classroom, which is a separate room or rooms dedicated solely to the education of students with special needs within a larger school that also provides general education. These classrooms are typically staffed by specially trained teachers, who provide specific, individualized instruction to individuals and small groups of students with special needs. Self-contained classrooms, because they are located in a general education school, may have students who remain in the self-contained classroom full-time, or students who are included in certain general education classes. In the United States a part-time alternative that is appropriate for some students is sometimes called a resource room.

History of Special Schools

One of the first special schools in the world was the Institut National des Jeunes Aveugles in Paris, which was founded in 1784. It was the first school in the world to teach blind students. The first school in U.K, for the Deaf was established 1760 in Edinburgh by Thomas Braidwood, with education for visually impaired people beginning in the Edinburgh and Bristol in 1765.

In the 19th Century, people with disabilities and the inhumane conditions where they were supposed to be housed and educated were addressed in the literature of Charles Dickens. Dickens characterized people with severe disabilities as having the same—if not more—compassion and insight in Bleak House and Little Dorrit.

Such attention to the downtrodden conditions of people with disabilities brought with it reforms in Europe including the re-evalutation of special schools. In the United States reform came slower. Throughout the mid half of the 20th century, special schools, termed institutions, were not only acceptable they were encouraged. Students with disabilites were housed with people with mental illness, and little if any education took place.

With the Amendments to the Individuals with Disabilities Act of 1997, school districts in the United States began to slowly integrate students with moderate and severe special needs into regular school systems. This changed the form and function of special education services in many school districts and special schools subsequently saw a steady decrease in enrollment as districts weighed the cost per student. It also posed general funding dilemmas to certain local schools and districts, changed how schools view assessments, and formally introduced the concept of inclusion to many educators, students and parents.

Instructional Strategies

Different instructional techniques are used for some students with special educational needs. Instructional strategies are classified as being either accommodations or modifications.

An *accommodation* is a reasonable adjustment to teaching practices so that the student learns the same material, but in a format that is accessible to the student. Accommodations may be classified by whether they change the presentation, response, setting, or scheduling. For example, the school may accommodate a student with visual impairments by providing a large-print textbook; this is a presentation accommodation.

A *modification* changes or adapts the material to make it simpler. Modifications may change what is learned, how difficult the material is, what level of mastery the student is expected to achieve, whether and how the student is assessed, or any another aspect of the curriculum. For example, the school may modify a reading assignment for a student with reading difficulties by substituting a shorter, easier book. A student may receive both accommodations and modifications.

Examples of Modifications

- Skipping subjects: Students may be taught less information than typical students, skipping over material that the school deems inappropriate for the student's abilities or less important than other subjects. For example, students whose fine motor skills are weak may be taught to print block letters, but not cursive handwriting.
- Simplified assignments: Students may read the same literature as their peers but have a simpler version, for example Shakespeare with both the original text and a modern paraphrase available.
- Shorter assignments: Students may do shorter homework assignments or take shorter, more concentrated tests, e.g. 10 math problems instead of 30.
- Extra aids: If students have deficiencies in working memory, a list of vocabulary words, called a *word bank*, can be provided during tests, to reduce lack of recall and increase chances of comprehension. Students might use a calculator when other students are not.
- Extended time: Students with lower processing speed may benefit from extended time in assignments and/or tests in order to comprehend questions, recall information, and synthesize knowledge.

Examples of Accommodations

- Response accommodations: Typing homework assignments rather than hand-writing them (considered a modification if the subject is learning to write by hand). Having someone else write down answers given verbally.

- Presentation accommodations: Listening to audio books rather than reading printed books. Agencies like Recording for the Blind and Dyslexic in America and RNIB National Library Service in the UK offer a variety of titles on tape and CD. These may be used as substitutes for the text, or as supplements intended to bolster the students' reading fluency and phonetic skills. Similar options include designating a person to read text to the student, or providing text to speech software. (Considered a modification if the purpose of the assignment is reading skills acquisition). Designating a person to take notes during lectures. Using a talking calculator rather than one with only a visual display.
- Setting accommodations: Taking a test in a quieter room. Moving the class to a room that is physically accessible, e.g., on the first floor of a building or near an elevator. Arranging seating assignments to benefit the student, e.g., by sitting at the front of the classroom.
- Scheduling accommodations: Students may be given rest breaks or extended time on tests (may be considered a modification, if speed is a factor in the test).

All developed countries permit or require some degree of accommodation for students with special needs, and special provisions are usually made in examinations which take place at the end of formal schooling.

In addition to how the student is taught the academic curriculum, schools may provide non-academic services to the student. These are intended ultimately to increase the student's personal and academic abilities.

Related services include developmental, corrective, and other supportive services as are required to assist a student with special needs and includes speech and language pathology, audiology, psychological services, physical therapy, occupational therapy, counselling services, including rehabilitation counselling, orientation and mobility services, medical services as defined by regulations, parent counselling and training, school health services, school social work, assistive technology services, other appropriate developmental or corrective support services, appropriate access to recreation and other appropriate support services. In some countries, most related services are provided by the schools; in others, they are provided by the normal healthcare and social services systems.

As an example, students who have autistic spectrum disorders, poor impulse control, or other behavioural challenges may learn self-management techniques, be kept closely on a comfortingly predictable schedule, or given extra cues to signal activities.

Issues

At-risk students (those with educational needs that are not associated with a disability) are often placed in classes with students who have disabilities. Critics assert that placing at-risk students in the same classes as students with disabilities may impede the educational progress of people with disabilities. Some special education classes have been criticized for a watered-down curriculum.

The practice of inclusion (in mainstream classrooms) has been criticized by advocates and some parents of children with special needs because some of these students require instructional methods that differ dramatically from typical classroom methods. Critics assert that it is not possible to deliver effectively two or more very different instructional methods in the same classroom. As a result, the educational progress of students who depend on different instructional methods to learn often fall even further behind their peers.

Parents of typically developing children sometimes fear that the special needs of a single "fully included" student will take critical levels of attention and energy away from the rest of the class and thereby impair the academic achievements of all students.

Some parents, advocates, and students have concerns about the eligibility criteria and their application. In some cases, parents and students protest the students' placement into special education programmes. For example, a student may be placed into the special education programmes due to a mental health condition such as obsessive compulsive disorder, depression, anxiety, panic attacks or ADHD, while the student and his parents believe that the condition is adequately managed through medication and outside therapy. In other cases, students whose parents believe they require the additional support of special education services are denied participation in the programme based on the eligibility criteria.

Whether it is useful and appropriate to attempt to educate the most severely disabled children, such as children who are in a persistent vegetative state, is debated. While many severely disabled children can learn simple tasks, such as pushing a buzzer when they want attention, some children may be incapable of learning. Some parents and advocates say that these children would be better served by substituting improved physical care for any academic programme. In other cases, they question whether teaching such non-academic subjects, such as pushing a buzzer, is properly the job of the school system, rather than the health care system.

Another large issue is the lack of resources enabling individuals with special needs to receive an education in the developing world. As a consequence, 98 percent of children with special needs in developing countries do not have access to education.

National Approaches

Africa

South Africa: White Papers in 1995 and 2001 discuss special education in the country. Local schools are given some independent authority. Both modifications and accommodations are recommended, depending on the student's individual needs.

Asia

China: Japan: Japanese students with special needs are placed in one of four different school arrangements: special schools, special classrooms with another school, in resource rooms (which are called *tsukyu*), or in regular classrooms.

Special schools are reserved for students whose severe disabilities cannot be accommodated in the local school. They do not use the same grading or marking systems as mainstream schools, but instead assess students according to their individualized plans.

Special classes are similar, and may vary the national curriculum as the teachers see fit. *Tsukyu* are resource rooms that students with milder problems use part-time for specialized instruction individually in small groups. These students spend the rest of the day in the mainstream classroom. Some students with special needs are fully included in the mainstream classroom, with accommodations or modifications as needed.

Training of disabled students, particularly at the upper-secondary level, emphasizes vocational education to enable students to be as independent as possible within society. Vocational training varies considerably depending on the student's disability, but the options are limited for some. It is clear that the government is aware of the necessity of broadening the range of possibilities for these students. Advancement to higher education is also a goal of the government, and it struggles to have institutions of higher learning accept more disabled students.

Singapore: Special education is regulated centrally by the Singapore Ministry of Education. Both special schools and integration into mainstream schools are options for students with special educational needs, but most students with disabilities are placed in special schools.

Students with special education who wish accommodations on national exams must provide appropriate documentation to prove that they are disabled. Accommodations, but not modifications (e.g., simpler questions) are normally approved if they are similar to the accommodations already being used in everyday schoolwork, with the goal of maintaining the exam's integrity while not having students unfairly disadvantaged by factors that are unrelated to what is being tested. The accommodations are listed on the Primary School Leaving Exam.

Australia

Australian Association of Special Education Inc (AASE)'s position is informed by the Disability Standards for Education 2005 which require that students with disabilities are treated on the same basis as other students in regards to enrolment and participation in education. With respect to standardized tests, special consideration procedures are in place in all states for students who are disabled. Students must provide documentation Not all desired forms of accommodations are available. For example, students who cannot read, even if the inability to read is due to a disability, cannot have the exam read to them, because the exam results should accurately show that the student is unable to read. Reports on matriculation exams do not mention whether the student received any accommodations in taking the test.

Europe

Each country in Europe has its own special education support structures.

Czech Republic: Schools must take students' special education needs into account when assessing their achievements.

Denmark

In Denmark, 99% of students with specific learning difficulties like dyslexia are educated alongside students without any learning challenges.

Finland

Schools adapt the national guidelines to the needs of individual students. Students with special educational needs are given an individualized plan. They may be exempted from some parts of school examinations, such as students with hearing impairments not taking listening comprehension tests.

If the student receives modifications to the school-leaving exams, this is noted on the certificate of achievement. If they are not following the national core curriculum, then they are tested according to the goals of their individual educational programme.

France

French students with disabilities are normally included in their neighbourhood school, although children may be placed in special schools if their personalized plan calls for it. Each student's personalized school plan describes teaching methods, psychological, medical and paramedical services that the school will provide to the student.

Germany

Figure: *A special school for children with special emotional needs in Kötitz, Germany*

Most students with special needs in Germany attend a special school that serves only children with special needs. These include:

- *Förderschule für Lernbehinderte* (special school for learning disabilities): for children who have challenges that impair learning
- *Förderschule mit dem Förderschwerpunkt Geistige Entwicklung* (school for cognitive development): for children with very severe learning challenges
- *Förderschule Schwerpunkt emotionale und soziale Entwicklung* (school for emotional and social development): for children who have special emotional needs
- *Förderschule für Blinde* (school for the blind): for blind children
- *Förderschule für Sehbehinderte* (school for the visually impaired): for children who are visually challenged
- *Förderschule für Gehörlose* (school for the deaf): for deaf children
- *Förderschule für Schwerhörige* (school for the hearing impaired): for children who are hearing impaired
- *Förderschule für Körperbehinderte* (school for children with physical disabilities): for children with physical disabilities
- *Förderschule für Sprachbehinderte* (school for children with language disorders): for children with language disorders
- *Förderschule für Taubblinde* (school for the deafblind): for children who are deafblind
- *Schule für Kranke* (school for ill children): for children who are too ill to attend school or are hospitalized for a longer
- *Förderschule für schwer mehrfach Behinderte* (school for children with severe and multiple disabilities): for children with severe and multiple disabilities who needn very special care and attention. Sometimes these children are only susceptible for very basic emotional and sensory stimulation. Thus teachers at these school (as well as at schools for the deafblind) are highly specialized professionals.

One in 21 German students attends a special school. Teachers at those schools are specially trained professionals who have specialized in special needs education while in university. Special schools often have a very favourable student-teacher ratio and facilities other schools do not have.

Some special needs children in Germany do not attend a special school, but are educated in a mainstream school such as a Hauptschule or Gesamtschule (comprehensive school).

Students with special educational needs may be exempted from standardized tests or given modified tests.

Greece

Greek students with special needs may attend either mainstream schools or special schools.

Students whose disabilities have been certified may be exempted from some standardized tests or given alternative tests. Accommodations are responsive to students' needs; for example, students with visual impairments may take oral tests, and students with hearing impairments take written tests. Accommodations and modifications are noted on the certificate of achievement.

Hungary

Special Education is Regulated Centrally: According to the 1993 Act on Public Education, students with special educational needs may be exempted from standardized tests or given modified tests. They have a right to extra time, a choice of formats for the tests (e.g., oral rather than written), and any equipment that they normally use during the school day.

As of 2006, students with disabilities received a significant bonus (eight points) on the university entrance examination, which has been criticized as unfair.

The Netherlands

As a general rule, students with special educational needs are integrated into their regular, mainstream schools with appropriate support, under the "Going to School Together" policy (*Weer Samen Naar School*). Four types of disability-specific special schools exist. The national policy is moving towards "suitable education" (*passend onderwijs*), based on the individual's strengths and weaknesses.

A strong emphasis is placed on the specific needs and positive capabilities of the individual, rather than on limitations. Disabilities are normally documented by experts.

Norway

The National Support System for Special Needs Education (Statped) is managed by the Norwegian Directorate for Education and Training. The general objective for Statped is to give guidance and support to those in charge of the education in municipalities and county administrations to ensure that children, young people and adults with major and special educational needs are secured well-advised educational and developmental provisions. The institutions affiliated with Statped offer a broad spectrum of services. Statped consists of 13 resource centres owned by the State, and 4 units for special education, where Statped buys services. These centres offer special educational guidance and support for local authorities and county administrations.

Portugal

Students with disabilities have a "guaranteed right" to appropriate accommodations on assessments. Schools are generally considered autonomous.

Slovenia

On national tests, the National Examination Centre normally grants most requests for accommodations that are supported by the local school's examination committee. Legislation opposes the use of modifications that would be unfair to non-disabled students.

Spain

Schools are required to provide services and resources to students with special educational needs so that they make progress and participate in school. If the local school is unable to provide appropriately for an individual student, then the student may be transferred to a special school.

Spanish non-governmental organizations like ONCE have traditionally provided significant services to students with disabilities.

Sweden

Local schools have significant autonomy, based on national guidelines. Schools are expected to help students meet the goals that are set for them.

There are special schools (Swedish: Särskola) for students with low abilities to attend normal education. There has in 2012-2013 been media criticism on the fact that students with light problems such as dyslexia have been placed in special schools, seriously hampering their chances on the labour market.

Switzerland

Education is controlled by the 26 cantons, and so special education programmes vary from place to place. However, integration is typical. Students are assessed according to their individual learning goals.

United Kingdom

In England and Wales the acronym *SEN* for Special Educational Needs denotes the condition of having special educational needs, the services which provide the support and the programmes and staff which implement the education. In England *SEN PPS* refers to the Special Educational Needs Parent Partnership Service. *SENAS* is the special educational needs assessment service, which is part of the Local Authority. *SENCO* refers to a special educational needs coordinator, who usually works with schools and the children within schools who have special educational needs.

The Special Educational Needs Parent Partnership Services help parents with the planning and delivery of their child's educational provision. The Department for Education oversees special education in England.

Most students have an individual educational plan, but students may have a group plan in addition to, or instead of, an individual plan. Groups plans are used when a group of students all have similar goals.

In Scotland the Additional Support Needs Act places an obligation on education authorities to meet the needs of all students in consultation with other agencies and parents.

In Scotland the term Special Educational Needs (SEN), and its variants are not official terminology although the very recent implementation of the Additional Support for Learning Act means that both *SEN* and *ASN* (Additional Support Needs) are used interchangeably in current common practice.

North America

In North America, special education is commonly abbreviated as *special ed*, *SpecEd*, *SPED*, or *SpEd* in a professional context.

Canada

Education in Canada is the responsibility of the individual provinces and territories. As such, rules vary somewhat from place to place. However, inclusion is the dominant model.

For major exams, Canadian schools commonly use accommodations, such as specially printed examinations for students with visual impairments, when assessing the achievements of students with special needs. In other instances, alternative assessments or modifications that simplify tests are permitted, or students with disabilities may be exempted from the tests entirely.

United States

All special-needs students receive an Individualized Education Programme (IEP) that outlines how the school will meet the student's individual needs. The Individuals with Disabilities Education Act (IDEA) requires that students with special needs be provided with a Free Appropriate Public Education in the Least Restrictive Environment that is appropriate to the student's needs. Government-run schools provide special education in varying degrees from the least restrictive settings, such as full inclusion, to the most restrictive settings, such as segregation in a special school.

The education offered by the school must be appropriate to the student's individual needs. Schools are not required to maximize the student's potential or to provide the best possible services. Unlike most of the developed world, American schools are also required to provide many medical services, such as speech therapy, if the student needs these services.

According to the Department of Education, approximately 6 million children (roughly 10 percent of all school-aged children) currently receive some type of special education services. As with most countries in the world, students who are poor, ethnic minorities, or do not speak the dominant language fluently are disproportionately identified as needing special education services. Poor, black and Latino urban schools are more likely to have limited resources and to employ inexperienced teachers that do not cope well with student behaviour problems, "thereby increasing the number of students they referred to special education."

During the 1960s, in some part due to the civil rights movement, some researchers began to study the disparity of education amongst people with disabilities. The landmark Brown v. Board of Education decision, which declared unconstitutional the "separate but equal" arrangements in public schools for students of different races, paved the way for PARC v. Commonwealth of Pennsylvania and Mills vs. Board of Education of District of Columbia, which challenged the segregation of students with special needs. Courts ruled that unnecessary and inappropriate segregation of students with disabilities was unconstitutional. Congress responded to these court rulings with the federal Education for All Handicapped Children Act in 1975 (since renamed the Individuals with Disabilities Education Act (IDEA)). This law required schools to provide services to students previously denied access to an appropriate education.

In US government-run schools, the dominant model is inclusion. In the United States, three out of five students with academic learning challenges spend the overwhelming majority of their time in the regular classroom.

Inclusion (Education)

Inclusion in education is an approach to educating students with special educational needs. Under the inclusion model, students with special needs spend most or all of their time with non-disabled students. Implementation of these practices varies. Schools most frequently use them for selected students with mild to severe special needs.

Inclusive education differs from previously held notions of *integration* and *mainstreaming*, which tended to be concerned principally with disability and 'special educational needs' and implied learners changing or becoming 'ready for' or deserving of accommodation by the mainstream. By contrast, inclusion is about the child's right to participate and the school's duty to accept the child. Inclusion rejects the use of special schools or classrooms to separate students with disabilities from students without disabilities. A premium is placed upon full participation by students with disabilities and upon respect for their social, civil, and educational rights. Inclusion gives students with disabilities skills they can use in and out of the classroom.

Fully inclusive schools, which are rare, no longer distinguish between "general education" and "special education" programmes; instead, the school is restructured so that all students learn together.

Classification

Inclusion has two sub-types: the first is sometimes called regular inclusion or partial inclusion, and the other is full inclusion.

"Inclusive practice" is not always inclusive but is a form of integration. For example, students with special needs are educated in regular classes for nearly all of the day, or at least for more than half of the day. Whenever possible, the students receive any additional help or special instruction in the general classroom, and the student is treated like a full member of the class. However, most specialized services are provided outside a regular classroom, particularly if these services require special equipment or might be disruptive to the rest of the class (such as speech therapy), and students are pulled out of the regular classroom for these services. In this case, the student occasionally leaves the regular classroom to attend smaller, more intensive instructional sessions in a resource room, or to receive other related services, such as speech and language therapy, occupational and/or physical therapy, and social work. This approach can be very similar to many mainstreaming practices, and may differ in little more than the educational ideals behind it.

In the "full inclusion" setting, the students with special needs are always educated alongside students without special needs, as the first and desired option while maintaining appropriate supports and services. Some educators say this might be more effective for the students with special needs. At the extreme, full inclusion is the integration of all students, even those that require the most substantial educational and behavioural supports and services to be successful in regular classes and the elimination of special, segregated special education classes. Special education is considered a service, not a place and those services are integrated into the daily routines and classroom structure, environment, curriculum and strategies and brought to the student, instead of removing the student to meet his or her individual needs.

However, this approach to full inclusion is somewhat controversial, and it is not widely understood or applied to date. Much more commonly, local educational agencies provide a variety of settings, from special classrooms to mainstreaming to inclusion, and assign students to the system that seems most likely to help the student achieve his or her individual educational goals. Students with mild or moderate disabilities, as well as disabilities that do not affect academic achievement, such as using wheelchair, are most likely to be fully included. However, students with all types of disabilities from all the different disability categories have been successfully included in general education classes, working and achieving their individual educational goals in regular school environments and activities (reference needed).

Alternatives

Students with disabilities who are not included are typically either mainstreamed or segregated.

A mainstreamed student attends some general education classes, typically for less than half the day, and often for less academically rigorous classes. For example, a young student with significant intellectual disabilities might be mainstreamed for physical education classes, art classes and storybook time, but spend reading and mathematics classes with other students that have similar disabilities. They may have access to a resource room for remediation of course content.

A segregated student attends no classes with non-disabled students. He or she might attend a special school that only enrolls other students with disabilities, or might be placed in a dedicated, self-contained classroom in a school that also enrolls general education students.

Some students may be confined to a hospital due to a medical condition and are thus eligible for tutoring services provided by a school district. Less common alternatives include homeschooling and, particularly in developing countries, exclusion from education.

Legal Issues

The new anti-discriminatory climate has provided the basis for much change in policy and statute, nationally and internationally. Inclusion has been enshrined at the same time that segregation and discrimination have been rejected. Articulations of the new developments in ways of thinking, in policy and in law include:

- The UN Convention on the Rights of the Child (1989) which sets out children's rights in respect of freedom from discrimination and in respect of the representation of their wishes and views.
- The Convention against Discrimination in Education of UNESCO prohibits any dicrimination, exclusion or segregation in education.
- The UNESCO Salamanca Statement (1994) which calls on all governments to give the highest priority to inclusive education.
- The UN Convention on the Rights of Persons with Disabilities (2006) which calls on all States Parties to ensure an inclusive education system at all levels.

For schools in the United States, the federal requirement that students be educated in the least restrictive environment that is reasonable encourages the implementation of inclusion for some students.

Frequency of Use

The proportion of students with disabilities who are *included* varies by place and by type of disability, but it is relatively common for students with milder disabilities and less common with certain kinds of severe disabilities. In Denmark, 99% of students with learning disabilities like dyslexia are placed in general education classrooms. In the United States, three out of five students with learning disabilities spend the majority of their time in the general education classroom.

Necessary Resources

Although once hailed as a way to increase achievement while decreasing costs, full inclusion does not save money, reduce students' needs, or improve academic outcomes; in most cases, it merely moves the special education professionals out of their own classrooms and into a corner of the general classroom. To avoid harm to the academic education of students with disabilities, a full panoply of services and resources is required, including:

- Adequate supports and services for the student
- Well-designed individualized education programmes
- Professional development for all teachers involved, general and special educators alike
- Time for teachers to plan, meet, create, and evaluate the students together
- Reduced class size based on the severity of the student needs
- Professional skill development in the areas of cooperative learning, peer tutoring, adaptive curriculum
- Collaboration between parents or guardians, teachers or para educators, specialists, administration, and outside agencies.
- Sufficient funding so that schools will be able to develop programmes for students based on student need instead of the availability of funding.

In principle, several factors can determine the success of inclusive classrooms:

- Family-school partnerships
- Collaboration between general and special educators
- Well-constructed plans that identify specific accommodations, modifications, and goals for each student
- Coordinated planning and communication between "general" and "special needs" staff
- Integrated service delivery
- Ongoing training and staff development

Common Practices

Students in an inclusive classroom are generally placed with their chronological age-mates, regardless of whether the students are working above or below the typical academic level for their age. Also, to encourage a sense of belonging, emphasis is placed on the value of friendships. Teachers often nurture a relationship between a student with special needs and a same-age student without a special educational need. Another common practice is the assignment of a buddy to accompany a student with special needs at all times (for example in the cafeteria, on the playground, on the bus and so on).

This is used to show students that a diverse group of people make up a community, that no one type of student is better than another, and to remove any barriers to a friendship that may occur if a student is viewed as "helpless." Such practices reduce the chance for elitism among students in later grades and encourage cooperation among groups.

Teachers use a number of techniques to help build classroom communities:

- Using games designed to build community
- Involving students in solving problems
- Sharing songs and books that teach community
- Openly dealing with individual differences by discussion
- Assigning classroom jobs that build community
- Teaching students to look for ways to help each other
- Utilizing physical therapy equipment such as standing frames, so students who typically use wheelchairs can stand when the other students are standing and more actively participate in activities
- Encouraging students to take the role of teacher and deliver instruction (e.g. read a portion of a book to a student with severe disabilities)
- Focusing on the strength of a student with special needs

Collaboration

Inclusion settings allow children with and without disabilities to play and interact every day, even when they are receiving therapeutic services. When a child displays fine motor difficulty, his ability to fully participate in common classroom activities, such as cutting, colouring, and zipping a jacket may be hindered.

While occupational therapists are often called to assess and implement strategies outside of school, it is frequently left up to classroom teachers to implement strategies in school. Collaborating with occupational therapists will help classroom teachers use intervention strategies and increase teacher's awareness about student's needs within school settings and enhance teacher's independence in implementation of occupational therapy strategies.

As a result of the 1997 re-authorization of the Individuals With Disabilities Education Act (IDEA), greater emphasis has been placed on delivery of related services within inclusive, general education environments. [Nolan, 2004] The importance of inclusive, integrated models of service delivery for children with disabilities has been widely researched indicating positive benefits. [Case-Smith& Holland, 2009] In traditional "pull out" service delivery models, children typically work in isolated settings one on one with a therapist, Case-Smith and Holland(2009) argue that children working on skills once or twice a week are "less likely to produce learning that leads to new behaviours and increased competence." [Case Smith &Holland, 2009, pg.419]. In recent years, occupational therapy has shifted from the conventional model of "pull out" therapy to an integrated model where the therapy takes place within a school or classroom.

Selection of Students for Inclusion

Educators generally say that some students with special needs are not good candidates for inclusion. Many schools expect a fully included student to be working at or near grade level, but more fundamental requirements exist: First, being included requires that the student is able to attend school. Students that are entirely excluded from school (for example, due to long-term hospitalization), or who are educated outside of schools (for example, due to enrollment in a distance education programme) cannot attempt inclusion.

Additionally, some students with special needs are poor candidates for inclusion because of their effect on other students. For example, students with severe behavioural problems, such that they represent a serious physical danger to others, are poor candidates for inclusion, because the school has a duty to provide a safe environment to all students and staff. Finally, some students are not good candidates for inclusion because the normal activities in a general education classroom will prevent them from learning. For example, a student with severe attention difficulties or extreme sensory processing disorders might be highly distracted or distressed by the presence of other students working at their desks. Inclusion needs to be appropriate to the child's unique needs.

Most students with special needs do not fall into these extreme categories, as most students do attend school, are not violent, do not have severe sensory processing disorders, etc.

The students that are most commonly included are those with physical disabilities that have no or little effect on their academic work (diabetes mellitus, epilepsy, food allergies, paralysis), students with all types of mild disabilities, and students whose disabilities require relatively few specialized services.

Bowe says that regular inclusion, but not full inclusion, is a reasonable approach for a significant majority of students with special needs. He also says that for some students, notably those with severe autism spectrum disorders or mental retardation, as well as many who are deaf or have multiple disabilities, even regular inclusion may not offer an appropriate education. Teachers of students with autism spectrum disorders sometimes use antecedent procedures, delayed contingencies, self-management strategies, peer-mediated interventions, pivotal response training and naturalistic teaching strategies.

Relationship to Progressive Education

Some advocates of inclusion promote the adoption of progressive education practices. In the progressive education or inclusive classroom, everyone is exposed to a "rich set of activities," and each student does what he or she can do, or what he or she wishes to do and learns whatever comes from that experience. Maria Montessori's schools sometimes named as an example of inclusive education.

Inclusion requires some changes in how teachers teach, as well as changes in how students with and without special needs interact with and relate to one another. Inclusive education practices frequently rely on active learning, authentic assessment practices, applied curriculum, multi-level instructional approaches, and increased attention to diverse student needs and individualization.

Arguments for Full Inclusion

Advocates say that even partial non-inclusion is morally unacceptable. Proponents believe that non-inclusion reduces the disabled students' social importance and that maintaining their social visibility is more important than their academic achievement. Proponents say that society accords disabled people less human dignity when they are less visible in general education classrooms. Advocates say that even if typical students are harmed academically by the full inclusion of certain special needs students, that the non-inclusion of these students would still be morally unacceptable, as advocates believe that the harm to typical students' education is always less important than the social harm caused by making people with disabilities less visible in society.

A second key argument is that everybody benefits from inclusion. Advocates say that there are many children and young people who don't fit in (or feel as though they don't), and that a school that fully includes all disabled students feels welcoming to all. Moreover, at least one author has studied the impact a diversified student body has on the general education population and has concluded that students with mental retardation who spend time among their peers show an increase in social skills and academic proficiency.

Advocates for inclusion say that the long-term effects of typical students who are included with special needs students at a very young age have a heightened sensitivity to the challenges that others face, increased empathy and compassion, and improved leadership skills, which benefits all of society.

A combination of inclusion and pull-out (partial inclusion) services has been shown to be beneficial to students with learning disabilities in the area of reading comprehension, and preferential for the special education teachers delivering the services.

Inclusive education can be beneficial to all students in a class, not just students with special needs. Some research show that inclusion helps students understand the importance of working together, and fosters a sense of tolerance and empathy among the student body.

Positive Effects

There are many positive effects of inclusions where both the students with special needs along with the other students in the classroom both benefit. Research has shown positive effects for children with disabilities in areas such as reaching individualized education programme (IEP) goal, improving communication and social skills, increasing positive peer interactions, many educational outcomes, and post school adjustments. Positive effects on children without disabilities include the development of positive attitudes and perceptions of persons with disabilities and the enhancement of social status with nondisabled peers.

Several studies have been done on the effects of inclusion of children with disabilities in general education classrooms. A study on inclusion compared integrated and segregated (special education only) preschool students. The study determined that children in the integrated sites progressed in social skills development while the segregated children actually regressed. Another study shows the effect on inclusion in grades 2 to 5. The study determined that students with specific learning disabilities made some academic and affective gains at a pace comparable to that of normal achieving students. Specific learning disabilities students also showed an improvement in self-esteem and in some cases improved motivation.

Criticism

Critics of full and partial inclusion include both educators, administrators and parents. Full and partial inclusion approaches neglect to acknowledge the fact most students with significant special needs require individualized instruction or highly controlled environments. Thus, general education classroom teachers often are teaching a curriculum while the special education teacher is remediating instruction at the same time. Similarly, a child with serious inattention problems may be unable to focus in a classroom that contains twenty or more active children. Although with the increase of incidence of disabilities in the student population, this is a circumstance all teachers must contend with, and is not a direct result of inclusion as a concept.

Full inclusion may in fact be a way for schools to placate parents and the general public, using the word as a phrase to garner attention for what are in fact illusive efforts to education students with special needs in the general education environment.

At least one study examined the lack of individualized services provided for students with IEPs when placed in an inclusive rather than mainstreamed environment.

Some researchers have maintained school districts neglect to prepare general education staff for students with special needs, thus preventing any achievement. Moreover, school districts often expound an inclusive philosophy for political reasons, and do away with any valuable pull-out services, all on behalf of the students who have no so say in the matter.

Inclusion is viewed by some as a practice philosophically attractive yet impractical. Studies have not corroborated the proposed advantages of full or partial inclusion. Moreover, "push in" servicing does not allow students with moderate to severe disabilities individualized instruction in a resource room, from which many show considerable benefit in both learning and emotional development. Parents of disabled students may be cautious about placing their children in an inclusion programme because of fears that the children will be ridiculed by other students, or be unable to develop regular life skills in an academic classroom.

Some argue that inclusive schools are not a cost-effective response when compared to cheaper or more effective interventions, such as special education. They argue that special education helps "fix" the special needs students by providing individualized and personalized instruction to meet their unique needs. This is to help students with special needs adjust as quickly as possible to the mainstream of the school and community. Proponents counter that students with special needs are not fully into the mainstream of student life because they are secluded to special education. Some argue that isolating students with special needs may lower their self-esteem and may reduce their ability to deal with other people. In keeping these students in separate classrooms they aren't going to see the struggles and achievements that they can make together. However, at least one study indicated mainstreaming in education has long-term benefits for students as indicated by increased test scores, where the benefit of inclusion has not yet been proved.

Broader Approach: Social and Cultural Inclusion

As used by UNESCO, inclusion refers to far more than students with special educational needs. It is centred on the inclusion of marginalized groups, such as religious, racial, ethnic, and linguistic minorities, immigrants, girls, the poor, students with disabilities, HIV/AIDS patients, remote populations, and more. In some places, these people are not actively included in education and learning processes. In the U.S. this broader definition is also known as "culturally responsive" education, and is promoted among the ten equity assistance centres of the U.S. Department of Education, for example in Region IX (AZ, CA, NV), by the Equity Alliance at ASU. Gloria Ladson-Billings points out that teachers who are culturally responsive know how to base learning experiences on the cultural realities of the child (e.g. home life, community experiences, language background, belief systems). Proponents argue that culturally responsive pedagogy is good for all students because it builds a caring community where everyone's experiences and abilities are valued.

Proponents want to maximize the participation of all learners in the community schools of their choice and to rethink and restructure policies, curricula, cultures and practices in schools and learning environments so that diverse learning needs can be met, whatever the origin or nature of those needs. They say that all students can learn and benefit from education, and that schools should adapt to the physical, social, and cultural needs of students, rather than students adapting to the needs of the school. Proponents believe that individual differences between students are a source of richness and diversity, which should be supported through a wide and flexible range of responses. The challenge of rethinking and restructuring schools to become more culturally responsive calls for a complex systems view of the educational system, where one can extend the idea of strength through diversity to all participants in the educational system (e.g. parents, teachers, community members, staff).

Although inclusion is generally associated with elementary and secondary education, it is also applicable in postsecondary education. According to UNESCO, inclusion "is increasingly understood more broadly as a reform that supports and welcomes diversity amongst all learners." Under this broader definition of inclusion, steps should also be taken to eliminate discrimination and provide accommodations for all students who are at a disadvantage because of some reason other than disability.

8

Problem-based Learning

Problem-based learning (PBL) is a student-centred pedagogy in which students learn about a subject through the experience of problem solving. Students learn both thinking strategies and domain knowledge. The PBL format originated from the medical school of thought, and is now used in other schools of thought too. The goals of PBL are to help the students develop flexible knowledge, effective problem solving skills, self-directed learning, effective collaboration skills and intrinsic motivation. Problem-based learning is a style of active learning.

Working in groups, students identify what they already know, what they need to know, and how and where to access new information that may lead to resolution of the problem. The role of the instructor (known as the tutor in PBL) is to facilitate learning by supporting, guiding, and monitoring the learning process. The tutor must build students' confidence to take on the problem, and encourage the students, while also stretching their understanding. PBL represents a paradigm shift from traditional teaching and learning philosophy, which is more often lecture-based. The constructs for teaching PBL are very different from traditional classroom/lecture teaching.

Definition

Barrows defines the Problem-Based Learning Model as:

1. Student Centred Learning
2. Learning is done in Small Student Groups, ideally 6-10 people
3. Facilitators or Tutors guide the students rather than teach
4. A Problem forms the basis for the organized focus of the group, and stimulates learning

5. The problem is a vehicle for the development of problem solving skills. It stimulates the cognitive process.
6. New knowledge is obtained through Self-Directed Learning(SDL)

History

PBL was pioneered in the medical school programme at McMaster University in Hamilton, Ontario, Canada in the late 1960s by Howard Barrows and his colleagues. Traditional medical education disenchanted students, who perceived the vast amount of material presented in the first three years of medical school as having little relevance to the practice of medicine and clinically based medicine. The PBL curriculum was developed in order to stimulate the learners, assist the learners in seeing the relevance of learning to future roles, maintain a higher level of motivation towards learning, and to show the learners the importance of responsible, professional attitudes.

Problem-based learning has subsequently been adopted by other medical school programmes, adapted for undergraduate instruction, as well as K-12. The use of PBL has expanded from its initial introduction into medical school programmes to include education in the areas of other health sciences, math, law, education, economics, business, social studies, and engineering. The use of PBL, like other student-centred pedagogies, has been motivated by recognition of the failures of traditional instruction. and the emergence of deeper understandings of how people learn. Unlike traditional instruction, PBL actively engages the student in constructing knowledge. PBL includes problems that can be solved in many different ways and have more than one solution.

Supporters

Advocates of PBL claim it can be used to enhance content knowledge while simultaneously fostering the development of communication, problem-solving, critical thinking, collaboration, and self-directed learning skills. PBL may position students in a simulated real world working and professional context which involves policy, process, and ethical problems that will need to be understood and resolved to some outcome. By working through a combination of learning strategies to discover the nature of a problem, understanding the constraints and options to its resolution, defining the input variables, and understanding the viewpoints involved, students learn to negotiate the complex sociological nature of the problem and how competing resolutions may inform decision-making.

Constructivism and PBL

Problem Based Learning addresses the need to promote lifelong learning through the process of enquiry and constructivist learning. PBL can be considered a constructivist approach to instruction, emphasizing collaborative and self-directed learning and being supported by flexible teacher scaffolding. Yew and Schmidt, Schmidt, and Hung elaborate on the cognitive constructivist process of PBL:

1. Learners are presented with a problem and through discussion within their group, activate their prior knowledge.
2. Within their group, they develop possible theories or hypotheses to explain the problem. Together they identify learning issues to be researched. They construct a shared primary model to explain the problem at hand. Facilitators provide scaffold, which is a frame work on which students can construct knowledge relating to the problem.
3. After the initial team work, students work independently in self directed study to research the identified issues.
4. The students re-group to discuss their findings and refine their initial explanations based on what they learned.

PBL follows a constructivist perspective in learning as the role of the instructor is to guide and challenge the learning process rather than strictly providing knowledge. From this perspective, feedback and reflection on the learning process and group dynamics are essential components of PBL. Students are considered to be active agents who engage in social knowledge construction. PBL assists in processes of creating meaning and building personal interpretations of the world based on experiences and interactions. PBL assists to guide the student from theory to practice during their journey through solving the problem.

Supporting Evidence

Several studies support the success of the constructivist problem-based and enquiry learning methods. One example is a study on a project called GenScope, an enquiry-based science software application, which found that students using the GenScope software showed significant gains over the control groups, with the largest gains shown in students from basic courses.

One large study tracked middle school students' performance on high-stakes standardized tests to evaluate the effectiveness of enquiry-based science.

The study found a 14 percent improvement for the first cohort of students and a 13 percent improvement for the second cohort. The study also found that enquiry-based teaching methods greatly reduced the achievement gap for African-American students.

A systematic review of the effects of problem-based learning in medical school on the performance of doctors after graduation showed clear positive effects on physician competence. This effect was especially strong for social and cognitive competencies such as coping with uncertainty and communication skills.

Another study from Slovenia looked at whether students who learn with PBL are better at solving problems and if their attitudes towards mathematics were improved compared to their peers in a more traditional curriculum.

The study found that students who were exposed to PBL were better at solving more difficult problems, however, there was no significant difference in student attitude towards mathematics.

Examples of PBL in Curricula

Malaysia: In Malaysia, an attempt is being made to introduce a problem-based learning model in secondary mathematics, with the aim of educating citizens to prepare them for decision-making in sustainable and responsible development.

This model called problem-based learning the four core areas (PBL4C) first sprouted in SEAMEO RECSAM in 2008, and as a result of training courses conducted, a paper was presented at the EARCOME5 conference in 2010, followed by two papers during the 15th UNESCO-APEID conference in 2011.

This model has since expanded in its use in the field of education management, Education for International & Intranational Understanding (EIU), and human resource management. Subsequently, many Malaysian universities began implementing PBL in their curricula in an effort to improve the quality of their education. In collaboration with Aalborg University of Denmark, PBL was introduced at University Tun Hussein Onn Malaysia (UTHM). Since then the PBL was widely used among engineering and as well as humanities lecturers at UTHM (Berhannudin, 2007). In Universiti

Malaya, the Bachelor of Medicine, Bachelor of Surgery and Bachelor of Dental Surgery courses included several sessions of problem-based learning in their curriculum as a way of teaching interactions between students.

Medical Schools

Several medical schools have incorporated problem-based learning into their curricula, using real patient cases to teach students how to think like a clinician. More than eighty percent of medical schools in the United States now have some form of problem-based learning in their programmes. Research of 10 years of data from the University of Missouri School of Medicine indicates that PBL has a positive effect on the students' competency as physicians after graduation.

Monash University was the second institution to adopt PBL within a medical school environment and continues to apply this within the Faculty of Medicine, Nursing and Health Sciences for the Bachelor of Medicine / Bachelor of Surgery (MBBS) programmes delivered in Australia and Malaysia.

Maastricht University offers its whole programme in PBL format only, as does the University of Limerick graduate entry medical school in Ireland.

In 1998, Western University of Health Sciences opened its College of Veterinary Medicine, with curriculum based completely on PBL.

In 2004, the Lake Erie College of Osteopathic Medicine founded a branch campus in Bradenton, Florida, using an entirely PBL format. From 2006 to 2010, this campus led the nation in COMLEX scores.

In 2002, Gadjah Mada University of Yogyakarta, Indonesia began offering an International Medicine programme based on problem-based learning.

In 2009, Libyan International Medical University of Benghazi, Libya started using PBL for all of its medical programmes.

High School

In 2008, Parramatta Marist High School a secondary Catholic school in Australia employed the methods of PBL in their teaching for year 9 and 10 boys. The learning system was a great success and since has been expanded to lower grades to challenge students to think outside of the box and relate content drive courses to problems in the real world.

North Lawndale College Prep High School (NLCP), on Chicago's west side, continues to refine its very high expectations Interdisciplinary Projects, or I-Projects. As they progress freshman through senior year, these vertically aligned projects involve increasingly rigorous Common Core State Standards in research, close reading, quantitative reasoning, argumentation, writing, and presentation skills. Each NLCP Junior and Senior Project derives itself from the student's own driving question (examples of driving questions include "How can genocide be stopped globally?" and "Does making obesity a disease help or harm obese people?").

Additionally and starting in 2014, all NLCP Senior Project Presentations will include the senior's creation of an artistic element that somehow expresses his/her argument, e.g., a documentary film, a website, a business proposal, a literary portfolio, a visual art portfolio, a unique oratory, or performative debate. Noodletools, "a powerful, integrated platform for research and literacy," is the assistive technology for North Lawndale's endeavour.

Ecological Economics

The transdisciplinary field of ecological economics has embraced problem-based learning as a core pedagogy. A workbook developed by Joshua Farley, Jon Erickson, and Herman Daly organizes the problem-solving process into

(1) building the problem base,

(2) analyzing the problem,

(3) synthesizing the findings, and

(4) communicating the results.

Building the problem base includes choosing, defining, and structuring an ecological economic problem. Analysis is breaking down of a problem into understandable components. Synthesis is the re-integration of the parts in a way that helps better understand the whole. Communication is the translation of results into a form relevant to stakeholders, broadly defined as the extended peer community.

Criticisms

Cognitive load: Sweller and others have published a series of studies over the past twenty years that is relevant to problem-based learning but concerning cognitive load and what they describe as the guidance-fading effect. Sweller et al. conducted several classroom-based studies with students studying algebra problems. These studies have shown that active problem solving early in the learning process is a less effective instructional strategy than studying worked examples (Sweller and Cooper, 1985; Cooper and Sweller, 1987).

Certainly active problem solving is useful as learners become more competent, and better able to deal with their working memory limitations. But early in the learning process, learners may find it difficult to process a large amount of information in a short amount of time.

Thus the rigors of active problem solving may become an issue for novices. Once learners gain expertise the scaffolding inherent in problem-based learning helps learners avoid these issues. These studies have however been conducted largely based on individual problem solving of well-defined problems.

Sweller (1988) proposed cognitive load theory to explain how novices react to problem solving during the early stages of learning. Sweller, et al. suggests a worked example early, and then a gradual introduction of problems to be solved.

They propose other forms of learning early in the learning process (worked example, goal free problems, etc.); to later be replaced by completions problems, with the eventual goal of solving problems on their own. This problem based learning becomes very useful later in the learning process.

Many forms of scaffolding have been implemented in problem based learning to reduce the cognitive load of learners. These are most useful to fade guidance during problem solving. As an example, consider the fading effect helps learners to slowly transit from studying examples to solving problems. In this case backwards fading was found to be quite effective and assisting in decreasing the cognitive load on learners.

Evaluation of the effects of PBL learning in comparison to traditional instructional learning have proved to be a challenge. Various factors can influence the implementation of PBL: extent of PBL incorporation into curriculum, group dynamics, nature of problems used, facilitator influence on group, and the motivation of the learners.

There are also various outcomes of PBL that can be measured including knowledge acquisition and clinical competence. Additional studies are needed to investigate all the variables and technological scaffolds, that may impact the efficacy PBL.

Demands of Implementing

Implementing PBL in schools and Universities is a demanding process that requires resources, a lot of planning and organization. Azer discusses the 12 steps for implementing the "pure PBL"

1. Prepare faculty for change
2. Establish a new curriculum committee and working group
3. Designing the new PBL curriculum and defining educational outcomes
4. Seeking Advice from Experts in PBL
5. Planning, Organizing and Managing
6. Training PBL facilitators and defining the objectives of a facilitator
7. Introducing Students to the PBL Programme
8. Using 3-learning to support the delivery of the PBL programme
9. Changing the assessment to suit the PBL curriculum
10. Encouraging feedback from students and teaching staff
11. Managing learning resources and facilities that support self directed learning
12. Continuing evaluation and making changes (pg. 809-812)

Hung reviews the various models of PBL, Barrow's original concept or "pure PBL", the Hybrid PBL and lecture based learning with problem solving activities. In general these models form a continuum where the level of instruction and lecture are inversely proportional to the amount of self-directed learning.

The individual Problem design, or "trigger" must ultimately guide students to obtain the learning objectives. Azer reviews the detailed objectives for constructing "the problem" for PBL. Facilitator selection, training and development is very important to PBL. Students respond better to motivated and enthusiastic facilitators. It is the facilitator's role to direct students during the tutorials. Guiding students learning entails much more time then simply giving students the answers. Kol et al.(2008) reported PBL facilitator-student contact time was 3-4 times greater than instructors in traditional methods.

Other Outcomes

One of the aims of PBL is the development of self-directed learning (SDL) skills. In Loyens, Magda & Rikers' discussion, SDL is defined as "a process in which individuals take the initiative...in diagnosing their learning needs, formulating goals, identifying human and material resources, choosing and implementing appropriate learning strategies, and evaluating learning outcomes."

By being invited into the learning process, students are also invited to take responsibility for their learning, which leads to an increase in self-directed learning skills. In Severiens and Schmidt's study of 305 first year college students, they found that PBL and its focus on SDL led to motivation for students to maintain study pace, led to social and academic integration, encouraged development of cognitive skills, and fostered more study progress than students in a conventional learning setting. PBL encourages learners to take a place in the academic world through inquiring and discovery that is central to problem-based learning.

PBL is also argued as a learning method that can promote the development of critical thinking skills. In PBL learning, students learn how to analyze a problem, identify relevant facts and generate hypotheses, identify necessary information/knowledge for solving the problem and make reasonable judgements about solving the problem.

Employers have appreciated the positive attributes of communication, teamwork, respect and collaboration that PBL experienced students have developed. These skills provide for better future skills preparation in the ever-changing information explosion. PBL curriculum includes building these attributes through knowledge building, written and interpersonal interactions and through the experience of the problem solving process.

Learning Styles

Learning style is an individual's natural or habitual pattern of acquiring and processing information in learning situations. A core concept is that individuals differ in how they learn. The idea of individualized learning styles originated in the 1970s, and has greatly influenced education.

Proponents of the use of learning styles in education recommend that teachers assess the learning styles of their students and adapt their classroom methods to best fit each student's learning style. Although there is ample evidence for differences in individual thinking and ways of processing various types of information, few studies have reliably tested the validity of using learning styles in education.

Critics say there is no evidence that identifying an individual student's learning style produces better outcomes. There is evidence of empirical and pedagogical problems related to the use of learning tasks to "correspond to differences in a one-to-one fashion". Well-designed studies contradict the widespread "meshing hypothesis", that a student will learn best if taught in a method deemed appropriate for the student's learning style.

Models

David Kolb's Model: The David A. Kolb styles model is based on the Experiential Learning Theory, as explained in his book *Experiential Learning.* The ELT model outlines two related approaches toward grasping experience: Concrete Experience and Abstract Conceptualization, as well as two related approaches toward transforming experience: Reflective Observation and Active Experimentation.

According to Kolb's model, the ideal learning process engages all four of these modes in response to situational demands. In order for learning to be effective, all four of these approaches must be incorporated. As individuals attempt to use all four approaches, however, they tend to develop strengths in one experience-grasping approach and one experience-transforming approach. The resulting learning styles are combinations of the individual's preferred approaches. These learning styles are as follows:

1. Converger;
2. Diverger;
3. Assimilator;
4. Accommodator;.

Convergers are characterized by abstract conceptualization and active experimentation. They are good at making practical applications of ideas and using deductive reasoning to solve problems.

Divergers tend toward concrete experience and reflective observation. They are imaginative and are good at coming up with ideas and seeing things from different perspectives.

Assimilators are characterized by abstract conceptualization and reflective observation. They are capable of creating theoretical models by means of inductive reasoning.

Accommodators use concrete experience and active experimentation. They are good at actively engaging with the world and actually doing things instead of merely reading about and studying them. Kolb's model gave rise to the Learning Style Inventory, an assessment method used to determine an individual's learning style. An individual may exhibit a preference for one of the four styles—Accommodating, Converging, Diverging and Assimilating—depending on their approach to learning via the experiential learning theory model.

Although Kolb's model is the most widely accepted with substantial empirical support, recent studies suggest the Learning Style Inventory (LSI) is seriously flawed

Peter Honey and Alan Mumford's Model

Two adaptations were made to Kolb's experiential model. Firstly, the stages in the cycle were renamed to accord with managerial experiences of decision making/problem solving. The Honey & Mumford stages are:

1. Having an experience
2. Reviewing the experience
3. Concluding from the experience
4. Planning the next steps.

Secondly, the styles were directly aligned to the stages in the cycle and named Activist, Reflector, Theorist and Pragmatist. These are assumed to be acquired preferences that are adaptable, either at will or through changed circumstances, rather than being fixed personality characteristics. The Honey & Mumford *Learning Styles Questionnaire* (LSQ) is a self-development tool and differs from Kolb's Learning Style inventory by inviting managers to complete a checklist of work-related behaviours without directly asking managers how they learn. Having completed the self-assessment, managers are encouraged to focus on strengthening underutilised styles in order to become better equipped to learn from a wide range of everyday experiences.

A MORI survey commissioned by The Campaign for Learning in 1999 found the Honey & Mumford LSQ to be the most widely used system for assessing preferred learning styles in the local government sector in the UK.

Anthony Gregorc's Model

Dennis W. Mills discusses the work of Anthony F. Gregorc and Kathleen A. Butler in his article entitled "Applying What We Know:

Student Learning Styles". Gregorc and Butler worked to organize a model describing how the mind works. This model is based on the existence of perceptions—our evaluation of the world by means of an approach that makes sense to us. These perceptions in turn are the foundation of our specific learning strengths, or learning styles.

In this model, there are two perceptual qualities

1) concrete and
2) abstract;

and two ordering abilities

1) random and
2) sequential.

Concrete perceptions involve registering information through the five senses, while abstract perceptions involve the understanding of ideas, qualities, and concepts which cannot be seen. In regard to the two ordering abilities, sequential involves the organization of information in a linear, logical way and random involves the organization of information in chunks and in no specific order. Both of the perceptual qualities and both of the ordering abilities are present in each individual, but some qualities and ordering abilities are more dominant within certain individuals.

There are four combinations of perceptual qualities and ordering abilities based on dominance:

1) Concrete Sequential;
2) Abstract Random;
3) Abstract Sequential;
4) Concrete Random.

Individuals with different combinations learn in different ways—they have different strengths, different things make sense to them, different things are difficult for them, and they ask different questions throughout the learning process.

Sudbury Model of Democratic Education

Some critics (Mazza) of today's schools, of the concept of learning disabilities, of special education, and of response to intervention, take the position that every child has a different learning style and pace and that each child is unique, not only capable of learning but also capable of succeeding.

Sudbury Model democratic schools in the United States assert that there are many ways to study and learn. They argue that learning is a process you do, not a process that is done to you, and that this is true of everyone; it's basic. The experience of *Sudbury model democratic schools* shows that there are many ways to learn without the intervention of teaching, that is to say, without the intervention of a teacher being imperative.

In the case of reading for instance in the Sudbury model democratic schools, some children learn from being read to, memorizing the stories and then ultimately reading them. Others learn from cereal boxes, others from games instructions, others from street signs. Some teach themselves letter sounds, others syllables, others whole words. Sudbury model democratic schools assert that in their schools no one child has ever been forced, pushed, urged, cajoled, or bribed into learning how to read or write.

None of their graduates are real or functional illiterates, and no one who meets their older students could ever guess the age at which they first learned to read or write. In a similar manner, students learn all the subjects, techniques, and skills in these schools.

Describing current instructional methods as homogenization and lockstep standardization, alternative approaches are proposed, such as the *Sudbury Model of Democratic Education schools*, an alternative approach in which children, by enjoying personal freedom thus encouraged to exercise personal responsibility for their actions, learn at their own pace and style rather than following a compulsory and chronologically-based curriculum. Proponents of unschooling have also claimed that children raised in this method learn at their own pace and style, and do not suffer from learning disabilities.

Gerald Coles asserts that there are partisan agendas behind the educational policy-makers and that the scientific research that they use to support their arguments regarding the teaching of literacy is flawed. These include the idea that there are neurological explanations for learning disabilities.

Neil Fleming's VAK/VARK Model

One of the most common and widely-used categorizations of the various types of learning styles is Fleming's VARK model (sometimes VAK) which expanded upon earlier Neuro-linguistic programming (VARK) models:

1. visual learners;
2. auditory learners;
3. reading-writing preference learners;
4. kinesthetic learners or tactile learners.

Fleming claimed that visual learners have a preference for seeing (think in pictures; visual aids such as overhead slides, diagrams, handouts, etc.). Auditory learners best learn through listening (lectures, discussions, tapes, etc.). Tactile/kinesthetic learners prefer to learn via experience—moving, touching, and doing (active exploration of the world; science projects; experiments, etc.).

Its use in pedagogy allows teachers to prepare classes that address each of these areas. Students can also use the model to identify their preferred learning style and maximize their educational experience by focusing on what benefits them the most.

Other Models

Cognitive approach to learning styles:

Anthony Grasha and Sheryl Reichmann, in 1974, formulated the Grasha-Reichmann Learning Style Scale. It was developed to analyze the attitudes of students and how they approach learning. The test was originally designed for college students. Grasha's background is in cognitive processes and coping techniques. The concepts of various learning styles are as follows:

- avoidant
- participative
- competitive
- collaborative
- dependent
- independent

The conclusion of this model was to provide teachers with insight on how to approach instructional plans.

Aiming to explain why aptitude tests, school grades, and classroom performance often fail to identify real ability, Robert J. Sternberg listed various cognitive dimensions in his book *Thinking Styles* (1997). Several other models are also often used when researching learning styles. This includes the Myers Briggs Type Indicator (MBTI) and the DISC assessment.

A More Recent Evidence-based Model of Learning

Chris J Jackson's neuropsychological hybrid model of learning in personality argues Sensation Seeking provides a core biological drive of curiosity, learning and exploration. A high drive to explore leads to dysfunctional learning consequences unless cognitions such as goal orientation, conscientiousness, deep learning and emotional intelligence re-express it in more complex ways to achieve functional outcomes such as high work performance.

The model aims to explain many forms of functional behaviour (such as entrepreneurial activity, work performance, educational success) as well as dysfunctional behaviour (such as delinquency and anti-social behaviour). The wide applicability of the model and its strong grounding in the academic literature suggests that this evidence based model of learning has much potential.

Latest research is summarized here. Evidence for this model is considerable. Siadaty and Taghiyareh (2007) report that training based on Conscientious Achievement increases performance but that training based on Sensation Seeking does not. These results strongly support Jackson's model since the model proposes that Conscientious Achievement will respond to intervention whereas Sensation Seeking (with its biological basis) will not. Jackson's papers can be downloaded here.

NASSP Learning Style Model

Learning style is a gestalt that tells us how a student learns and prefers to learn. Keefe (1979) says that: "Learning styles are characteristic cognitive, affective, and physiological behaviours that serve as relatively stable indicators of how learners perceive, interact with, and respond to the learning environment."

There are three broad categories of learning style characteristics:

- Cognitive styles are preferred ways of perception, organization and retention.
- Affective styles represent the motivational dimensions of the learning personality; each learner has a personal motivational approach.
- Physiological styles are traits deriving from a person's gender, health and nutrition, and reaction to school physical surroundings, such as preferences for levels of light, sound, and temperature.

Styles are hypothetical constructs that help to explain the learning (and teaching) process. Because learning is an internal process, we know that it has taken place only when we observe a relatively stable change in learner behaviour resulting from what has been experienced" (Keefe, 1979). Similarly, learning style reflects underlying learning behaviour. We can recognize the learning style of an individual student only by observing his or her behaviour.

Assessment Methods

Learning Style Inventory: The Learning Style Inventory (LSI) is connected with Kolb's model and is used to determine a student's learning style. The LSI assesses an individual's preferences and needs regarding the learning process. It does the following:

(1) allows students to designate how they like to learn and indicates how consistent their responses are,

(2) provides computerized results which show the student's preferred learning style,

(3) provides a foundation upon which teachers can build in interacting with students,

(4) provides possible strategies for accommodating learning styles,

(5) provides for student involvement in the learning process;

(6) provides a class summary so students with similar learning styles can be grouped together.

A completely different Learning Styles Inventory is associated with a binary division of learning styles, developed by Felder and Silverman. In this model, learning styles are a balance between four pairs of extremes: Active/Reflective, Sensing/Intuitive, Verbal/Visual and Sequential/Global. Students receive four scores describing these balances. Like the LSI mentioned above, this inventory provides overviews and synopses for teachers.

NASSP Learning Style Profile

The NASSP Learning Style Profile (LSP) is a second-generation instrument for the diagnosis of student cognitive styles, perceptual responses, and study and instructional preferences. The Profile was developed by the NASSP research department (Keefe and Monk, 1986) in conjunction with a national task force of learning style experts. The task force spent almost a year reviewing the available literature and instrumentation before deciding to develop a new instrument. The Profile was developed in four phases with initial work undertaken at the University of Vermont (cognitive elements), Ohio State University (affective elements), and St. John's University (physiological/environmental elements).

Rigid validation and normative studies were conducted using factor analytic methods to ensure strong construct validity and subscale independence.

The Learning Style Profile contains 24 scales representing four higher order factors: cognitive styles, perceptual responses, study preferences and instructional preferences (the affective and physiological elements). The LSP scales are as follows:

- Analytic Skill
- Spatial Skill
- Discrimination Skill
- Categorizing Skill
- Sequential Processing Skill
- Simultaneous Processing Skill
- Memory Skill
- Perceptual Response: Visual
- Perceptual Response: Auditory
- Perceptual Response: Emotive
- Persistence Orientation
- Verbal Risk Orientation;
- Verbal-Spatial Preference
- Manipulative Preference
- Study Time Preference: Early Morning
- Study Time Preference: Late Morning
- Study Time Preference: Afternoon
- Study Time Preference: Evening
- Grouping Preference
- Posture Preference
- Mobility Preference
- Sound Preference
- Lighting Preference
- Temperature Preference

The LSP is a first-level diagnostic tool intended as the basis for comprehensive style assessment. Extensive readability checks, reliability and validity studies, and factor analyses of the instrument, combined with the supervisory efforts of the task force, ensure valid use of the instrument with students in the sixth to twelfth grades.

Other Methods

Other methods (usually questionnaires) used to identify learning styles include Fleming's VARK Learning Style Test, Jackson's Learning Styles Profiler (LSP), and the NLP meta programmes based iWAM questionnaire. Many other tests have gathered popularity and various levels of credibility among students and teachers.

Ilene Thiel introduced LLL as a preferred method of learning style otherwise known as Lifelong Love of Learning.

Criticism

Learning style theories have been criticized by many scholars and researchers. Some psychologists and neuroscientists have questioned the scientific basis for and the theories on which they are based. According to Susan Greenfield the practice is "nonsense" from a neuroscientific point of view: "Humans have evolved to build a picture of the world through our senses working in unison, exploiting the immense interconnectivity that exists in the brain."

Many educational psychologists believe that there is little evidence for the efficacy of most learning style models, and furthermore, that the models often rest on dubious theoretical grounds. According to Stahl, there has been an "utter failure to find that assessing children's learning styles and matching to instructional methods has any effect on their learning." Guy Claxton has questioned the extent that learning styles such as VARK are helpful, particularly as they can have a tendency to label children and therefore restrict learning.

Critique Made by Coffield, et al.

A non-peer-reviewed literature review by authors from the University of Newcastle upon Tyne identified 71 different theories of learning style. This report, published in 2004, criticized most of the main instruments used to identify an individual's learning style.

In conducting the review, Coffield and his colleagues selected 13 of the most influential models for closer study, including most of the models cited on this page. They examined the theoretical origins and terms of each model, and the instrument that purported to assess individuals against the learning styles defined by the model. They analyzed the claims made by the author(s), external studies of these claims, and independent empirical evidence of the relationship between the learning style identified by the instrument and students' actual learning.

Coffield's team found that none of the most popular learning style theories had been adequately validated through independent research, leading to the conclusion that the idea of a learning cycle, the consistency of visual, auditory and kinesthetic preferences and the value of matching teaching and learning styles were all "highly questionable."

One of the most widely known theories assessed by Coffield's team was the learning styles model of Dunn and Dunn, a VAK model. This model is widely used in schools in the United States, and 177 articles have been published in peer-reviewed journals referring to this model. The conclusion of Coffield et al. was as follows:

Despite a large and evolving research programme, forceful claims made for impact are questionable because of limitations in many of the supporting studies and the lack of independent research on the model.

Coffield's team claimed that another model, Gregorc's Style Delineator (GSD), was "theoretically and psychometrically flawed" and "not suitable for the assessment of individuals."

The Critique Regarding Kolb's Model

Mark K. Smith compiled and reviewed some critiques of Kolb's model in his article, "David A. Kolb on Experiential Learning". According to Smith's research, there are six key issues regarding the model. They are as follows:

1) the model doesn't adequately address the process of reflection;
2) the claims it makes about the four learning styles are extravagant;
3) it doesn't sufficiently address the fact of different cultural conditions and experiences;
4) the idea of stages/steps doesn't necessarily match reality;
5) it has only weak empirical evidence;
6) the relationship between learning processes and knowledge is more complex than Kolb draws it.

Other Critiques

Coffield and his colleagues and Mark Smith are not alone in their judgements. Demos, a UK think tank, published a report on learning styles prepared by a group chaired by David Hargreaves that included Usha Goswami from Cambridge University and David Wood from the University of Nottingham. The Demos report said that the evidence for learning styles was "highly variable", and that practitioners were "not by any means frank about the evidence for their work."

Cautioning against interpreting neuropsychological research as supporting the applicability of learning style theory, John Geake, Professor of Education at the UK's Oxford Brookes University, and a research collaborator with Oxford University's Centre for Functional Magnetic Resonance Imaging of the Brain, commented that

We need to take extreme care when moving from the lab to the classroom. We do remember things visually and aurally, but information isn't defined by how it was received.

2009 APS Critique

In late 2009, the journal *Psychological Science in the Public Interest* of the Association for Psychological Science (APS) published a report on the scientific validity of learning styles practices (Pashler et al., 2009). The panel was chaired by Hal Pashler (University of California, San Diego); the other members were Mark McDaniel (Washington University), Doug Rohrer (University of South Florida), and Robert Bjork (University of California, Los Angeles).

The panel concluded that an adequate evaluation of the learning styles hypothesis—the idea that optimal learning demands that students receive instruction tailored to their learning styles—requires a particular kind of study. Specifically, students should be grouped into the learning style categories that are being evaluated (e.g., visual learners vs. verbal learners), and then students in each group must be randomly assigned to one of the learning methods (e.g., visual learning or verbal learning), so that some students will be "matched" and others will be "mismatched".

At the end of the experiment, all students must sit for the same test. If the learning style hypothesis is correct, then, for example, visual learners should learn better with the visual method, whereas auditory learners should learn better with auditory method. Notably, other authors have reached the same conclusion (e.g., Massa & Mayer, 2006).

As disclosed in the report, the panel found that studies utilizing this essential research design were virtually absent from the learning styles literature. In fact, the panel was able to find only a few studies with this research design, and all but one of these studies were negative findings—that is, they found that the same learning method was superior for all kinds of students (e.g., Massa & Mayer, 2006).

Furthermore, the panel noted that, even if the requisite finding were obtained, the benefits would need to be large, and not just statistically significant, before learning style interventions could be recommended as cost-effective. That is, the cost of evaluating and classifying students by their learning style, and then providing customized instruction would need to be more beneficial than other interventions (e.g., one-on-one tutoring, after school remediation programmes, etc.).

As a consequence, the panel concluded, "at present, there is no adequate evidence base to justify incorporating learning styles assessments into general educational practice. Thus, limited education resources would better be devoted to adopting other educational practices that have strong evidence base, of which there are an increasing number."

The article incited critical comments from some defenders of learning styles. *The Chronicle of Higher Education* reported that Robert Sternberg from Tufts University spoke out against the paper: "Several of the most-cited researchers on learning styles, Mr. Sternberg points out, do not appear in the paper's bibliography." This charge was also discussed by *Science*, which reported that Pashler said, "Just so...most of [the evidence] is 'weak.'"

Learning Styles in the Classroom

Various researchers have attempted to hypothesize ways in which learning style theory can be used in the classroom. Two such scholars are Dr. Rita Dunn and Dr. Kenneth Dunn, who follow a VARK approach.

Although learning styles will inevitably differ among students in the classroom, Dunn and Dunn say that teachers should try to make changes in their classroom that will be beneficial to every learning style. Some of these changes include room redesign, the development of small-group techniques, and the development of Contract Activity Packages. Redesigning the classroom involves locating dividers that can be used to arrange the room creatively (such as having different learning stations and instructional areas), clearing the floor area, and incorporating student thoughts and ideas into the design of the classroom.

Their so-called "Contract Activity Packages" are educational plans that use:

1) a clear statement of the learning need;
2) multisensory resources (auditory, visual, tactile, kinesthetic);
3) activities through which the newly-mastered information can be used creatively;
4) the sharing of creative projects within small groups;
5) at least three small-group techniques;
6) a pre-test, a self-test, and a post-test.

Another scholar who believes that learning styles should have an effect on the classroom is Marilee Sprenger in *Differentiation through Learning Styles and Memory*. Sprenger bases her work on three premises:

1) Teachers can be learners, and learners teachers. We are all both.
2) Everyone can learn under the right circumstances.
3) Learning is fun! Make it appealing.

She details various ways of teaching, visual, auditory, or tactile/kinesthetic. Methods for visual learners include ensuring that students can see words written, using pictures, and drawing time lines for events. Methods for auditory learners include repeating words aloud, small-group discussion, debates, listening to books on tape, oral reports, and oral interpretation. Methods for tactile/kinesthetic learners include hands-on activities (experiments, etc.), projects, frequent breaks to allow movement, visual aids, role play, and field trips. By using a variety of teaching methods from each of these categories, teachers cater to different learning styles at once, and improve learning by challenging students to learn in different ways.

James W. Keefe and John M. Jenkins (2000; 2008) have incorporated learning style assessment as a basic component in their "Personalized Instruction" model of schooling. Six basic elements constitute the culture and context of personalized instruction. The cultural components - - teacher role, student learning characteristics, and collegial relationships - -establish the foundation of personalization and ensure that the school prizes a caring and collaborative environment. The contextual factors—interactivity, flexible scheduling, and authentic assessment—establish the structure of personalization.

These six elements constitute the state of the art in personalized instruction. Cognitive and learning style aanlysis have a special role in the process of personalizing instruction. Style elements are relatively persistent qualities in the behaviour of individual learners.

They reflect genetic coding, personality, development, motivation, and environmental adaptation. Second only to the more flexible teacher role, the assessment of student learning style, more than any other element, establishes the foundation for a personalized approach to schooling: for student advisement and placement, for appropriate retraining of student cognitive skills, for adaptive instructional strategy, and for the authentic evaluation of learning.

Some learners respond best in instructional environments based on an analysis of their perceptual and environmental style preferences. Most individualized and personalized teaching methods reflect this point of view. Other learners, however, need help to function successfully in any learning environment. If a youngster cannot cope under conventional instruction, enhancing his cognitive skills may make successful achievement possible.

Many of the student learning problems that learning style diagnosis attempts to solve relate directly to elements of the human information processing system. Processes such as attention, perception and memory, and operations such as integration and retrieval of information are internal to the system. Any hope for improving student learning necessarily involves an understanding and application of information processing theory. Learning style assessment is an important window to understanding and managing this process.

Some research evaluating teaching styles and learning styles, however, has found that congruent groups have no significant differences in achievement from incongruent groups (Spoon & Schell, 1998).

Furthermore, learning style in this study varied by demography, specifically by age, suggesting a change in learning style as one gets older and acquires more experience. While significant age differences did occur, as well as no experimental manipulation of classroom assignment, the findings do call into question the aim of congruent teaching-learning styles in the classroom.

Theory of Multiple Intelligences

The theory of multiple intelligences was proposed by Howard Gardner in his 1983 book *Frames of Mind: The Theory of Multiple Intelligences* as a model of intelligence that differentiates it into specific (primarily sensory) "modalities", rather than seeing it as dominated by a single general ability. Gardner articulated seven criteria for a behaviour to be considered an intelligence.

These were that the intelligences showed: potential for brain isolation by brain damage, place in evolutionary history, presence of core operations, susceptibility to encoding (symbolic expression), a distinct developmental progression, the existence of savants, prodigies and other exceptional people, and support from experimental psychology and psychometric findings.

Gardner chose eight abilities that he held to meet these criteria: musical - rhythmic, visual - spatial, verbal - linguistic, logical - mathematical, bodily - kinesthetic, interpersonal, intrapersonal, and naturalistic. He later suggested that existential and moral intelligence may also be worthy of inclusion.

Musical - rhythmic & Harmonic

This area has to do with sensitivity to sounds, rhythms, tones, and music. People with a high musical intelligence normally have good pitch and may even have absolute pitch, and are able to sing, play musical instruments, and compose music. Since there is a strong auditory component to this intelligence, those who are strongest in it may learn best via lecture.

They will sometimes use songs or rhythms to learn. They have sensitivity to rhythm, pitch, metre, tone, melody or timbre.

Visual – spatial

This area deals with spatial judgement and the ability to visualize with the mind's eye. Spatial ability is one of the three factors beneath *g* in the hierarchical model of intelligence.

Verbal – linguistic

People with high verbal-linguistic intelligence display a facility with words and languages. They are typically good at reading, writing, telling stories and memorizing words along with dates. Verbal ability is one of the most *g*-loaded abilities. This type of intelligence is associated with the Verbal IQ in WAIS-III.

Logical – mathematical

This area has to do with logic, abstractions, reasoning, numbers and critical thinking. This also has to do with having the capacity to understand the underlying principles of some kind of causal system. Logical reasoning is closely linked to fluid intelligence and to general intelligence (*g* factor).

Bodily – kinesthetic

The core elements of the bodily-kinesthetic intelligence are control of one's bodily motions and the capacity to handle objects skillfully. Gardner elaborates to say that this also includes a sense of timing, a clear sense of the goal of a physical action, along with the ability to train responses. People who have bodily-kinesthetic intelligence should learn better by involving muscular movement (e.g. getting up and moving around into the learning experience), and be generally good at physical activities such as sports, dance, acting, and making things.

Gardner believes that careers that suit those with this intelligence include: athletes, dancers, musicians, actors, builders, police officers, and soldiers. Although these careers can be duplicated through virtual simulation, they will not produce the actual physical learning that is needed in this intelligence.

Interpersonal

This area has to do with interaction with others. In theory, individuals who have high interpersonal intelligence are characterized by their sensitivity to others' moods, feelings, temperaments and motivations, and their ability to cooperate in order to work as part of a group. According to Gardner in *How Are Kids Smart: Multiple Intelligences in the Classroom*, "Inter- and Intra- personal intelligence is often misunderstood with being extroverted or liking other people..." Those with this intelligence communicate effectively and empathize easily with others, and may be either leaders or followers. They typically learn best by working with others and often enjoy discussion and debate.

Gardner believes that careers that suit those with this intelligence include sales persons, politicians, managers, teachers, counsellors and social workers.

Intrapersonal

This area has to do with introspective and self-reflective capacities. This refers to having a deep understanding of the self; what your strengths/ weaknesses are, what makes you unique, being able to predict your own reactions/emotions. Personality refers to the pattern of thoughts, feelings, social adjustments, and behaviours consistently exhibited over time that strongly influences one's expectations, self-perceptions, values, and attitudes. It also predicts human reactions to other people, problems, and stress.

There is still no universal consensus on the definition of "personality" in psychology. Gordon Allport (1937) described two major ways to study personality: the nomothetic and the idiographic. *Nomothetic psychology* seeks general laws that can be applied to many different people, such as the principle of self-actualization or the trait of extraversion. *Idiographic psychology* is an attempt to understand the unique aspects of a particular individual.

Naturalistic

This area has to do with nurturing and relating information to one's natural surroundings. Examples include classifying natural forms such as animal and plant species and rocks and mountain types. This ability was clearly of value in our evolutionary past as hunters, gatherers, and farmers; it continues to be central in such roles as botanist or chef. In the December 15, 2004 NSTA Reports, Anne Tweed (President of the National Science Teachers Association NSTA), concluded that a variety of teaching strategies, including enquiry-based learning and direct instruction techniques are what is best for students (Tweed, 2004).

Existential

Some proponents of multiple intelligence theory proposed spiritual or religious intelligence as a possible additional type. Gardner did not want to commit to a spiritual intelligence, but suggested that an "existential" intelligence may be a useful construct. The hypothesis of an existential intelligence has been further explored by educational researchers.

Critical Reception

Gardner argues that there is a wide range of cognitive abilities, but that there are only very weak correlations among them. For example, the theory postulates that a child who learns to multiply easily is not necessarily more intelligent than a child who has more difficulty on this task. The child who takes more time to master multiplication may best learn to multiply through a different approach, may excel in a field outside mathematics, or may be looking at and understanding the multiplication process at a fundamentally deeper level. Such a fundamental understanding can result in slowness and can hide a mathematical intelligence potentially higher than that of a child who quickly memorizes the multiplication table despite possessing a shallower understanding of the process of multiplication..

Intelligence tests and psychometrics have generally found high correlations between different aspects of intelligence, rather than the low correlations which Gardner's theory predicts, supporting the prevailing theory of general intelligence rather than multiple intelligences (MI). The theory has been widely criticized by mainstream psychology for its lack of empirical evidence, and its dependence on subjective judgement. Certain models of alternative education employ the approaches suggested by the theory.

Definition of Intelligence

One major criticism of the theory is that it is *ad hoc*: that Gardner is not expanding the definition of the word "intelligence", but rather denies the existence of intelligence as traditionally understood, and instead uses the word "intelligence" where other people have traditionally used words like "ability" and "aptitude". This practice has been criticized by Robert J. Sternberg, Eysenck, and Scarr. White (2006) points out that Gardner's selection and application of criteria for his "intelligences" is subjective and arbitrary, and that a different researcher would likely have come up with different criteria.

Defenders of MI theory argue that the traditional definition of intelligence is too narrow, and thus a broader definition more accurately reflects the differing ways in which humans think and learn. They would state that the traditional interpretation of intelligence collapses under the weight of its own logic and definition, noting that intelligence is usually defined as the cognitive or mental capacity of an individual, which by logical necessity would include all forms of mental qualities, not just the ones most transparent to I.Q. tests.

Some criticisms arise from the fact that Gardner has not provided a test of his multiple intelligences. He originally defined it as the ability to solve problems that have value in at least one culture, or as something that a student is interested in. He then added a disclaimer that he has no fixed definition, and his classification is more of an artistic judgement than fact:

Ultimately, it would certainly be desirable to have an algorithm for the selection of an intelligence, such that any trained researcher could determine whether a candidate's intelligence met the appropriate criteria. At present, however, it must be admitted that the selection (or rejection) of a candidate's intelligence is reminiscent more of an artistic judgement than of a scientific assessment.

Gardner argues that by calling linguistic and logical-mathematical abilities intelligences, but not artistic, musical, athletic, etc. abilities, the former are needlessly aggrandized. Certain critics balk at this widening of the definition, saying that it ignores "the connotation of intelligence ... [which] has always connoted the kind of thinking skills that makes one successful in school."

Gardner writes "I balk at the unwarranted assumption that certain human abilities can be arbitrarily singled out as intelligence while others cannot." Critics hold that given this statement, any interest or ability can be redefined as "intelligence". Thus, studying intelligence becomes difficult, because it diffuses into the broader concept of ability or talent. Gardner's addition of the naturalistic intelligence and conceptions of the existential and moral intelligences are seen as fruits of this diffusion. Defenders of the MI theory would argue that this is simply a recognition of the broad scope of inherent mental abilities, and that such an exhaustive scope by nature defies a one-dimensional classification such as an IQ value.

The theory and definitions have been critiqued by Perry D. Klein as being so unclear as to be tautologous and thus unfalsifiable. Having a high musical ability means being good at music while at the same time being good at music is explained by having a high musical ability.

Neo-Piagetian Criticism

Andreas Demetriou suggests that theories which overemphasize the autonomy of the domains are as simplistic as the theories that overemphasize the role of general intelligence and ignore the domains. He agrees with Gardner that there are indeed domains of intelligence that are relevantly autonomous of each other. Some of the domains, such as verbal, spatial, mathematical, and social intelligence are identified by most lines of research in psychology.

In Demetriou's theory, one of the neo-Piagetian theories of cognitive development, Gardner is criticized for underestimating the effects exerted on the various domains of intelligences by processes that define general processing efficiency, such as speed of processing, executive functions, working memory, and meta-cognitive processes underlying self-awareness and self-regulation. All of these processes are integral components of general intelligence that regulate the functioning and development of different domains of intelligence.

The domains are to a large extent expressions of the condition of the general processes, and may vary because of their constitutional differences but also differences in individual preferences and inclinations. Their functioning both channels and influences the operation of the general processes. Thus, one cannot satisfactorily specify the intelligence of an individual or design effective intervention programmes unless both the general processes and the domains of interest are evaluated.

IQ tests

Gardner argues that IQ tests only measure linguistic and logical-mathematical abilities. Psychologist Alan S. Kaufman points out that IQ tests have measured spatial abilities for 70 years. Modern IQ tests are greatly influenced by the Cattell-Horn-Carroll theory which incorporates a general intelligence but also many more narrow abilities. While IQ tests do give an overall IQ score, they now also give scores for many more narrow abilities.

Lack of Empirical Evidence

According to a 2006 study many of Gardner's "intelligences" correlate with the *g* factor, supporting the idea of a single dominant type of intelligence. According to the study, each of the domains proposed by Gardner involved a blend of *g*, of cognitive abilities other than *g*, and, in some cases, of non-cognitive abilities or of personality characteristics.

Linda Gottfredson (2006) has argued that thousands of studies support the importance of intelligence quotient (IQ) in predicting school and job performance, and numerous other life outcomes. In contrast, empirical support for non-*g* intelligences is lacking or very poor. She argued that despite this the ideas of multiple non-*g* intelligences are very attractive to many due to the suggestion that everyone can be smart in some way.

A critical review of MI theory argues that there is little empirical evidence to support it:

To date there have been no published studies that offer evidence of the validity of the multiple intelligences. In 1994 Sternberg reported finding no empirical studies. In 2000 Allix reported finding no empirical validating studies, and at that time Gardner and Connell conceded that there was "little hard evidence for MI theory" (2000, p. 292). In 2004 Sternberg and Grigerenko stated that there were no validating studies for multiple intelligences, and in 2004 Gardner asserted that he would be "delighted were such evidence to accrue", and admitted that "MI theory has few enthusiasts among psychometricians or others of a traditional psychological background" because they require "psychometric or experimental evidence that allows one to prove the existence of the several intelligences."

The same review presents evidence to demonstrate that cognitive neuroscience research does not support the theory of multiple intelligences:

... the human brain is unlikely to function via Gardner's multiple intelligences. Taken together the evidence for the intercorrelations of subskills of IQ measures, the evidence for a shared set of genes associated with mathematics, reading, and g, and the evidence for shared and overlapping "what is it?" and "where is it?" neural processing pathways, and shared neural pathways for language, music, motor skills, and emotions suggest that it is unlikely that each of Gardner's intelligences could operate "via a different set of neural mechanisms" (1999, p. 99).

Equally important, the evidence for the "what is it?" and "where is it?" processing pathways, for Kahneman's two decision-making systems, and for adapted cognition modules suggests that these cognitive brain specializations have evolved to address very specific problems in our environment. Because Gardner claimed that the intelligences are innate potentialities related to a general content area, MI theory lacks a rationale for the phylogenetic emergence of the intelligences.

Several articles have surveyed the use of Gardner's ideas and conclude that there is little to no academically substantiated evidence that his ideas work in practice. Steven A. Stahl found that most of the previous studies which claimed to show positive results had major flaws:

Among others, Marie Carbo claims that her learning styles work is based on research. (I discuss Carbo because she publishes extensively on her model and is very prominent in the workshop circuit ...) But given the overwhelmingly negative findings in the published research, I wondered what she was citing, and about a decade ago, I thought it would be interesting to take a look. Reviewing her articles, I found that out of 17 studies she had cited, only one was published. Fifteen were doctoral dissertations and 13 of these came out of one university—St. John's University in New York, Carbo's alma mater. None of these had been in a peer-refereed journal. When I looked closely at the dissertations and other materials, I found that 13 of the 17 studies that supposedly support her claim had to do with learning styles based on something other than modality.

The theory of multiple intelligences has been widely used as an example of pseudoscience, because it lacks empirical evidence or falsifiability.

Use in Education

Gardner defines an intelligence as "biopsychological potential to process information that can be activated in a cultural setting to solve problems or create products that are of value in a culture." According to Gardner, there are more ways to do this than just through logical and linguistic intelligence. Gardner believes that the purpose of schooling "should be to develop intelligences and to help people reach vocational and avocational goals that are appropriate to their particular spectrum of intelligences. People who are helped to do so, [he] believe[s], feel more engaged and competent and therefore more inclined to serve society in a constructive way."

Gardner contends that IQ tests focus mostly on logical and linguistic intelligence. Upon doing well on these tests, the chances of attending a prestigious college or university increase, which in turn creates contributing members of society. While many students function well in this environment, there are those who do not.

According to Helding (2009), "Standard IQ tests measure knowledge gained at a particular moment in time, they can only provide a freeze-frame view of crystallized knowledge. They cannot assess or predict a person's ability to learn, to assimilate new information, or to solve new problems." Gardner's theory argues that students will be better served by a broader vision of education, wherein teachers use different methodologies, exercises and activities to reach all students, not just those who excel at linguistic and logical intelligence. It challenges educators to find "ways that will work for this student learning this topic".

James Traub's article in *The New Republic* notes that Gardner's system has not been accepted by most academics in intelligence or teaching. Gardner states that "while Multiple Intelligences theory is consistent with much empirical evidence, it has not been subjected to strong experimental tests ... Within the area of education, the applications of the theory are currently being examined in many projects. Our hunches will have to be revised many times in light of actual classroom experience."

George Miller, a prominent cognitive psychologist, wrote in *The New York Times Book Review* that Gardner's argument consisted of "hunch and opinion". Jerome Bruner called Gardner's "intelligences" "at best useful fictions," and Charles Murray and Richard J. Herrnstein in *The Bell Curve* (1994) called Gardner's theory "uniquely devoid of psychometric or other quantitative evidence."

Thomas Armstrong argues that Waldorf education engages all of Gardner's original seven intelligences. In spite of its lack of general acceptance in the psychological community, Gardner's theory has been adopted by many schools, where it is often used to underpin discussion about learning styles, and hundreds of books have been written about its applications in education. Gardner himself has said he is "uneasy" with the way his theory has been used in education. The No Child Left Behind test legislation in the United States does not encompass the multiple intelligences framework in the exams' design or implementation.

Life skills-based Education

Life skills have been defined by the World Health Organization (WHO) as "abilities for adaptive and positive behaviour that enable individuals to deal effectively with the demands and challenges of everyday life". They represent the psycho-social skills that determine valued behaviour and include reflective skills such as problem-solving and critical thinking, to personal skills such as self-awareness, and to interpersonal skills.

Practicing life skills leads to qualities such as self-esteem, sociability and tolerance, to action competencies to take action and generate change, and to capabilities to have the freedom to decide what to do and who to be. Life skills are thus distinctly different from physical or perceptual motor skills, such as practical or health skills, as well as from livelihood skills, such as crafts, money management and entrepreneurial skills . Health and livelihood education however, can be designed to be complementary to life skills education, and vice versa.

Life Skills-Based Education (LSBE) has a long history of supporting child development and health promotionin many parts In 1986, the

Ottawa Charter for Health Promotion recognized life skills in terms of making better health choices. The 1989 Convention on the Rights of the Child (CRC) linked life skills to education by stating that education should be directed towards the development of the child's fullest potential.

The 1990 Jomtien Declaration on Education for All took this vision further and included life skills among essential learning tools for survival, capacity development and quality of life. The 2000 Dakar World Education Conference took a position that all young people and adults have the human right to benefit from "an education that includes learning to know, to do, to live together and to be", and included life skills in two out of the six EFA Goals.

Life skills-based education is now recognized as a methodology to address a variety of issues of child and youth development and thematic responses including as expressed in UNGASS on HIV/AIDS (2001), UNGASS on Children (2002), World Youth Report (2003), World Programme for Human Rights Education (2004), UN Decade on Education for Sustainable Development (2005), UN Secretary General's Study on Violence Against Children (2006), 51st Commission on the Status of Women (2007), and the World Development Report (2007).

Expected learning outcomes include a combination of knowledge, values, attitudes and skills with a particular emphasis on those skills that related to critical thinking and problem solving, self-management and communication and inter-personal skills.

Concept Learning

Concept learning, also known as category learning, concept attainment, and concept formation, is largely based on the works of the cognitive psychologist Jerome Bruner. Bruner, Goodnow, & Austin (1967) defined concept attainment (or concept learning) as "the search for and listing of attributes that can be used to distinguish exemplars from non exemplars of various categories."

More simply put, concepts are the mental categories that help us classify objects, events, or ideas, building on the understanding that each object, event, or idea has a set of common relevant features. Thus, concept learning is a strategy which requires a learner to compare and contrast groups or categories that contain concept-relevant features with groups or categories that do not contain concept-relevant features.

Concept learning also refers to a learning task in which a human or machine learner is trained to classify objects by being shown a set of example objects along with their class labels. The learner simplifies what has been observed by condensing it in the form of an example. This simplified version of what has been learned is then applied to future examples.

Concept learning may be simple or complex because learning takes place over many areas. When a concept is difficult, it is less likely that the learner will be able to simplify, and therefore will be less likely to learn. Colloquially, the task is known as *learning from examples.* Most theories of concept learning are based on the storage of exemplars and avoid summarization or overt abstraction of any kind.

Types of Concepts

Not a Concept. Concept learning must be distinguished from learning by reciting something from memory (recall) or discriminating between two things that differ (discrimination).

However, these issues are closely related, since memory recall of facts could be considered a "trivial" conceptual process where prior exemplars representing the concept are invariant. Similarly, while discrimination is not the same as initial concept learning, discrimination processes are involved in refining concepts by means of the repeated presentation of exemplars.

Concrete or Perceptual Concepts vs Abstract Concepts

Defined (or Relational) and Associated Concepts: Complex Concepts. Constructs such as a schema and a script are examples of complex concepts. A schema is an organization of smaller concepts (or features) and is revised by situational information to assist in comprehension. A script on the other hand is a list of actions that a person follows in order to complete a desired goal. An example of a script would be the process of buying a CD. There are several actions that must occur before the actual act of purchasing the CD and a script provides a sequence of the necessary actions and proper order of these actions in order to be successful in purchasing the CD.

Methods of learning a concept

Discovery - Every baby discovers concepts for itself, such as discovering that each of its fingers can be individually controlled or that care givers are individuals. Although this is perception driven, formation of the concept is more than memorizing perceptions.

Examples - Supervised or unsupervised generalizing from examples may lead to learning a new concept, but concept formation is more than generalizing from examples.

Words - Hearing or reading new words leads to learning new concepts, but forming a new concept is more than learning a dictionary definition. A person may have previously formed a new concept before encountering the word or phrase for it.

Exemplars comparison - Another efficient way to learn new categories and induce new categorization rules is to compare a few objects when their categorical relation is known. For example, comparing two exemplars while being informed that the two are from the same category allows the attributes shared by the category members to be identified, and illustrates the variability permitted within this category.

On the other hand, comparing two exemplars while being informed that the two are from different categories may allow an identification of attributes which has diagnostic value. Interestingly, within a category and between categories comparisons are not always similarly useful for category learning, and the capacity to use either one of these two forms of learning by comparison is subject to change during early childhood (Hammer et al., 2009).

Invention - When prehistoric people who lacked tools used their fingernails to scrape food from killed animals or smashed melons, they noticed that a broken stone sometimes had a sharp edge like a fingernail and was therefore suitable for scraping food. Inventing a stone tool to avoid broken fingernails was a new concept.

Theoretical Issues

In general, the theoretical issues underlying concept learning are those underlying induction. These issues are addressed in many diverse publications, including literature on subjects like Version Spaces, Statistical Learning Theory, PAC Learning, Information Theory, and Algorithmic Information Theory. Some of the broad theoretical ideas are also discussed by Watanabe (1969,1985), Solomonoff (1964a,1964b), and Rendell (1986).

Modern Psychological Theories of Concept Learning

It is difficult to make any general statements about human (or animal) concept learning without already assuming a particular psychological theory of concept learning. Although the classical views of concepts and concept learning in philosophy speak of a process of abstraction, data compression, simplification, and summarization, currently popular psychological theories of concept learning diverge on all these basic points. The history of psychology has seen the rise and fall of many theories about concept learning. Classical conditioning (as defined by Pavlov) created the earliest experimental technique. Reinforcement learning as described by Watson and elaborated by Clark Hull created a lasting paradigm in behavioural psychology. Cognitive psychology emphasized a computer and information flow metaphor for concept formation.

Neural network models of concept formation and the structure of knowledge have opened powerful hierarchical models of knowledge organization such as George Miller's Wordnet. Neural networks are based on computational models of learning using factor analysis or convolution. Neural networks also are open to neuroscience and psychophysiological models of learning following Karl Lashley and Donald Hebb.

Rule-based Theories of Concept Learning

Rule-based theories of concept learning began with cognitive psychology and early computer models of learning that might be implemented in a high level computer language with computational statements such as if:then production rules. They take classification data and a rule-based theory as input which are the result of a rule-based learner with the hopes of producing a more accurate model of the data (Hekenaho 1997). The majority of rule-based models that have been developed are heuristic, meaning that rational analyses have not been provided and the models are not related to statistical approaches to induction.

A rational analysis for rule-based models could presume that concepts are represented as rules, and would then ask to what degree of belief a rational agent should be in agreement with each rule, with some observed examples provided (Goodman, Griffiths, Feldman, and Tenenbaum). Rule-based theories of concept learning are focused more so on perceptual learning and less on definition learning. Rules can be used in learning when the stimuli are confusable, as opposed to simple. When rules are used in learning, decisions are made based on properties alone and rely on simple criteria that do not require a lot of memory (Rouder and Ratcliff, 2006).

Example of Rule-based Theory: "A radiologist using rule-based categorization would observe whether specific properties of an X-ray image meet certain criteria; for example, is there an extreme difference in brightness in a suspicious region relative to other regions? A decision is then based on this property alone."

Prototype Theory of Concept Learning

The prototype view of concept learning holds that people abstract out the central tendency (or prototype) of the examples experienced and use this as a basis for their categorization decisions.

The prototype view of concept learning holds that people categorize based on one or more central examples of a given category followed by a penumbra of decreasingly typical examples. This implies that people do not categorize based on a list of things that all correspond to a definition, but rather on a hierarchical inventory based on semantic similarity to the central example(s).

To illustrate, imagine the following mental representations of the category: Sports

The first illustration demonstrates a mental representation if we were to categorize by definition:

Definition of Sports: an athletic activity requiring skill or physical prowess and often of a competitive nature.

Basketball Football Bowling
Baseball Skiing
Track and field
Snowboarding
Lacrosse
rugby
Soccer Sports
Skateboarding
Golf
Bike-Racing
Hockey
Surfing
Weightlifting Tennis

The second illustration demonstrates a mental representation that prototype theory would predict:

1. Baseball
2. Football
3. Basketball
4. Soccer
5. Hockey
6. Tennis
7. Golf

...

15. Bike-racing
16. Weightlifting
17. Skateboarding
18. Snowboarding
19. Boxing
20. Wrestling

...

32. Fishing
33. Hunting
34. Hiking
35. Sky-diving
36. Bungee-jumping

...

62. Cooking
63. Walking

...

82. Gatorade
83. Water
84. Protein
85. Diet

It is evident that prototype theory hypothesizes a more continuous (less discrete) way of categorization in which the list to things that match the category's definition is not limited.

Exemplar Theories of Concept Learning

Exemplar theory is the storage of specific instances (exemplars), with new objects evaluated only with respect to how closely they resemble specific known members (and nonmembers) of the category. This theory hypothesizes that learners store examples *verbatim*. This theory views concept learning as highly simplistic. Only individual properties are represented. These individual properties are not abstract and they do not create rules.

An example of what exemplar theory might look like is, "water is wet". It is simply known that some (or one, or all) stored examples of water have the property wet. Exemplar based theories have become more empirically popular over the years with some evidence suggesting that human learners use exemplar based strategies only in early learning, forming prototypes and generalizations later in life. An important result of exemplar models in psychology literature has been a de-emphasis of complexity in concept learning. One of the best known exemplar theories of concept learning is the Generalized Context Model (GCM).

A problem with exemplar theory is that exemplar models critically depend on two measures: similarity between exemplars, and having a rule to determine group membership. Sometimes it is difficult to attain or distinguish these measures.

Multiple-prototype Theories of Concept Learning

More recently, cognitive psychologists have begun to explore the idea that the prototype and exemplar models form two extremes. It has been suggested that people are able to form a multiple prototype representation, besides the two extreme representations. For example, consider the category 'spoon'. There are two distinct subgroups or conceptual clusters: spoons tend to be either large and wooden, or small and made of metal.

The prototypical spoon would then be a medium-size object made of a mixture of metal and wood, which is clearly an unrealistic proposal. A more natural representation of the category 'spoon' would instead consist of multiple (at least two) prototypes, one for each cluster. A number of different proposals have been made in this regard (Anderson, 1991; Griffiths, Canini, Sanborn & Navarro, 2007; Love, Medin & Gureckis, 2004; Vanpaemel & Storms, 2008). These models can be regarded as providing a compromise between exemplar and prototype models.

Explanation-based Theories of Concept Learning

The basic idea of explanation-based learning suggests that a new concept is acquired by experiencing examples of it and forming a basic outline. Put simply, by observing or receiving the qualities of a thing the mind forms a concept which possesses and is identified by those qualities.

The original theory, proposed by Mitchell, Keller, and Kedar-Cabelli in 1986 and called explanation-based generalization, is that learning occurs through progressive generalizing. This theory was first developed to programme machines to learn. When applied to human cognition, it translates as follows: the mind actively separates information that applies to more than one thing and enters it into a broader description of a category of things. This is done by identifying sufficient conditions for something to fit in a category, similar to schematizing.

The revised model revolves around the integration of four mental processes – generalization, chunking, operationalization, and analogy.

- Generalization is the process by which the characteristics of a concept which are fundamental to it are recognized and labelled. For example, birds have feathers and wings. Anything with feathers and wings will be identified as 'bird'.
- When information is grouped mentally, whether by similarity or relatedness, the group is called a chunk. Chunks can vary in size from a single item with parts or many items with many parts.
- A concept is operationalized when the mind is able to actively recognize examples of it by characteristics and label it appropriately.
- Analogy is the recognition of similarities among potential examples.

This particular theory of concept learning is relatively new and more research is being conducted to test it.

Bayesian Theories of Concept Learning

Bayes' theorem is important because it provides a powerful tool for understanding, manipulating and controlling data that takes a larger view that is not limited to data analysis alone. The approach is subjective, and this requires the assessment of prior probabilities, making it also very complex.

However, if Bayesians show that the accumulated evidence and the application of Bayes' law are sufficient, the work will overcome the subjectivity of the inputs involved. Bayesian inference can be used for any honestly collected data and has a major advantage because of its scientific focus.

One model that incorporates the Bayesian theory of concept learning is the ACT-R model, developed by John R. Anderson. The ACT-R model is a programming language that defines the basic cognitive and perceptual operations that enable the human mind by producing a step-by-step simulation of human behaviour. This theory exploits the idea that each task humans perform consists of a series of discrete operations. The model has been applied to learning and memory, higher level cognition, natural language, perception and attention, human-computer interaction, education, and computer generated forces.

In addition to John R. Anderson, Joshua Tenenbaum has been a contributor to the field of concept learning; he studied the computational basis of human learning and inference using behavioural testing of adults, children, and machines from Bayesian statistics and probability theory, but also from geometry, graph theory, and linear algebra. Tenenbaum is working to achieve a better understanding of human learning in computational terms and trying to build computational systems that come closer to the capacities of human learners.

Component Display Theory

M. D. Merrill's Component Display Theory (CDT) is a cognitive matrix that focuses on the interaction between two dimensions: the level of performance expected from the learner and the types of content of the material to be learned. Merrill classifies a learner's level of performance as: find, use, remember, and material content as: facts, concepts, procedures, and principles. The theory also calls upon four primary presentation forms and several other secondary presentation forms.

The primary presentation forms include: rules, examples, recall, and practice. Secondary presentation forms include: prerequisites, objectives, helps, mnemonics, and feedback. A complete lesson includes a combination of primary and secondary presentation forms, but the most effective combination varies from learner to learner and also from concept to concept. Another significant aspect of the CDT model is that it allows for the learner to control the instructional strategies used and adapt them to meet his or her own learning style and preference. A major goal of this model was to reduce three common errors in concept formation: over-generalization, under-generalization and misconception.

Machine Learning Approaches to Concept Learning

This is a budding field due to recent progress in algorithms, computational power, and the expansion of information on the Internet. Unlike the situation in psychology, the problem of concept learning within machine learning is not one of finding the 'right' theory of concept learning, but of finding the most effective method for a given task. As such, there has been a huge proliferation of concept learning theories. In the machine learning literature, this concept learning is more typically called supervised learning or supervised classification, in contrast to unsupervised learning or unsupervised classification, in which the learner is not provided with class labels.

In machine learning, algorithms of exemplar theory are also known as instance learners or lazy learners.

There are three important roles for machine learning.

1. Data Mining: using historical data to improve decisions. An example is looking at medical records and then applying one's medical knowledge to make a diagnosis.
2. Software applications that cannot be programmed by hand: examples are autonomous driving and speech recognition
3. Self-customizing programmes: an example is a newsreader that learns a reader's particular interests and highlights them when the reader visits the site.

Machine learning has an exciting future. Some potential advantages include: learning across full mixed-media data, learning across multiple internal databases (including the Internet and news feeds), learning by active experimentation, learning decisions rather than predictions, and the possibility of programming languages with embedded learning.

Minimum Description Length Theories

The minimum description length principle is a formalization of Occam's Razor in which the best hypothesis for a given set of data is the one that leads to the largest compression of the data. In short, data that show many regularities and/or patterns may be compressed without losing any important information.

Applied to learning, the conclusion is that the more regularity and/or patterns can be found within data, the more has been learned about the data.

Meaning and Importance of Technical and Vocational Education and Training

A particularly important area of work and employment consists of those occupations which centre on the application of technical and vocational skills to the world of work. It is estimated that world-wide some 80% of all occupations are of this type (UNESCO-UNEVOC & UNESCO-UIS, 2006).

Technical and vocational education and training (TVET) has fuelled phenomenal economic growth in some countries and fallen short of expectations in others; while globalization is prompting governments to take renewed interest in this branch of education, still perceived by some as second-class. The purpose of this double, special edition (volume 9/1-2) of the *International Journal of Training Research* (also released for separate sale as a book; ISBN 978-1-921729-10-2) is to explore key aspects of the current development of TVET in various countries.

The field of technical and vocational education and training (TVET) has changed throughout history, usually in response to the demands made upon it by the societies it serves. The current term - TVET - requires both definition and differentiation from other designations. Vocational education and training are probably as old as humanity, and knowledge, skills and belief systems have been transmitted from one generation to the next since the origins of humankind.

Over time, various terms have been used to describe elements of the field that are now conceived as comprising TVET. These include: apprenticeship training, vocational education, industrial arts, technical education, technical/ vocational education (TVE), occupational education (OE), vocational education and training (VET), career and technical education (CTE), etc. Several of these terms are commonly used in specific geographical areas. For example, in Europe the term vocational education and training (VET) is in common usage, while in the United States the current term is career and technical education (CTE). In addition, many in the field are advocating the use of continuing vocational education and training (CVET). There are also several different dimensions that can be used to define vocational education and training - for example: its venue (company-based, apprenticeship, school-based), character (initial, continuing), etc.

At the second International Congress on Technical and Vocational Education, held in the Republic of Korea in 1999, UNESCO and ILO (in consultation with their respective Member States and partner agencies) jointly agreed upon using the term technical and vocational education and training (TVET) in future in order to unite the field. There has also been discussion to add TVET to the UNESCO 'Education for All' (EFA) and 'Education for Sustainable Development' (ESD) initiatives. Strengthening and upgrading TVET is also regarded as important for achieving the Millennium Development Goals (MDGs). The definition of TVET adopted at the Korean Congress is:

Those aspects of the educational process involving, in addition to general education, the study of technologies and related sciences, and the acquisition of practical skills, attitudes, understanding and knowledge relating to occupants in various sectors of economic and social life (UNESCO, 1999).

Key Global Trends: Increasing Importance of Lifelong Learning; Bridging Academic and Vocational Learning

The many designations for the field are probably a by-product of practitioners' responses to changes in demand over time for skills and technologies used in workplaces, the globalization of production, the increasing utilization of information and communication technologies (ICTs) and related matters. Similarly, changes in TVET policy and practice reflect differences in opinion among practitioners and researchers. What has not changed, and appears to be increasing, is the growing emphasis on lifelong learning - and relearning - associated with TVET.

Jacques Delors wrote that 'the concept of learning throughout life emerges as one of the keys to the twenty-first century'. He further noted that the concept 'goes beyond the traditional distinction between initial and continuing education [and] meets the challenges posed by a rapidly changing world' (Delors et al., 1996, p. 22).

According to Finch and Crunkilton (1999), TVET refer to education and training that prepares persons for gainful employment. TVET can take place either in formal schools (i.e. kindergarten through to grade 12 or 13), or increasingly in post-secondary community and/or technical colleges, or informally by means of training at the workplace and increasingly by distance media. Many TVET educators favour the integration of academic and technical/technological curricula. The education and training of so-called knowledge workers suggests that this integration trend will predominate in the twenty-first century. This is because learning sophisticated technological concepts requires a sound foundation in mathematics, science and communications skills, and also an understanding of technology.

Globally, currently almost 50 million students are enrolled in technical and vocational education in 2002. Nine out of ten are enrolled at the upper secondary level, typically designed to serve youth aged 15 to 20 years (Maclean & Wilson, 2009).

The global average is that one in five upper secondary students is enrolled in technical and vocational programmes. However, the enrolment rates vary widely by regions. In Europe and East Asia, including China, such programmes account for 50% and 33%, respectively, of upper secondary enrolment. In the other regions, technical and vocational enrolment is far less common. In Africa and South America, the share is less than 20%, and in North America and West Asia less than 10% and 4%, respectively (Maclean & Wilson, 2009).

A recent trend is the enrolment of recent university graduates at community and technical colleges, to add occupation-specific credentials to their Bachelor of Arts degrees which have not led to their employment. Since many of these (mainly liberal arts) graduates are choosing TVET courses in the community and technical colleges, this trend - called *reverse transfer* - is important and is quite likely to become even more pronounced in the years to come.

One trend, noted earlier, has been the impact of *academic* and *mission drift* upon TVET. While these phenomena have probably always been operative, what seems to have changed during the past few decades has been the *pace* of these phenomena. Notably, the transformation of ninety British polytechnics into universities in 1995 is viewed as the beginning of this accelerated pace. The impact upon quality TVET has not been viewed in a favourable light. This is because when there is a change in status, prestige, funding, etc., priorities and quality also appear to change - often not for the better.

The education and training of *knowledge workers* requires different educational policies, facilities, curricula and, above all, teachers. Teachers must be transformed from those who *impart knowledge* to those who *facilitate learning*. Curricula must be transformed from mechanisms to deliver facts into mechanisms to promote and facilitate learning and thinking.

Some writers assert that a competency- based approach to curriculum development can facilitate this transformation. TVET curricula have been in transition from its *Industrial Age* 'mix' of 50% theory and 50% practical to one that is 80% theory and 20% practical, paralleling the transition from the *Industrial* to the *Information Age*. This shift from a *manipulative* to a *cognitive* focus accompanies the convergence of 'academic' and TVET curricula.

Knowledge workers may be defined as those who use logical-abstract thinking to diagnose problems, research and apply knowledge, propose solutions, and design and implement those solutions, often as a team member.

The impact of technological modernization upon many aspects of education - and particularly upon curricula - necessitates basing the education of future *knowledge workers* upon a firm foundation. This foundation should include provision of a sound understanding of mathematics, science, technology and communication skills.

Rather than compartmentalizing knowledge, technology affects all aspects of life and necessitates a broader understanding of what technologies are, how they work, how they have been applied to real-world problems, and how they affect our lives. This *technological education* foundation at the elementary and secondary school levels should then be augmented with a broad-based curriculum, prior to the commencement of specialization in post-secondary education.

To avoid 'cluttering' curricula, many education systems have adopted a cross-curricular approach to infuse common themes in as many curricular areas as possible. Moreover, specialization has increasingly differentiated upward from the second to third level of education.

A policy encouraging *continuous,* lifelong learning should supplement the 'basic training' of *knowledge workers* by the delivery of 'just-in-time' education and training when new knowledge is required at the workplace. Many assert that individuals are likely to have three or more different occupations and/or careers during their lifetime. This necessitates workers *learning how to learn* in order to recycle themselves when moving from one position or workplace to another.

Originally, the direct preparation for work was the main goal of TVET and this remains prominent in many developing nations. However, with the technological revolutions and innovations in science and technology during the twentieth century, new domains of knowledge and new disciplines have become important at all levels of education and training.

Further, the *upward differentiation* of TVET from the first to the second level and then to the third level of education was an important development of the twentieth century and set the stage for the twenty-first century. The current focus is increasingly upon preparing *knowledge workers* to meet the challenges posed during the transition from the *Industrial Age* to the *Information Age*, with its concomitant post-industrial human-resource requirements and the changing world of work.

TVET is currently faced with the challenges posed by the displacement of the traditionally strong focus upon manual work in favour of mental work, or at least the changing mixture of competencies required in the workplace. The boundaries between manual and mental work are fading away, as many traditional forms of work and the respective preparation processes for learning to work undergo change.

Key problems in the field of TVET include pathways and content leading to generic or very specific professions and jobs. The dual system in Germany, for example, is an artefact of the German *Berufskultur* concept, while in many other countries a culture (or approach) developed to match labour-market needs with individual education and training in a mixed model of qualifications.

In addition to pathways and content in terms of generic and specific competencies, and the way these goals are being justified at local, national and international levels, new demands in terms of employability, re-training, lifelong learning, personal growth and flexibility, transferability and mobility are imminent.

The terms 'education' and 'training' also require elaboration. Essentially, the goal of education is 'to create independent problem solvers [with] sufficient depth of understanding'. In contrast, the goal of training 'is to teach people to follow prescribed procedures and to perform in a standardized manner' (Gray & Herr, 1998, p. 159). What appears to be taking place in the changing 'world of work' is a convergence between these two - formerly distinct - points of view. This convergence is important for the future of education, particularly TVET.

Draxler and Haddad (2002, p. 4) observed that *knowledge,* 'both basic and applied, is being generated very quickly and is growing exponentially'. They claimed that 'more new information has been produced within the last three decades than in the last five millennia'. Their forecast was that 'we should be poised for dramatic technological advances and breakthroughs in the macro frontiers of the universe on the one hand, and microscopic secrets of the human body on the other hand'.

Key Issues and Challenges Concerning TVET

In order to establish an overall context for a consideration of the articles contained in this special issue on 'The future of technical and vocational education and training: Global challenges and possibilities' reference will now be made in summary form to the main issues and challenges facing skills development for employability, and in particular TVET, worldwide.

The Image and Status of TVET

TVET has consistently faced problems stemming from the negative image commonly held by students, parents and many sectors of societies. This is also related to the lack of student motivation to enrol in TVET programmes. These difficulties must be met with a renewed effort to raise the public perception of TVET. There are available some excellent examples of the promotion of TVET for employment. One aspect of this promotion has to do with the following issue.

After 'basic education', what?

As nations implement Universal Primary Education and proceed to consolidate nine or more years of 'basic education', other countries have already achieved universal access to secondary education and are increasing participation in post-secondary education. This progression results in the *upward differentiation* of TVET from primary to secondary and secondary to post-secondary levels of their education systems. Issues of *access* to education and *equality* of treatment within education become increasingly important.

An important question concerns the fact that after nations have implemented basic education they must then effectively address the question of student flows into 'academic' and/or TVET streams, which is also an *access* and *equity* issue.

In nations where unemployment is endemic, TVET, particularly in areas fostering entrepreneurship and small enterprises, becomes increasingly important for the future. Tilak (2003) characterizes TVET as an 'equity measure' because it promotes 'equity with a rural bias and serves the needs of relatively poor people', as well as being an 'antidote to urban-biased elite education' (p. 675).

The Promotion of TVET for Girls and Women

This is essentially an issue of *access* to TVET and, once girls and women enter TVET institutions, how they are received and accommodated. While many exemplary programmes have been developed and implemented during the past several decades, there still remains considerable work to be done. Changing the 'macho' image of TVET participants and workers has not been easy, but it has taken place.

One of the best examples was the programme developed by the Canadian International Development Agency for SENAI in Brazil in the 1990s. The extension of TVET to occupations that are relevant to girls and women has also contributed to the increased participation of women and girls. Attracting more female instructors and administrators into TVET is going to be a major challenge in the future. However, as good as previous aid and development initiatives were, an evaluation of aid provided by DANIDA (2002) noted 'the weak involvement of women in Danish-supported VET activities'. This suggests that these initiatives need to be increased in the future.

TVET Planning

It is imperative to recognize that countries are at different stages of social and economic development. This has a direct bearing upon TVET needs and training systems; therefore, each nation must plan relevant TVET institutions and programmes to meet its current and projected future needs.

The length of compulsory schooling, the percentage of participation in education, the locus of TVET and many other factors reinforce the necessity to plan for the specific conditions existing in each nation. Abrahart and Verme (2001) stress that labour-market policies should 'fit in with education priorities' and 'should be directed towards basic education or towards adult re-education and retraining' (p. 127). Although there has historically been a time lag in the collection, processing and analysis of labour-market information (LMI), the rapid pace of workplace change necessitates its timely provision to TVET institutions in order to prepare workers with new skills and to re-train existing employees. Moreover, the acceleration of globalization and the outsourcing of both blue- and white-collar employment have made both human-resource planning and TVET planning more difficult.

Several developing nations have addressed problems of youth unemployment, the vocationalization of secondary education and population growth by promoting *entrepreneurship* education and training. The DANIDA evaluation carried out in 2002 noted that entrepreneurship training is an important activity in private-sector development and much training is provided for this in DANIDA-supported programmes.

They cite the Micro-Enterprise Development Project for the *jua kali* (informal) sector in Kenya, the innovative Manufacturing Advisory Centre (MAC) in South Africa, the small and medium enterprise (SME) sector in Uganda, including the introduction of entrepreneurship curricula in both schools and polytechnics, in collaboration with DANIDA and the Japan International Co-operation Agency. Similar initiatives have been undertaken in Botswana by the Department of Vocational Education in the Ministry of Education.

TVET institutions should improve their capacity to make use of LMI, including market signals, indicators and intelligence, for planning and curriculum modernization. Governments should develop strategies to help TVET sectors respond effectively to labour-market needs and to deliver training programmes to respond to these needs. TVET institutions should also maintain and enhance their linkages with employers and develop capacity to gather LMI to contribute to the curriculum development process.

TVET Facilities and Equipment

A perennial problem in TVET is the high cost of construction, equipment, maintenance and the provision of consumable training materials. Routine and preventive maintenance have also constituted perennial problems. These issues have implications for TVET finance, instructor training, curriculum development and the delivery of instruction.

If one of these attributes is diminished, the others are affected. Many TVET systems have utilized cost-recovery, industrial levies, linkage with enterprises and employer participation mechanism to address this issue.

Workplace Health and Safety

The impact of HIV/AIDS upon youth and working- age populations is a major challenge to be faced by TVET. If the very youth and workers educated and trained in TVET programmes are rendered incapable of working due to HIV/AIDS, then the investment in their future is lost. Moreover, since teachers and instructors have also suffered a high incidence of HIV/AIDS, the very educative process is in jeopardy.

The lack of sustainability for both populations is poignant. An evaluation by DANIDA (2002) noted that 'HIV/Aids awareness-raising activities have been integrated into all DANIDA-funded VET programmes'. This newest challenge has overshadowed traditional issues of workplace health and safety that have always concerned TVET personnel. However, all of these issues will continue to be of extreme importance in the near future.

The Organization and Administration of TVET

There are many systems and variations for the organization, governance and administration of TVET. While the majority of TVET systems are public in nature, others are para-statal and still others are private. Within some governments, the locus of TVET has alternated between the ministries of education, labour and specifically TVET. *Dual systems* merge public and private organization, administration, finance and delivery. During the past two decades, an increasing number of national TVET systems have been restructured under the aegis of national training boards or authorities. It is likely that this trend will continue in the future.

The *management of change* is important to ensure that TVET systems keep pace with technological change and the needs of each nation. This is equally important in the organization and administration of TVET to prevent ossification. CINTERFOR (2000) highlighted 'the importance of management training' for TVET administrators. Similarly, the DANIDA (2002) evaluation noted 'the shift in recent years in the focus of VET programmes, from technical skills to organisational and management issues.' This will continue to be an important issue in the future.

TVET Curriculum Reform and Development

In many nations TVET curricula have lost their relevance to the requirements of the labour market. In other nations, for a variety of reasons, employers prefer to employ untrained youth or 'academic' graduates and provide on-the-job training. One salient trend is the growing convergence between TVET and 'academic' curricula, resulting from technological change.

In addition, the 'traditional' curricular balance between *theory* and *practice* has shifted in recent years. TVET curricula need to respond to these trends by enhancing the 'foundation' provided to students in mathematics, science, communications and an understanding of technology.

Some exemplary new curricula have been developed in *mechatronics,* biotechnology, ICTs, robotics, rapid prototyping and similar 'new' fields. A related issue concerns *who* participates in curriculum development. If the needs of the workplace are to be met, then workplace participation in curriculum development - through advisory boards or other mechanisms - is even more relevant than in the past. Another curricular issue is the movement to competency-based curriculum development and instruction.

Teaching and Learning

As TVET becomes increasingly more knowledge oriented, the role of the teachers and instructors must change from the didactic imparting of skills and knowledge to the *facilitation of learning*. This requires a quantum change on the part of TVET teachers and instructors, but is an essential step in the education and training of *knowledge workers* for the workplaces of the future.

The changing role of TVET instructors involves 'linking occupational related (academic) studies with technical subjects', according to CINTERFOR (2000). The increasing use of ICT and other media also contributes to this shift in teaching and learning methodologies. Since many nations have developed dedicated institutions for training TVET and polytechnic personnel, change should also take place in these institutions in order to foster the desired teaching and learning methodologies.

TVET Teacher Education

The second International Congress on TVET in Seoul (UNESCO, 1999) called for 'a new breed of TVET teachers and a new paradigm of training them'. A round-table held by UNESCO-APEID in 2002 called for 'the development of prototype training materials that model effective and responsive content and the application of learner-centred approaches'.

The Philippine Technical Education and Skills Development Authority (TESDA) highlighted 'inadequacies in knowledge, skills and industrial experience' of TVET teachers and noted that they 'must be able to transmit to the trainees' actual occupational and practical skills which are relevant to present practices in the workplace'.

Similarly, CINTERFOR (2000) noted that 'broadening the role for instructors will require changes in the way TVET instructors are educated in teacher training courses.' In addition to modernizing pre-service TVET teacher education, increasing attention must be devoted to the in-service education of existing TVET personnel, otherwise these desired changes may not be achieved - and so will be lost.

TVET Teachers' Conditions of Service

In some nations TVET teachers and instructors are not treated in the same manner as are 'academic' teachers with regard to their various conditions of service. In particular, issues of different terms for remuneration, promotion and benefits are a source of frustration.

This often leads to alienation and high teacher turnover; especially when highly qualified TVET personnel can be tempted away by higher salaries in commercial enterprises.

Relationship between TVET and Enterprises

Employer participation in curriculum development has become increasingly important. In addition, TVET personnel need to be encouraged to participate in industrial attachments in order to both maintain viable relationships with employers and to enhance their knowledge and competencies.

Similarly, the development of viable student attachments is increasingly important. The improvement of linkages with enterprises can be accomplished in many ways - one important mechanism being through public/private sector partnerships.

The DANIDA (2002) evaluation highlighted the importance of private sector development programmes that link Danish enterprises with enterprises in partner countries in which DANIDA finances related training activities with up to 9% of the total cost of training. This new departure in bilateral development assistance might contribute much to addressing issues of industry/TVET linkages and finance in the future.

The Growing Importance of ICTs for TVET

Information and communications technologies (ICTs) have become increasingly important for TVET, both in terms of content and delivery. The addition of ICTs to TVET programmes and curricula (preferably as part of a cross-curricular focus) will assist modernization of the field. The use of ICTs to deliver TVET courses, in both formal and informal settings, will assume even greater importance in the near future.

The ICT contribution to the development of teaching and learning resources has been phenomenal and, if anything, is likely to continue to increase in the near future. One important example is the increasing usage of simulation software, which some claim can substitute for some of the 'hands-on' manipulative workshop training in TVET. Another important aspect of ICTs has been the exchange of TVET information between nations through the UNESCO-UNEVOC network, the ILO network and other multi-lateral and nongovernmental networks.

TVET Finance

With even traditionally well-funded TVET institutions experiencing financial difficulties, it is and will increasingly be necessary to develop additional sources of finance. The issue of public/

private sector partnerships noted above is one avenue for broadening participation in TVET funding. Cost-recovery has traditionally been an available option and is becoming even more attractive in the new Information Age.

Abrahart and Verme (2001) stress the importance of 'the use of student or trainee fees for TVET' with exemptions for unemployed and government-sponsored trainees (p. 127). They are sceptical about rate-of-return studies, noting that higher returns to general education 'may say just as much about excessive costs and the poor structure of vocational education systems as it does about the subsequent benefits to students'. Here, they mirror our own scepticism about World Bank rate-of-return-based policies favouring decreased investment in TVET.

The traditional 'levy finance' systems remain viable options. Many post-secondary TVET institutions have developed new sources of finance during the past few decades. One example is the national training funds referred to earlier. Part of these initiatives also involves donations of expensive and rapidly obsolete equipment to TVET institutions by cooperating enterprises. Tilak (2003) notes that TVET is 'necessarily expensive' and cautions that 'poor investments cannot yield attractive returns'.

Testing and Certification

While national systems of testing and certification remain necessary and continue to require improvement, one salient impact of globalization has been the international recognition of qualifications. The establishment of national training frameworks in a large number of nations has begun the broader recognition of competencies and qualifications.

A UNESCO-UNEVOC (2001) round-table identified many important issues concerning the role of national occupational standards in TVET curriculum development. These issues are also of major importance in the design and development of testing and certification mechanisms and will continue to be of importance in the future.

The CINTERFOR (2000) and UNESCO-UNEVOC (2001) small island States' meetings added the issue of 'accreditation framework(s) for national, sub-regional' and regional recognition of TVET qualifications.

This issue is related to the larger regional accreditation systems in Europe and elsewhere. Both types of regional recognition will continue to be important in the future.

The impact of international student testing - the International Association for Educational Achievement (IEA), the Trends in International Mathematics and Science Study (TIMSS) and the Programme of International Student Assessment (PISA) - while more visible upon 'academic' education, is also having an impact upon TVET.

Also, the desire of international/ multinational employers to hire persons with recognized qualifications is affecting (and will increasingly continue to affect) hiring practices. While this is current practice at the university level, it has also become increasingly important at the technician, technologist and skilled-trades levels.

Overview of This Special Edition of the International Journal of Training Research

Although this special issue of the *International Journal of Training Research* is a large, double issue, it is clearly beyond the scope of this volume to examine all, or even most, of the trends, issues and challenges currently facing TVET worldwide at the current time, which have been referred to above.

However, this Special Issue does address some of these matters, and the authors of this special issue refer to issues and concerns in their various countries from different regions of the world.

Kenneth King (2011), Professor Emeritus from the University of Edinburgh opens the issue with 'Skills and Education for All from Jomtien (1990) to the GMR of 2012. A Policy History'. The paper examines 'the different aspects of skill as found in the literature associated with the World Conferences in Jomtien and Dakar'.

The difficulties of incorporating skills in the Education for All movement are examined by tracing the treatment of skills in global monitoring reports (GMRs) since 2002. One such difficulty, according to King (2011), is to recognise the development of the capacities of young people and adults to fully work and participate in society as an entitlement or a right.

Despite a lack of consensus on this issue, the increasing prominence of skills development as a policy measure for governments to 'support economic growth, combat poverty and overcome social marginalization' has prompted renewed interest in reconsidering the role of skills development and examining issues that are related to the provision of skills. Questions such as who should provide skills or who should pay for the provision, and issues on certification and assessment of skills are themes that will be examined in the GMR 2012 and will also appear in different papers in the special issue.

Amidst this renewed interest in vocational education and skills training as a way to equip and upskill the workforce for intense global competition, Simon McGrath's 'Where to now for Vocational Education and Training in Africa' (2011) not only offers critical and sober reflections on the direction of TVET development in Africa, it also outlines three areas in which a new approach might be developed.

One of the major insights of the article is to refute the common notion that vocational education and training is primarily to prepare students for employment, or what has been come to call, an increase in the 'employability' of the students. McGrath (2011), who follows the German tradition, argues that vocation education can include concern for 'technical, moral and social qualities' and that 'the workplace is a site of moral engagement, where engaging with the traditions and standards of the occupation leads to character formation'.

This affirmation of the moral purpose and value of vocation education places considerable emphasis on the workplace as a site of moral engagement to which graduates of TVET should relate not only as an economic player, but as a socially responsible citizen. This provides a solid non-economic justification for the purpose of vocational education and will certainly have implications in the debate about why vocational education should be provided and who should provide this form of education.

Turning to the issue of teacher education in TVET, the paper 'New Paradigm in Teacher Education in TVET' by Shyamal Majumdar (2011), Director General of the Colombo Plan Staff College in the Philippines (and the new Head - designate - of the UNESCO-UNEVOC International Centre for TVET in Bonn, Germany), discusses in detail, five macro changes that constitute to a paradigm shift in teacher training in TVET.

They are: globalisation, the shift to a knowledge-based society, climate change, sustainable development and the information and communication technology (ICT) revolution. Majumdar (2011) argues that the new paradigm requires teachers to take up new roles which facilitate students to acquire knowledge, interact with students to stimulate their intellectual curiosity, and change the mode of curriculum delivery from content-based to enquiry-based.

As suggested, the situation of skill acquisition is a concern for many developing countries. The paper entitled 'Is Skills Training a

Good Investment for the Poor? Evidence from Pakistan' by Shehryar Janjua (2011) from the Mahboub ul Hag Human Development Centre [the Pakistan partner of the Research Consortium on Educational Outcomes and Poverty (RECOUP)] utilises three sources of data to argue for the case that 'the poor are excluded from the formal training system, and even in the informal sector, they are marginalised as training is dependent on social and community connections'.

The result is a highly informative paper that is packed with revealing facts as well as direct quotations from poor skilled workers in four communities from two different provinces in Pakistan. Aside from successfully enumerating the policy context for the acquisition of skills in Pakistan, Janjua (2011) offers convincing findings which prove that the poor, being much more likely to be uneducated, has much more difficulties in accessing formal skills training due to entry requirements related to qualifications and fees.

Such barriers are noteworthy in a nation where 44% of the workforce is illiterate. The paper also offers an interesting finding about women's access to skills in a Muslim country, in which 20.6% of the women in a household survey indicated some form of skills training, but only 18% had utilised the skills to generate income. Janjua (2011) attributes this phenomenon to the concept of *purdah*, which requires women to stay away from male strangers.

This revealing finding confirms the importance of culture and gender sensitivity when designing a vocational education system that will maintain a subtle balance between tradition and new economic imperatives, and one which will take care to widen, rather than circumscribe, individual choices. Similarly, the paper by Claire Noronha and Tanuka Endow (2011) from the Collaborative Research and Development (CORD) organisation [the Indian partner of Research Consortium on Educational Outcomes and Poverty (RECOUP)] based at the University of Cambridge, reports a qualitative research study that investigated the informal and non-formal skills training experiences of 66 skilled workers, including drivers, tailors, electricians and *murtikars* (a type of statue maker) from four communities in two states in India. Issues such as access, process of training and employment outcomes of training were the central themes.

The paper 'Informal training for skilled workers: Issues arising from a qualitative study in four sites in Rajasthan and Madhya Pradesh' (2011) reports that informal and non-formal skills trainings are important means for people to earn a livelihood.

However, low entry requirements, prolonged periods of low-paid training and lack of standardisation often lead to oversupply of skilled workers and issues related to occupational safety and sliding standards of craftsmanship. There is also some evidence that the caste system serves to fence off the poor from acquiring certain traditional skills. On the whole, having one skill appears to be insufficient for providing the poor with sufficient earnings. There is the need to learn a diversity of skills in order to acquire enough different types of work to earn a decent living.

The paper written by Stephen Lamb (2011) from the University of Melbourne investigates the prospects and challenges of TVET development in an advanced-economy. In 'TVET and the Poor: Challenges and Possibilities', Lamb (2011) provides ample evidence to prove his case that TVET is an important device to encourage social inclusiveness in education, actualise the potential of instruction and provide a safety net for students from lower socio-economic backgrounds so that they become engaged and active in an ever-changing economy. Nevertheless, all these good points are offset by challenges such as the low status of TVET, high non-completion rate and poor funding of TVET despite large growths in full-time enrollments and the number of delivered hours. These recurrent themes on the problems of TVET, however, should not make one lose sight of the fact that, as Lamb skillfully shows, TVET has already a stronger purchase among the poor, the early school leavers and people coming from lower socio-economic backgrounds in Australia. Any government which is concerned about the principles of equality and democratic participation of its populace will not only strive for the betterment of TVET, but will also be concerned about how the receiving end of the labour-market is collaborating and interacting with the education sector to realise the potential and value of work as a vocation.

Taking up the specific issue of credentialism or 'skill-squeezing' in the development of vocational education in Australia, in 'The implications of skills deepening for vocational education and training in Australia, Tom Karmel (2011) from the National Centre for Vocational Education and Research uses a primary data set derived from the Census of Population and Housing for 1996 and 2006 to order occupations based on skill levels and analyse how the occupational structure and the distribution of qualifications within an occupation has changed over the period. Comparisons of the relationship between qualifications and occupations for various age cohorts are also made and his findings indicate there is evidence to suggest that skill deepening, that is, 'an increasing qualification levels within occupations' has affected diploma holders the most as 'a diploma no longer being the entry qualification into high skill jobs that it once was'. Karmel (2011) suggests that with the government's drive to continually increase the proportion of workforce with qualifications, TVET providers should consider moving 'upmarket' and 'offering degrees as a standard entry level qualification' or else the TVET providers are 'likely to become residualised, offering certificate level of education targeted at low to middle skill level jobs'.

Although such a move has all sorts of implications for the positioning and self-definition of TVET in Australia, the overall government goal to increase the number of students from low socio-economic backgrounds or indigenous backgrounds who undertake degrees is regarded by Karmel as constituting positive advantages for the TVET providers to offer degrees. He reckons that degrees offered by TVET institutions are likely to be attractive to this group of students because these institutions are less intimidating and have 'a larger regional footprint not shared by universities'. Whether such a development will really lead to a form of higher education provision which is more locally embedded and better cater to the poor and the marginalised, remains something to be seen and anticipate.

In anticipation of the implementation of the ASEAN Free Trade Area (AFTA) in 2015 and the actual wide disparity that exists between the countries within the ASEAN, mobility of skilled labour within the region becomes an issue which according to Paryono (2011), who belongs to the Regional Centre of Vocational and Technical Education and Training under the Southeast Asian Ministers of Education Organization (SEAMEO), is triggering various regional initiatives which has implications for TVET development.

The paper entitled 'TVET initiatives in Southeast Asian countries in response to increasing labour mobility' enumerates a few such initiatives, such as negotiation of regional skills recognition agreements, development of a regional qualification framework, and development of regional skills standards. While different international organisations and regional agencies appear to be involved in these processes, Paryono (2011) argues that these regional initiatives are important 'to enhance labour mobility by way of skills upgrading, re-tooling, and training in new skills' and will 'enhance social and economic integration and cooperation in the region'.

However, the situation may not be so straightforward, as the suggestion that in the absence of adequate employment in the local labour market, TVET in relatively less well-off countries should help train employees for other more developed economies in the region, such as Singapore and Malaysia, is controversial. This is inviting an old question with a new twist, that is, who should really pay for TVET provision: the sending government, the receiving government, or the businesses or industries which hire the workers at the destination?

This complements the next paper by Roslyn Cameron and Terry O'Hanlon-Rose (2011) entitled 'Global skills and mobility challenges and possibilities for VET: A cross-border, cross-sectoral case study' which is essentially a perspective from an advanced economy which are absorbing skilled migrants. The paper discusses the macro forces that constitute to global labour mobility which is emergence of a global market, supply chain productions and global labour markets. The authors focus on Australia (Cameron & O'Hanlon-Rose, 2011), where they suggest that an aging population and skills shortages have contributed to the implementation of a skilled migration policy, which primarily aims to plug the skills gaps to maintain the productivity and innovative abilities of the country. Cameron and O'Hanlon-Rose (2011) argue that these influences act as drivers in creating growing demand for TVET educators, curriculum and TVET students with global perspectives and competencies. Cameron and O'Hanlon-Rose (2011) then present a case study of a cross-border, cross-sectoral alliance between Australia and the Philippines to deliver 'higher education courses' that 'include cross-border TVET qualifications to produce a globally-ready workforce'. Hence the question on who should pay for TVET provision is answered here by collaboration between a migrant sending country and a migrant receiving country at the institutional level. The cost presumably is borne by the Filipino TVET students who will receive skills training recognised by both countries. This leaves the question about whether such cross-border TVET initiatives should be encouraged and promoted, and presumably, the migrant sending country, migrant receiving country, institutions and students involved, will have very different answers to that question.

While the above seven articles more or less assumed the importance of skills training to economic development, Georgia Lysaght and Peter Kell (2011) question this assumption, in their article, 'Building future sustainability and democratic practices: The role of adult education in post-conflict communities'. They argue that the role of adult education in post-conflict or developing societies has largely been overlooked in education initiatives and development programmes in the world or most of these programmes have been misconstrued. Lysaght and Kell (2011) propose alternative international approaches to adult education in post-conflict countries. The authors first clearly define the different categories of conflict; the difficulties of reinstating an education system in a post-conflict environment are explored. The authors then elevate the discussion by questioning what exactly is development and what is the relationship between education and development in post-conflict societies; the assumption that the reconstruction of an education system (especially one that prioritizes primary and secondary education) will necessarily lead to economic development is questioned (Lysaght & Kell, 2011). Even where adult/ vocational education programmes are implemented, they are criticized as tying 'adult education with wage-based labour and economic development' and prone to serve western interest, reinforce ideologies espoused by international financial institutions and international NGOs, reproduce exploitative working conditions, and perpetuate poverty within society (Lysaght & Kell, 2011). The authors advocate 'bottom up', participatory research strategies and critical action research as a form of 'socially transformative practices in adult education' which would allow authentic and democratic rebuilding of social and economic infrastructures, and can promote inclusion (Lysaght & Kell, 2011).

The paper by Michael Bailey (2011) entitled 'Notes from the South Pacific: Vocational education and training teaching practice at the Australia- Pacific Technical College' offers an interesting case study which echoes the themes addressed in the article by Lysaght and Kell (2011). Bailey (2011) examines teaching practices in an official development assistance (ODA) programme funded by the government of Australia and administered by the Australian Agency for International Development (AusAID) through the Australia-Pacific Technical College (APTC).

The mission of the programme is to train Pacific Islanders into skilled workers 'in targeted industry sectors so that they graduate with Australian qualifications which can help improve their local, regional and international employment opportunities'. An online survey and structured interviews were carried out with the teachers of the programme to examine among other things, their experiences of overseas assignments, adjustments of their teaching practices in the development context and their identification with the development programme.

As the APTC has drawn its teaching workforce mainly from VET institutions in Australia, it is not surprising that most of the teachers were found to be ill prepared for their development role. Difficulties with translating previous VET teaching experience into the new environment were revealed and only one teacher out of the 16 surveyed identifies him or herself as a 'development worker' while none identify themselves as 'VET development workers' (Bailey, 2011). A majority prioritise their teacher identity and regard themselves as 'VET teachers working on an international/aid development programme' (Bailey 2011). This leads us back to the point made by Lysaght and Kell (2011): when vocational education programmes are implemented top-down by western governments and aid agencies with the explicit goal of serving and 'developing' certain countries, are the frontline 'development workers' conscious of what they are doing and can they really aid 'development' simply by bringing western standards and practices into the developing world? This question will probably never have a clear cut answer, but by constantly prodding and examining the practices of aid agencies, perhaps adjustments can be made and more 'bottom up', participatory and democratic programme design procedures can be implemented, or more diverse standards and practices can be introduced to truly make a meaningful difference to the developing world.

Bibliography

Anderson, D.: *The Discipline and the Profession,* Wm. C. Brown Publishers, Dubuque, IA, 1989.

Anthony Landale: *Gower Handbook of Training and Development*, Gower Publishing, Ltd., UK, 1999.

Babbie, E.R.: *The Practice of Social Research,* Belmont, CA: Wadsworth, 1995.

Bottery, M. : *The Ethics of Educational Management: Personal, Social and Political Perspectives on School Organization*, London, Cassell, 1992.

Choudhary, Prem Shanker : *Encyclopaedia of Research Methodology in Social Sciences and Humanities*, Anmol, Delhi, 2009.

Dent, K.S.: *Informal Agencies of Education: Proceedings of the 1977 Annual Conference of the History of Education Society of Great Britain*, Leicester, History of Education Society, 1979.

Elliott, J. : *Action Research for Educational Change*, Milton Keynes, Open University, 1991.

Goodlad, John I. : *Educational Renewal: Better Teachers, Better Schools*, San Francisco, Jossey-Bass, 1994.

Hughes, John J.: *Bits, Bytes and Biblical Studies*, Grand Rapids, Mi.: Zondervan, 1987.

Jack Murrin, *Valuation: Measuring and Managing the Value of Companies,* New York, Wiley, 1994.

Jeffs, T. and Smith, M.: *Using Informal Education*, Milton Keynes, Open University Press, 1990.

Kirkwood, G. and Kirkwood, C.: *Living Adult Education, Freire in Scotland,* Milton Keynes, Open University Press, 1989.

Malone, Michael S.: *The Microprocessor: A Biography*, Santa Clara, CA: TELOS, 1995.

Martha H. Verbrugge: *Active Bodies: A History of Women's Physical Education in Twentieth-Century America,* Oxford University Press, New York, 2012.

Mayer, R. E.: *Learning and Instruction,* Pearson Education, Inc., New Jersey, 2008.

Nurullah, S. and J.P. Naik: *A Students History of Education in India,* New Delhi, Macmillan, 1974.

Omvedt, Gail : *Reinventing Revolution: New Social Movements and the Socialist Tradition in India,* New York, Sharpe, 1993.

Poster, C. and Kruger, A. : *Community Education in the Western World,* London, Routledge, 1990.

Prentice, William: *Principles of Athletic Training: A Competency-Based Approach,* McGraw Hill, New York, 2011.

Ramanujan, A.K. : *Hymns for the Drowning: Poems for Visnu of Nammalvar,* Princeton, Princeton University Press, 1981.

Smith, M.: *Developing Youth Work, Informal Education, Mutual aid and Popular Practice,* Milton Keynes, Open University Press, 1988.

Southworth, G.: *Looking into Primary Headship: A Research based Interpretation,* London, Falmer, 1995.

Starratt, R.J.: *Centering Educational Administration: Cultivating Meaning, Community and Responsibility,* Mahwah, Lawrence Earlbaum, 2003.

Thrupp, J. & Willmott. : *Educational Management in Managerialist Times: Beyond the Textual Apologists,* Maidenhead, UK, 2003.

White, P. : *Civic Virtues and Public Schooling: Educating Citizens for a Democratic Society,* New York, Teachers College, 1996.

Williams G. : *Paying for Education beyond Eighteen: An Examination of Issues and Options,* Council for I0ndustry in Higher Education, London, 1996.

Wolfgang Banzhaf; Peter Nordin, Robert E. Keller, and Frank D. Francone: *Genetic Programming: An Introduction,* Morgan Kaufmann Publishers, Inc., NJ, 1998.

Index

H

I

L

M

N

O

P

R

S

T

V

W

❑❑❑